D1274745

DAT

SEP 20 '0)

EVERYBODY'S GRANDMOTHER
AND NOBODY'S FOOL

42960852

HQ
1438
.G4
N37
2000

Everybody's Grandmother and Nobody's Fool

*Frances Freeborn Pauley and the
Struggle for Social Justice*

Kathryn L. Nasstrom

With a foreword by Julian Bond

CORNELL UNIVERSITY PRESS

ITHACA AND LONDON

DISCARDED

NORMANDALE COMMUNITY COLLEGE
LIBRARY
9700 FRANCE AVENUE SOUTH
BLOOMINGTON, MN 55431-4399

MAR 15 2001

Copyright © 2000 by Cornell University

All rights reserved. Except for brief quotations in a review, this book, or parts thereof, must not be reproduced in any form without permission in writing from the publisher. For information, address Cornell University Press, Sage House, 512 East State Street, Ithaca, New York 14850.

First published 2000 by Cornell University Press.

Printed in the United States of America

Library of Congress Cataloging-in-Publication Data

Nasstrom, Kathryn L.
  Everybody's grandmother and nobody's fool: Frances Freeborn Pauley and the struggle
for social justice / Kathryn L. Nasstrom; foreword by Julian Bond.
    p. cm.
  Includes bibliographical references and index.
  ISBN 0-8014-3782-2
    1. Pauley, Frances Freeborn, 1905- 2. Women social reformers--Georgia--Biography.
  3. Women civil rights workers--Georgia--Biography.

HQ1438.G4 N37 2000
303.48'4'092--dc21
  [B]   99-059993

Cornell University Press strives to use environmentally responsible suppliers and materials to the fullest extent possible in the publishing of its books. Such materials include vegetable-based, low-VOC inks and acid-free papers that are recycled, totally chlorine-free, or partly composed of nonwood fibers. Books that bear the logo of the FSC (Forest Stewardship Council) use paper taken from forests that have been inspected and certified as meeting the highest standards for environmental and social responsibility. For further information, visit our website at www.cornellpress.cornell.edu

Cloth printing   10 9 8 7 6 5 4 3 2 1

FSC FSC Trademark © 1996 Forest Stewardship Council A.C.
     SW-COC-098

® GCIU

Contents

Foreword

It is difficult to write about Frances Pauley—difficult because there is so much to say and small space to say it in and because words cannot properly convey who she is and what her life has meant to so many who never will know her.

Long before I met her, she was fighting the good fight—steadily, steadfastly, laboring without reward toward the ideal her faith taught her.

Our paths intersected in the early 1960s, and she was everywhere there was racial conflict then, but when her name is mentioned today I think of her in one place—the second-floor hallways of the Georgia State Capitol, outside one of the legislative chambers, calmly buttonholing legislators one by one, explaining how a proposed amendment to the budget or the budget itself would wreak havoc on Georgia's defenseless poor.

When I arrived there in 1966, she had been haunting those halls for a quarter of a century. Everyone knew Mrs. Pauley.

Sometimes, she won. Sometimes she convinced a reluctant lawmaker, conditioned by his life's experiences to think poverty was genetic, that the state did bear a responsibility to children and to those who could not care for themselves. She opened eyes and hearts in a place where most were closed to the tragedy of poverty in Georgia.

Frances Pauley has plodded steadily on for most of her ninety-plus years. Working for equality in Georgia in the 1940s—even in the 1980s—was laborious work. It was great toil; she did real drudgery, work few wanted to do.

The dictionary unattractively says people who "plod" work laboriously; they toil and drudge. Drudgery's definition is wearisome work, but here she defies the dictionary, for if she ever got weary, or disappointed, no one ever knew.

Through it all, she managed to retain a cheerfulness and optimism that must have been her motivation—the sure knowledge that little efforts produce great rewards.

She will indignantly deny it, but she is the best of Southern Ladyhood—that combination of sweetness and steel, magnolias and muscle that melts opposition with a smile and reasoned argument—not a crinolined Scarlett O'Hara facsimile, but an iron-willed amazon in pantsuit and sneakers.

If we'd had more Frances Pauleys, who can dream of where we would all be now?

Her life stories are an injunction to those who ask, "What can I do?" and "How can I possibly change things?"

Frances Pauley asked herself these questions, and provided her own answers. I once said she was "everybody's grandmother and nobody's fool."

As a child, she relates, her favorite song was "Give Your Best to the Master." She has never stopped giving her best.

Let this book serve as introduction to a great soul.

JULIAN BOND

Washington, D.C.

Acknowledgments

My first debt is to the historians, both professional and popular, who interviewed Frances Pauley before she and I began working together and who generously allowed me to draw on their interviewing and research talent. They are: Jacquelyn Dowd Hall, Cliff Kuhn, Paul Mertz, Albert McGovern, Lenecia L. Bruce, and Murphy Davis. In "Notes on Sources," I acknowledge their work more formally and point interested researchers to the locations of their interviews. Here I thank them for recognizing the importance of recording an oral history of Frances's activist career. This book would not have been possible without them.

Also important to the creation of this oral history record were those friends and colleagues of Frances who joined us for joint interviews: Harry Boardman, Paul Rilling, Buren Batson, Betsey Stone, and Muriel Lokey. Along with formal interviews, they helped me understand Frances through our numerous conversations and correspondence and cheered me and this project along its way. Harry deserves special thanks. I remember clearly the day that Harry flew into Atlanta to check me out and decide if he would lend his support to this project. I am grateful that I passed muster, not only because of his contributions, but also because he became a friend as well. Thanks also to Jean Boardman for hospitality at the Whetstone Inn.

Frances's family is a gift to a researcher. They have always been interested and willing to help, but also content to let my professional judgments shape the book's final form. First among these is Frances's daughter Marylin Beittel; without her, this book would not have come together. From the moment she answered my out-of-the-blue phone call in June 1995, Marylin has been this project's mainstay. She read the manuscript twice, collected photographs, tracked down odd bits of information, and entertained and informed me during visits to Atlanta and Lancaster. Thanks also to Frances's daughter Joan Lamb and son-in-law Jim Beittel.

On my regular research trips to Atlanta, I came to know a number of Frances's friends and colleagues. For hospitality, encouragement, and insight into Frances, I thank: Lewis Sinclair, Buren Batson, Muriel Lokey, Betsey Stone, Paul Rilling, Austin Ford, and Murphy Davis. Special thanks to Murphy for always taking time from her important work at the Open Door Community to have long conversations with me when I visited Atlanta and for her unfailing enthusiasm for this project. She first saw the need to pull Frances's stories together into published form and did so in *Frances Pauley: Stories of Struggle and Triumph.*

Frances's personal papers are on deposit at the Special Collections Department of Woodruff Library at Emory University. I used her papers long before I had any notion of a book about Frances. Any researcher who has had the pleasure of working at Emory knows that there isn't a more helpful archival staff around. Thanks to Linda Matthews, Director of Special Collections, and the staff that worked most closely with Frances's materials: Beverly Allen, Kathy Knox Shoemaker, and Ellen Nemhauser.

A number of colleagues read the manuscript of this book for me. I benefitted from their suggestions and from their enthusiastic response to Frances's life story. Thanks to: Tracy K'Meyer, Gail Kurtz, Steve Friedman, Alicia Rouverol, Teresa Walsh, Tony Fels, Marge Lasky, Linda Shopes, Cliff Kuhn, Grey Osterud, and Jacquelyn Hall. Jacquelyn has a special place among these: she was the first to interview Frances, back in 1974; she was my graduate advisor at the University of North Carolina at Chapel Hill, where I began the intellectual journey that led me to take up Frances's life story; and she read the manuscript, as she has with most of my work, with just the right combination of support and criticism. Grey Osterud also deserves extra thanks, as she read the manuscript twice, both times with a speedy turnaround that kept me on track and with a rare combination of attention to its smallest details and its widest implications.

I have also enjoyed a great deal of institutional support for this project. The University of San Francisco allowed me to take leave time to work on the manuscript and offered financial support through the Faculty Development Fund, the College of Arts and Sciences, and the Catholic Social Thought Project. Jorge Rojas, my research assistant during the final frenzy of completing the book, tracked down items large and small. The National Endowment for the Humanities and the Virginia Foundation for the Humanities also supported my larger research project on women in the civil rights movement, of which this book with Frances is one part. Harry Boardman coordinated a fundraising project for the book, and I thank those who responded generously to his solicitation: Judge Clarence Seeliger, John R. Bertrand, Anne Wells White, Frank Samford, Dan Swinney, Joan Cates, Fran Breedan, Charles Demere, Paul Rilling, and Betsey Stone.

Peter Agree at Cornell University Press picked up this project at just the right time. I will always be grateful for that, and for his shepherding of a first-time author through the publishing process.

Finally, I thank Frances for the pleasures of four years of personal and professional collaboration and our growing friendship. I count myself among the lucky not only to know of her work, but also to know her.

Kathryn L. Nasstrom

EVERYBODY'S GRANDMOTHER
AND NOBODY'S FOOL

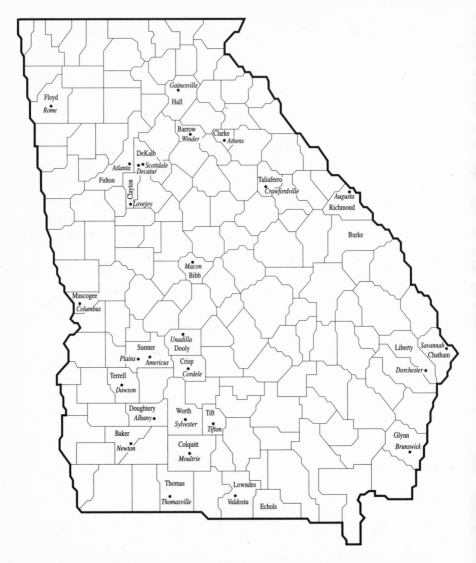

FRANCES PAULEY'S GEORGIA. OVER THE COURSE OF HER ACTIVIST
CAREER, FRANCES WORKED IN ALL OF THE STATE'S 159 COUNTIES.

Introduction

"At 83, Still Showing Poor People They Count."

So ran the headline of a brief article profiling Frances Freeborn Pauley in the July 10, 1989, issue of *Newsweek* magazine. A special section honored fifty Americans, one from each state, who were making a difference in their communities. Frances Pauley represented Georgia.

The *Newsweek* feature introduced Frances's story—largely a southern story—to a national audience. Fittingly, it came just as the lifetime of activism it chronicled was winding down, "at 83." A brief summary of Frances's work highlighted four actions: "set up a hot-lunch program for the schools," "struck the bylaws clause limiting membership to whites," was "jailed during the '60s for helping to desegregate schools and organizing interracial committees in small towns," and "founded the Georgia Poverty Rights Organization." The feature might have added that Frances tells good stories. She has much more to say about the "60-year devotion to social activism" for which *Newsweek* recognized her.

> One of my earliest memories is my mother telling me that when people call you a "damn Yankee," just smile. That was a good lesson for me, because I always talked too much. And I remember being proud that I was a "damn Yankee."

Frances Emma Freeborn, born in small-town Ohio in 1905, moved with her mother, father, and elder brother to the South in 1908; the family settled in Decatur, Georgia, just outside of Atlanta. By the early twentieth century, the "New South" was in transition from a rural, agricultural past to an urban, industrial future. Decatur offered a good vantage point from which to view the emergence of this New South. As late as 1907, the streets were unpaved, the school system consisted of a single building, and there was no city water works, although electricity had arrived. Agriculture remained the backbone of the economy in surrounding DeKalb County. Yet Decatur sat at the edge of Atlanta, an expanding metropolis whose population doubled between 1900 and 1920. On many occasions, Frances rode the streetcar from Decatur into Atlanta with the family's shopping list in hand, clutching an additional fifteen cents for an ice cream soda. Business boomed in early twentieth-century Atlanta, and when Scottdale Mills, manufacturers of textiles, opened in 1909 a few miles from the Freeborn home, the industrial age came to DeKalb County as well.

The New South was marked by rigid racial segregation and discrimination. By the time the Freeborns arrived in Georgia, Jim Crow had a firm hold: laws denied African Americans the right to vote and required that they use separate and inferior public facilities; custom dictated deferential behavior toward whites; and lynching and other acts of terror enforced white supremacy. As Frances grew up, stories of Atlanta's 1906 race riot, a signal event in the city's history, circulated around her. In September of that year, a white mob, whipped into a frenzy of racial violence by rumors of black misconduct, descended on African American neighborhoods in a three-day rampage. Rioters killed more than twenty African Americans and burned numerous black businesses to the ground.

Jim Crow relegated most African Americans to unskilled manual labor and service jobs, and Frances's first direct experience of segregation was in a domestic setting. Like virtually every southern white child growing up in a family of some means, Frances's household included African American domestic help, in the Freeborn's case an all-purpose cook who provided meals and general household help. Josephine Andrews Freeborn, Frances's mother, departed from neighborhood custom by paying a higher wage, limiting the hours she required of her domestic workers, and (in a nearly unthinkable act for a southerner) inviting them to enter through the front door. Frances admired her mother's willingness to challenge custom, and the summers Frances spent in the North offered an annual reminder of less oppressive race relations. These personal examples, small but significant in the context of a racially segregated society, were seeds for a much deeper social critique that would develop over a lifetime. They also taught Frances that the actions of individuals mattered.

The racial exclusion of Jim Crow shaped lives on both sides of the color line and exacted costs from the white working class as well: occupational discrimination against African Americans depressed the wage structure of the state and region as a whole. As an impressionable ten year old, Frances visited the Fulton Bag and Cotton Mills, Atlanta's largest textile manufacturing enterprise, where she was horrified by the sight and smell of the poverty that plagued the white working class in the largely unregulated textile industry. As she passed from childhood into adolescence, visits to nearby Scottdale Mills with a Methodist youth group put a human face on poverty. It was also in the Methodist church that Frances met some of the South's homegrown reformers, southerners whose commitment to social change matched that of her family. Social activism bred in the church, along with the individual examples of family members, suggested to Frances the possibility of greater justice in the New South, laying the foundation for the activist career that she recounts in these pages.

What almost immediately impresses anyone who learns of Frances Pauley is the longevity of her activism and the tenacity of her resolve. Beginning in the 1930s, a core set of commitments to public education, health and welfare, the civil rights of the oppressed, and the needs of the poor animated a lifetime of educating, organizing, and lobbying. Frances's career takes us from the depths of the Great Depression, when Franklin Roosevelt's New Deal offered hope of ameliorating human misery, through the early (and lesser known) stages of the civil rights movement of the 1940s and early 1950s, into the movement in full swing in the tumultuous 1960s, and, finally, into campaigns against poverty and homelessness in the 1970s and 1980s. Over these decades, Frances developed a thoroughgoing pragmatism. Once she identified a problem, she searched tirelessly for its solution and turned for assistance to elected officials, government agencies, and the public at large. Nothing pleased Frances more than to bring together people of good will and *their* government (the emphasis is hers) to address a social problem. Frances believes in both the power of individuals to affect their own lives and the efficacy of wise and generous government. That she never viewed these as mutually exclusive bespeaks a levelheadedness only too rare in today's public discourse, where those who insist on an atomized individual responsibility and those who defend government programs seem to find too little common ground. Frances never assumed any such incompatibility. Searching out what was possible was her life's work for over five decades. Only as she approached her nineties did Frances slow down.

I first met Frances Pauley on August 9, 1991. Like so many other researchers interested in the events of the twentieth-century South that she saw and shaped, I made my way to her door. A year into my doctoral research, I was already grateful that Frances had been a pack rat throughout her decades of political work. Her papers, donated to Emory University's Special Collections Department in 1984, were available to researchers, and I had read them avidly. I was also a budding oral historian, with my tape recorder tucked under my arm.

One image of that first meeting remains fixed in my mind: Frances's car sported a bumper sticker, "Fight AIDS, Not People with AIDS." I remember being impressed that an elderly woman was taking a stand on such a controversial issue. After the interview, I wrote in my notes: "Pauley is 85 years old. She seems to have boundless amounts of energy. We had no problem talking for two hours, and she was just as clear and energetic at the end as at the beginning." I was soon to learn that Frances's stamina was legendary.

This book took shape somewhat later. While working in Atlanta in the summer of 1995, I approached Frances about the possibility of recording her life history. We talked at length that summer, and the tape recorder has only recently stopped turning. Over the years, many people have suggested to Frances that she write a book about her life. She never did, but she has spoken volumes to interested friends, colleagues, and scholars. Our collaboration preserves a portion of that orally delivered life story. The interviews I conducted with Frances over a three-year period constitute roughly one-half of the material I used. Others who interviewed Frances generously shared their work with me, and these contributors are recognized in the acknowledgments. The earliest interview dates from 1974, the most recent from 1998. Most of these were individual interviews, and the text that follows most often features Frances's first-person narration. To record some aspects of Frances's activism, however, we relied on friends and colleagues to prompt memories, and portions of the text are in the form of conversations. Frances's work, shaped by the commitment of a seasoned political organizer, was never solitary. The social character of her activism is evident throughout the text but especially in the collective voice of these conversations.

Autobiographical writings and other documents from Frances's collection constitute a second body of material that I used to flesh out Frances's memories. These documents allow for some aspects of her work to be included that she could no longer, in the mid-1990s, remember and narrate in sufficient detail. They also often function as a counterpoint to Frances's oral histories, capturing the spontaneity of response that no longer lingers in memory, as in a letter to her children in which Frances exclaimed over then–Georgia Governor Ernest Vandiver's role in desegregating Atlanta's schools in 1961: "Old Vandiver says in his news conference that the most important thing he did was to keep the schools open. That he was the brain! Such a world!" In reproducing these documents, I have corrected obvious typographical errors and altered punctuation and usage when necessary for clarity. In general, however, I avoided too heavy an editorial hand in an effort to retain a sense of Frances as she hurried about her work. Frances's writings often had a dashed-off quality, and they let us see her on the run, which she usually was.

Often, however, it is Frances's retrospective storytelling that carries the past into the present with its full emotional force. If I have a single favorite story, it is Frances's description of her grueling interrogation in 1954 at the hands of another Georgia Governor, Herman Talmadge, concerning her position on racial desegregation. (The story appears in context in chapter 3.)

I was the last one to be questioned. It was a very hot day and the capitol was not air-conditioned at that time, and I was dressed in navy blue trimmed with white, and white gloves, white shoes, and white hat. I went forth very sedately. I was called, and Talmadge's lawyer, named Buck Murphy, started questioning me, and he questioned and questioned. One of his first questions was, "I suppose you want your daughter to marry a 'nigger'?" That was the tone of the interview. I was determined they weren't going to get the best of me. I stood there, and I can remember how hot I was, and I can remember how I felt the perspiration trickle down, and I was wondering if it was dropping on the floor, and I had this vision of a pool of water because I was that hot. The day was so hot and then the questions were so hot.

Talmadge picked up and asked meaner questions. He already knew me and hated me from the county unit fight. They would go back and forth, and finally they gave out of questions and I still stood there. Finally at the end I said, "And gentlemen, are there any other questions?" That took all I had. That took everything I had to ask that. I was so scared they'd have another question, and I was just simply done in. But I was always so proud of myself for being able to just stand up there, because they had the church women and the different people that had been on our side, and they had just practically made them dissolve in tears, and sit down one after another. I just was determined they weren't going to do me that way, and they didn't.

Here is classic Frances Pauley: prepared, proper (when she needed to be), but steeled to do difficult work in the face of sometimes fierce opposition. Her narration, alive with the specificity of individual experience, also resonates with some of the central themes of twentieth-century U.S. history: the evolution of race relations, the growing political participation of women, the consequences of economic change, and the social movements of the oppressed. In recording, editing, and commenting on her life story, I have sought to preserve both its literary quality and its historical value.

One final word by way of introducing Frances: I have avoided heavy annotation within the chapters that are Frances's story, electing instead to save my commentary for later sections. Readers who wish to know more about my analysis of Frances's activism may turn to the interpretive essay that follows her narrative, and those interested in a fuller description of my editorial practice may consult the chapter on method. Frances has, I believe, provided sufficient explanation of people, places, and events to guide the general reader, who may be unfamiliar with Georgia and southern history, through her story. Readers who know this history will find many familiar characters and will, I hope, enjoy learning about them through Frances's words. All readers, however, will come to know Frances best.

THE LIFE STORY OF FRANCES
FREEBORN PAULEY

1 Born in Ohio, Raised in Georgia

*Like many children raised in small southern towns of the early twentieth century,
Frances experienced a childhood firmly rooted in family and church. The Freeborns were new to the South, having relocated from Ohio in 1908 when Frances
was only three years old. Family ties to the North remained strong for many
years, and Frances learned about the South through a continual process of
regional comparison. Labeled a "damn Yankee" by others, she in turn often found
the South to be lacking in comparison to the North. The Methodist church provided the basis for the family's social life, yet the Freeborns combined faith with
dissent, particularly when it came to the customs and mores of the racially segregated society that surrounded them. Frances learned about prejudice and injustice early but also about activism for social change, finding inspiration in both her
family and religion. As she passed from adolescence into early adulthood, education and the theater expanded her horizons and encouraged the further development of a social conscience.*

I was born in 1905, September 11, in a little town in northern Ohio,
Wadsworth, which is between Akron and Cleveland. My family name is
Freeborn. I was the second baby, and I was greatly cherished because
there were lots and lots of boys in my family, but I was the first girl in a
long, long time. So I know I had more hair ribbons, and cared for them the
least, of any little girl that ever was born.

In that section of Ohio, my mother and my father's people were settlers
in the early 1800s. They founded the town. McDonough was the county
seat, and that was where my great grandfather lived. I had an uncle that
lived in Cleveland, and I had some relatives that lived in Akron. It was
farming country, and I think pretty good farming country.

They cut down trees to build their little frontier town. After they got
their own cabins built, they built a town hall, a little cabin that was to be
the town hall, the meeting place. There they were going to have church and
schools and public meetings. Everyone that had a child had to make a
bench to put in the building, because the main thing they wanted was a

school. That showed an early emphasis on education. Ohio was a leader in the early days, had very good educational systems. But the benches didn't fit the child. They must have made the benches to fit the adults, so I can see all those poor little children sitting there with their legs dangling down.

My father had two sisters, and one was a schoolteacher, Della Freeborn. In fact, she was the first woman principal in Cleveland, because in those days men were principals. She was very small, very petite, and very feminine, but she used to coach the football team. They used to tease her about it, and she said she really didn't know anything about it. But she had this one wonderful football player, and she would ask him how to do everything, and he would tell her.

My father's family used to go to Florida, to Interlachen, Florida. My father used to tell me those were the happiest days of his life because there he learned to swim and learned all the outdoor sports that he hadn't had in Ohio. My aunt Pearl—my father's sister—met Mr. H. G. Hastings there. The Hastings also were from Ohio, from Springfield, Ohio. They went to the same little town in Florida in the wintertime. My aunt married Mr. H. G. Hastings, and his father was a retired newspaper man. He was very concerned about the plight of the southern farmer because they were so poor, and they farmed so poorly in comparison with the way they farmed in Ohio. So they started a newspaper, the *Southern Ruralist*, which lasted for years. From what I've heard, it was a wonderful newspaper; it had widespread circulation. Then they started the Hastings Seed Company, because the farmers didn't have decent seeds. They started it in Florida, but about the turn of the century they moved it up to Atlanta.

My father, meanwhile, was in the clothing business. He had Freeborn's Gents Furnishing Store in Wadsworth. His store burned one Saturday night. It had a poolroom in the basement, and it caught on fire and burned. So my uncle in Atlanta asked him if he didn't want to come to Atlanta and go into business with him, which he did. That's why my family moved South in 1908. I was three.

They started out with a real mission, the Hastings Company did, and that was to really help the Georgia farmer. They perfected seeds, worked with the U.S. experiment station in Tifton developing seeds. I remember one was "Hastings Prolific Corn," a corn that did well in this area. My father was very upset when they started selling things like flower seeds and shrubbery. He thought they were getting away from the mission.

My father was in charge of mail-order distribution. However, he used to do inspections. In the earlier days, they hired various farmers to grow their seeds. I remember going with him once to Florida to inspect the watermelon crop. I was just a kid. We would go out in the field, and Papa

FRANCES FREEBORN, AGE THREE.
(Photograph courtesy of Frances Pauley.)

would drop a melon to break it and take a taste out of the heart of the melon. How good that watermelon used to taste! It tasted so cool, in spite of the fact that we were there in the hot, hot sun.

When we moved to Decatur, we bought a lot for our house from the Hastings. My two grandfathers came from Ohio and helped build the house, and I lived in that house until the early 1950s. But we used to go back to Ohio, because my mother was homesick when we first came. Also she didn't like the heat, so we'd go back every summer. My brother, Elbridge, used to say that we went back until we both had to pay train fare and then it cost too much. I remember loving to visit Cleveland, because the lake was always so fascinating to me. My uncle's home was not far from the lake. We'd walk down to the edge of the lake and see all of the drawbridges and the city. I used to just love Cleveland. Then we'd visit my grandparents. At that time, all my grandparents were still living in Wadsworth. So we would make our headquarters with them, stay with one part of the time, and the other part of the time.

One year we got sick, when I was about age six or seven. We had typhoid fever, so we didn't come home in time for school to start. My brother had it first, and so I started to school in Ohio because they made me. They had compulsory school attendance. I remember enjoying that too, going to school there. Several years later, I got the flu, and that was in the big, bad flu epidemic in 1918. We went to Cleveland for the weekend, and I must have gotten exposed there because I came back with the flu. In Wadsworth, they hadn't had any flu, and everybody was just furious with us because they said that we brought the flu. People used to walk on the other side of the street from us. I remember how sick we were too. We were really sick. It wasn't just a case of the flu like you have now.

When we first moved to the South, people didn't like us. That was 1908 and they didn't like Yankees. One of my earliest memories is my mother telling me that when people call you a "damn Yankee," just smile. That was a good lesson for me, because I always talked too much. And I remember being proud that I was a "damn Yankee." That was early in this century, and people had a lot of very bitter and hard memories about the Civil War. Yet they didn't, in many cases. I remember my grandfather, William Freeborn, who fought in the U.S. Army in the Civil War. On Sundays, he would talk about the war with an old man named Mr. Hammond at church. They would stand out under the tree and fight the war all over again, and then go arm in arm into Sunday School and sit down together. They were the best of friends. That was so interesting.

I was lucky not to have been brought up in a prejudiced home. My parents had come up in the North, and I'm sure the two or three blacks in the town went to their school. A woman named Auntie Lee—although Mama called her Mrs. Lee—still did my grandmother's washing, but she wasn't treated any much different. The day she came to do the washing she sat at the table and ate with the family. Little things like that made a difference in my upbringing. I didn't have the old master-servant mentality; I didn't come up with that handicap. I've talked to a number of people at length who have told me how difficult it was to get rid of that.

I also experienced discrimination, being from a northern family. I don't think unless you've been discriminated against, at least a little bit, in some way, that it would be very easy for you to understand discrimination. But if you had faced a little discrimination, as we had, being northerners in a southern community, it makes you understand. It bothered my brother more than it did me. I remember one time he said to mother, "What's the matter with us anyway? When we're at home, we're northerners, and when we're up here in Ohio, we're southerners." All of his life it bothered him what people thought of him.

It was hard for Mama to adjust to the South. When she came here, she was in the habit of taking care of her own kids, which was her family custom. The neighbors all had nursemaids that took care of the children, and Mama wasn't used to blacks. So she didn't trust us to be left with somebody else. If she left us with anybody, she left us with her sister.

Another thing that was different, and I am so thankful for, was that my mother thought the long hours that people worked as servants were not right. We had what we called a cook, but she did everything. The custom in the neighborhood was for the cook to come in the morning, before breakfast, and stay until after dinner. Mama thought that was bad, so she worked for Mama for eight hours. The neighbors didn't like that much. Also Mama said it was further to the back door than it was to the front door, and consequently the cook came in the front door. The neighbors thought that was terrible.

Mama also paid our servants a little bit more than the neighbors did, because she thought the wages were way too low. That, of course, ended up meaning that we always had the pick of the community, practically. I remember that once we had the wife of the man who was the head cook at Agnes Scott College, which was nearby, and she cooked for us for a long time. How wonderful she was! Her name was Fannie Brooks, and the Brooks family was a prominent black family in Decatur. They owned quite a bit of property and were really quite well-to-do for the black community. I think we came out ahead on that, but that wasn't what Mama was thinking about. That taught me something at an early age about caring about other people. I think that today it means that if I see a certain person that I feel is being oppressed, it makes me notice them a little bit more, I hope. So I'm thankful my mother taught me that.

If there was somebody sick, I can't remember us having a whole lot of talk about it, but if they didn't have any medicine, Mama saw that they got the medicine. In our church, Decatur Methodist, the women worked with a day nursery at the Fulton Bag and Cotton Mills in Atlanta. The church had one day a week when they went and helped with the day nursery. They would take the lunch for the children and would take care of them. Mama took me along once to help play with the kids when I was ten or so. I was so horrified. I still can smell how the room smelled, and I can see how dirty those children were. Cotton mills were awful, just awful. You know, poverty and its degradation are something you have to see and touch and smell. Even if you're a thoughtful and kind person, you just don't get it from reading. I went home and was sick all night, so Mama never took me back again.

My mother died at a young age from leukemia and that meant I had a lot of responsibility growing up. She taught me to do the shopping. I'd go to town, to Atlanta, starting when I was about twelve. If you were going to Atlanta you went "to town," and if you went to Decatur you went "uptown." In Decatur, there wasn't anything but a grocery store, a drug store, and a meat market. So if you wanted to buy clothes or anything, you had to go to Atlanta. We would go twice a year when I was little to buy clothes and go to the dentist. Those were big occasions, because we would eat lunch downtown. It was wonderful to eat lunch in a restaurant. Then as I got older and did the shopping, I went whenever something needed to be done. I'd feel so grown up and also a little bit scared. They didn't have any traffic lights, and I remember worrying about crossing streets because of how much traffic there was. Mama would give me a quarter, that was ten cents for the streetcar fare and fifteen cents for an ice cream soda. I had a lot of responsibility and I had it young. But I took a lot of pride in it. I was allowed to do things that my friends didn't do. They couldn't go to Atlanta on the streetcar by themselves. So I felt a little superior.

Mama had a lot of leadership qualities. We were Methodists, and she was president of the Woman's Missionary Society, and she was one of the first women on the Board of Stewards. Shortly after that, it was in the twenties, the problem of unification of the Methodist church in the North and the Methodist church in the South came up. Mama, when she came here, didn't know there were two churches. She thought she was coming to the same church that she went to in the North. Bishop Warren Candler was our bishop, and he was opposed to unification because he was very much a segregationist. Mama, being very political minded, in a certain sense, knew it wasn't any use for her to fight at the level where she was, so she didn't bring up the subject of segregation. It wasn't brought up that it was good, but she didn't bring up that it was bad, either. She simply didn't bring it up in the ladies' society and wasn't working against it. So one morning, publicly, the preacher put her off the Board of Stewards, said she wasn't loyal to the church. That was awful. She was so upset because we were so upset, and she didn't want us to get upset about it. I don't have much respect for the organized church, and I'm sure it goes back to things like that.

Of my parents, Mama maybe was more religious, but they both took an active part in the church. They weren't, though, "churchy" kind of folks. It was all right if you didn't go to church. Also they weren't the hellfire and damnation kind of religion at all, although at that time you heard a lot of that preached. Mama would usually see that we didn't get there a second time, if it was that kind of preacher.

I was very religious. I was trying to lead what I thought was a Christian life. The church played a very important part in my early life. A lot of my social life was around the church, through young people's groups. When I was in college, a bunch of us organized a Tithers Association. It was headed by Ernest C. ("Pomp") Caldwell, a theological student at Emory who later became head of one of the seminaries. None of us had much money, but by tithing every month, we'd have a nice little sum. We'd do things like buy widow so-and-so some new glasses, and so-and-so some feed for the cow. We gave half to the church and spent half on other things. The first year we gave to the church, Pomp preached and told about the organization. He was so brilliant, words just flowed. The organization was well thought of, so the preacher thought he should join. So did the head of the Sunday School. But, let me tell you something, neither one of them ever paid their tithe. We had never had anybody until then who didn't pay their tithe. And here was the preacher saying to everyone he was a member. We disbanded. That really got to me. People don't realize what they do to young people, do they? I thought about that a lot afterwards.

It was in the Methodist church that I met Mrs. Dorothy Tilly. She was an organizer of women in the Methodist church and got them interested in doing things outside of the church. She was in charge of juniors, and I came from a church where we had a youth group. So she was often taking me here, there, and yonder for me to make a speech. Evidently I could speak well, and that was good training for me, probably one of the reasons I went on and took speech when I went to college.

As I got older, many of the Emory theological students used to come to our church, and many of the boyfriends I had were theological students. I came pretty near marrying one, but I never thought I would be a very good preacher's wife.

My family was always interested in politics. Since they came from Ohio, they were brought up in a two-party state. They had been Republicans, but of course there wasn't any such thing here. Papa was on the city council for a time, and I always heard political conversations. I have a letter that my grandmother Freeborn wrote about why women should vote. That's going back a long time! She was visiting us the first time she had a chance to vote in Ohio. She went home so she could vote, went home before she had intended to go. I was brought up with the idea that women ought to vote.

My mother and father each had a sister that lived nearby. My mother's sister, Bess Andrews, first lived with us. She came down, and she lived with us and had a job with Rich's Department Store. That was unheard of because women weren't supposed to work, but Yankee women didn't have that same idea about work that southern women did. Aunt Bess married a southern man, and Uncle John was a member of the Ku Klux Klan. I remember seeing his robe. If something racial was happening, Papa would go over there to see if their car was in the yard, to see if John had gone with the Klan. Still, he and my father were really good friends. It was just something they never discussed. Never argued with each other in the slightest. He was southern and Papa was Yankee, and that was just part of them, as I remember it.

I started school in Decatur when I was five. When my older brother started to school was one of the first years they had any public school in Decatur. Before that, girls went to Agnes Scott—it had an elementary school—and boys went to a Presbyterian boys' school called Donald Fraser. My family thought it was so terrible that there were no public schools, because they had moved from Ohio where public schools had been great. To move to a place where they didn't even have a public school! You can imagine how hard they worked for public schools in Decatur.

Decatur's first public school was just in a little cottage on the square. Soon after they built a schoolhouse. I started to school in the new schoolhouse. Decatur always had the reputation of having a good school system, though. I think that the people were interested in education, and better people were on the school board than were on in some towns.

When the school year started, they had school on Saturday and not on Monday. This was because it was such a staunch Presbyterian town that they kept the Sabbath. I mean, they really kept the Sabbath! They did not want the children to study on Sunday, so they had school on Saturday and a holiday on Monday. I also remember distinctly my neighbors not cooking on the Sabbath. The other reason they had school on Saturday was to keep the Jews out. I don't remember any conversation about it when I was a child, but I've heard people are doing research on it. Keeping the Jews out of Decatur was one of the reasons for school on Saturday. We were friends with one Jewish family, and one of the family members came back years later and said we were the only family to ever invite them over.

School was fun and a place to play, and I remember we would usually not come back from Ohio until after school started. When I came back, everybody was so glad to see me because I seemed to be able to organize the play better than anybody else in the class. I never remember having, like some children in the South, black children that I played with, probably because of where we lived. And I never played with our servants' children. We didn't have any contacts like that, unless it was some special occasion that we had been invited to come to their church, or something special at their house, like a death. But just on regular occasions we didn't get together.

I liked school and remember that I always did all right in school. I was always kind of ahead, particularly in math. When my brother was coming along, my father would be teaching him his multiplication tables, and I learned them at the same time. A lot of things I learned when he learned them, just because they were helping him at home. Since I was good in math, the math teacher would look at my name and not look at what I had written and open the book and give me a hundred and then move on to the next one. It used to make people mad, and they would try to see if I had a mistake somewhere. But I didn't.

I was the first girl at Decatur High School to bob my hair. This was in 1921, at the end of my sophomore year. My brother was graduating, and we were the sister class. We were going to enter into the class night activities, and I had a new dress. It was red organdy, and I thought it was beautiful. And I decided I'd have my hair cut, and Mama let me. Boy, did it make a splash. We had to march with the seniors, so I remember how tickled I was. Everybody was saying, "Oh, look, she's cut her hair! She's cut her hair." That was my new freedom, to cut my hair. It was in the atmosphere and being talked about that people were cutting their hair. My cousin was in college and lived next door. His girlfriend had cut her hair, and I knew about that and had seen her, and I liked the way it looked.

All of my schooling was in Decatur. I went on to Agnes Scott College and graduated in 1927. By the time I was in college, my mother wasn't well, and I really was needed at home. Money was short because Mama

FRANCES FREEBORN, AT THE TIME OF HER HIGH SCHOOL
GRADUATION.
(Photograph courtesy of Frances Pauley.)

was sick. I think it would have been difficult for the family to send me away to school. Although I know I missed a lot by not being away from home and in college, I'm so glad I had those four years because they were the last four years of my mother's life. She died in 1928 from leukemia.

I majored in math, and I think the teacher that meant the most to me was Miss Gaylord, who was a math teacher, an absolutely excellent teacher. I always admired her so much. I was also interested in drama, but they didn't have a major in drama. Still, I took all the drama they had and playwriting. We put on our own plays, and I directed, acted, and wrote. I got to know Miss Gooch, in the Department of Spoken English, real well because I took all the speech classes. She had a fit when I went into civil rights work. She called me up, tried to dissuade me. She thought I was just throwing my life away. But, overall, Agnes Scott certainly taught me to be a serious student, a very serious citizen, that life is real, life is earnest. This was the attitude of the faculty as a whole.

Miss Nan Stephens was the playwriting teacher. I liked her the best, and I learned a lot from her that I have been grateful for. It ought to be a required subject for everyone to take drama, to have to play a role, be somebody else. I think it teaches you so much about walking in somebody else's shoes, and gives you a lot of insight into working with people and much more sympathy for any kind of person. It also adds so much to the enjoyment of your life.

Margaret Bland taught French at Agnes Scott. She wrote good plays, and she wrote one that we took to New York to enter in the Belasco Cup Tournament. And we won. There were four prizes, two prizes for published plays and two prizes for unpublished plays. We had two plays that went from Georgia. One was taken by some players from Savannah, and we took the other one from here. Those two won. That was fun because it meant that we got to stay in New York over the weekend, because the four winners played on Friday night and Saturday and Sunday. This was wonderful for us because it was my first, and I think most of our first, trip to New York. We got to go to other plays and go backstage and meet the actresses. That was very thrilling for us.

I played Touchstone from *As You Like It* one time. I usually played things like the fool! Miss Hopkins, the dean, was very precise and proper. She came to see dress rehearsal, and we had regular rental Shakespeare costumes. I had on the regular fool's costume, and she said that I couldn't wear it with the pants that short. So I went backstage and came out, and I had pulled them down to my knees. You can imagine how awful they looked. "Now, Miss Hopkins, is that all right?"

"Yes, that's fine. That's fine," she said.

Of course, the night of the play, you know very well that I wore them up.

The summer after I graduated from Agnes Scott, I took French at Emory. I was trying to get off my language requirements and decided I'd go ahead and get a master's. I was thinking particularly of drama and English. That fall I went into teaching in order to make some money. I figured it was time I was getting on my own and the family not providing all my needs. For two or three years, I taught in the Decatur schools. The high school gave me a room where I would teach private students during the day, if I would direct their dramatic club. I directed their senior play and maybe one other. It gave me a chance to direct, and we did well. We had packed houses.

I kept studying playwriting with the same teacher from Agnes Scott. She had a class in her home of people who had graduated. We kept writing, in that group, which was a wonderful group of people. We formed a Drama Workshop in Atlanta, and we were very successful. We had big crowds. I wrote one play, "The Poor Farm," about a lady from the poor farm who ran away to the fair. When she came home, she had won a goose, and I remember in the play we had her come on stage with a live goose. That made quite a hit with the audience. DeKalb County had a poor farm with little cottages where the people lived and kept house. The young people in my church used to go out there and have a religious service. I got to know the people a little bit, know them as individuals. Not real well, but it was personal. I didn't look down upon them as cast-off folks. It helped me understand poor people. In "The Poor Farm," I wanted to picture them as interesting people, not as dregs or failures in life. These were very interesting people who just happened to be poor.

At that time, a lot of folk plays were being written, plays that depicted different areas of our society, like the very poor, rather than just having a love story or something like that. The North Carolina Playmakers were an outstanding example of this. I used to go to North Carolina in the summertime a lot, so I got particularly interested in the poor people in North Carolina. My mother never did like the heat here, so we often would go somewhere where it was cooler, for a month or two. Also we would go for hay fever season, because my brother had hay fever and Mama had an idea that he had it less in the mountains than he had it here.

One year, in 1930, we sold season tickets for the Drama Workshop. We practically sold the house out and put the money in the bank, and the bank failed in the Depression. There we were with people having the tickets and us no money. We just couldn't bear the thought of not fulfilling our obligations to the people, and so we did it. You can imagine how hard it was, when nobody had any money, how difficult it was for us to put on the productions. We put on every one, but it was so difficult that when the last curtain went down, all of us threw in the towel. It took all the fun out of it. I don't think we ever wanted to think about producing another play as long as we lived. But, of course, nobody had any money then, and the Depression really was in its depth. So that ended that.

I also married in 1930. In fact, I met my husband while I was directing a play for St. Philip's Cathedral. It had already been cast, and so when I got there, the woman who had cast the play gave me a list of the characters, with little notations by each name. Next to Bill Pauley it said, "You won't like him. He's not dependable." So that was my introduction to my husband! Every time I would start to fuss at him a little bit after we were married, he said, "Now, you remember you were warned." We were married for fifty-four years, so I guess he turned out to be pretty dependable after all.

2 "About this time I began to hate the rich": The Depression and World War II

In 1929, Georgia and the rest of the nation plunged into the Great Depression. In the metropolitan Atlanta area, manufacturing dropped off by a third and wage-earning jobs by almost twenty percent in the first three years of the economic downturn. For many, hunger and homelessness followed. The Pauley family counted itself among the lucky; they kept their home and always had food on the table. For them, riding out the Depression meant living on a limited income and bartering for goods and services when cash was short.

Whether a family suffered greatly or lived on reduced but sufficient means, a partial antidote for economic hardship came with Franklin D. Roosevelt's New Deal. Bill Pauley maintained his landscape architect business only through work sponsored by the Works Progress Administration (WPA) and Public Works Administration (PWA), two of the New Deal agencies designed to provide work for the unemployed. Frances, raising two small daughters born during the Depression, was grateful for the "good eating money" the government provided. Like many, she became a fan of Franklin Roosevelt; she had seen firsthand what the government could do.

For Frances, the lesson of the New Deal was that the government had tremendous potential to supplement the church-based private charity that she witnessed in her youth. Indeed, it accomplished what charity could not. Although the Salvation Army, Red Cross, and local churches set up soup lines and doled out relief, only the New Deal made a significant dent in the suffering of the 1930s. As Frances embarked on her lifetime of civic and political work in the context of the Great Depression, a pragmatic mix of private and public initiatives followed quite naturally from the examples set by her family and her government.

Speech in support of the DeKalb Clinic
1941

A very unusual thing has happened in our community. A man felt that it was God's will that a piece of work be done. The way opened and he did the work. He feels that the Holy Spirit moved him to do it. He has faith that it will come out all right.

Last February I went to a meeting. This man stood
before us as president of the DeKalb Clinic. In his
report of the new clinic he told of the malnutrition
of our county children which had come to his
attention. 1/3 of them definitely hungry. He told of 30
children who had 75 teeth pulled in the new white dental clinic. He said if only there was a way to serve
one hot meal--perhaps it would pay.

Women started working. A plan was worked out with
the cooperation of my county superintendent, a man
with an endless amount of energy which he exercises
constantly for the good of children of this county. It
was found that we could have surplus commodities from
the federal government--tons of flour, oatmeal, butter,
grits, prunes, apples, oranges. It was found we could
have help from the WPA to prepare and serve these
meals. Then there was a wall--equipment. None of this
would be possible without the required stoves, refrig-
erators, dishes, etc. This man of great faith
obligated himself for this equipment. He worked out
with each individual school to handle their individual
situation and then provided them with the necessities.

I feel proud and happy to tell you that over 5000
hot meals are being served daily, 1000 of these free.

We feel we will have better citizens. We feel that
we are saving bodies--saving minds--for one can't
think well when one is hungry.

So to-day I come before you to tell you what one man
has done. And to ask you what you will do. $30,000 is
needed.

To me this is a challenge to our Christianity. I have
a practical mind, I'm afraid. To me this is a practical
way to serve our master. If Jesus were to come to
Decatur to-day would he not say, "Give ye them to eat"?
Did he not know the children? What would he do to-day
about the ill clad, ill housed, ill nourished third?
This clinic that we have needed so long, a place for
our good citizens who are unable to pay. Either you or
I--if the necessity should arise--might go.

Do you not think we as church people should stand
back of this clinic and help it in its struggle for
existence?

MARYLIN, FRANCES, PAPA, BILL, AND JOAN, IN FRONT OF
THE FREEBORN-PAULEY HOME, CA. 1938.
(Photograph courtesy of Frances Pauley.)

I married Bill in 1930, which was crazy, but I didn't understand the Depression was coming. I'm glad we did it. I guess we just felt that for our happiness we had to live together. He moved in, and I had a husband and a brother and a father and a couple of dogs, all in the same house. My husband loved it, because he'd been an only child and never had a family, and we always had a real good time at home. My brother, who lived with us until he got married in 1936, had lots of company, and my husband loved company. But he wasn't the type that would invite people over. He loved it when somebody else invited them. So he and my brother were real good friends, and he and my father were real good friends.

Another lucky thing for me was that my husband's mother hadn't liked to cook or clean house. So he thought the way I cooked and kept house—which was not much!—was just *fine*.

My two daughters were born during the Depression, Joan in 1931 and Marylin in 1935. It was a struggle. How were you going to make ends meet, and how were you going to feed your family well, and how were you going to clothe the kids? My husband was a landscape architect. His business was with the rich, and nobody was using his services. My father's business, the seed business, was hanging on by a thread, and there'd be times when they wouldn't receive their salaries. What little we had was in the bank which failed.

Still, we weren't alone in it. All the neighbors got together and tried to figure out the cheapest way to buy the best food and feed our families. There was quite a lot of bartering that went on in the Depression. Dr. Bartholomew was the obstetrician that delivered our babies, and so Bill landscaped their yard. He did work for Mathis Dairy, and we got paid in milk. We were all in it together, and we had to get out of it together.

Everybody was out of work. It's not like now. In the Depression it was everybody: rich and poor, black and white, old and young. The whites were suffering just as much as the blacks, just like the rich were jumping out the window. So you didn't have any feelings that it was individual failure on your part. It was just what was happening in the world. Today, the person who doesn't have something feels like a failure, because here's this person or that person who has a good job.

My husband came from Indiana, Lafayette, Indiana. He went to Purdue University and then the Massachusetts Agricultural College for his graduate work in landscape architecture. After he graduated as a landscape architect, he was looking for a place where he wanted to set up practice. He was in the army in World War I, and when they got out of the army, they were allowed to travel very cheaply, a cent a mile or something like that, to decide where they were going to settle down. He chose Atlanta,

THE FREEBORN-PAULEY HOME ON CLAIRMONT AVENUE IN
DECATUR, CA. 1938.
(Photograph courtesy of Frances Pauley.)

because here you can plant year 'round. A landscape architect had a lot more chance of making a living if he could plant the year 'round. He was very busy with his work, which was all over the South, so he traveled a lot. When he came to Atlanta, he was the only licensed landscape architect here, because we had no school of landscape architecture in the South at that time. Eventually, Bill helped establish one at the University of Georgia. He took pride in being a real landscape architect. He didn't like the idea that practically anybody could hang out a shingle and say they were a landscape architect, which they did. When he became a fellow in the American Society of Landscape Architects, they said that it was very unusual that he could have been made a fellow in so many different areas, like parks or playgrounds or homes or businesses or subdivisions, because he had done such a variety of work. That was simply because there were so few landscape architects.

This was great for us in the Depression when the WPA and PWA came down, because it meant that we got all the government work that we could do. The government required that the architects and the landscape architects be licensed. But the government work that Bill had, it paid very little. It didn't pay like private work. In fact, it paid only a little bit more than it paid for the manual work, which I think was perfectly okay, and I never remember Bill feeling that was wrong. We were just glad to have that money; it was good eating money. His business had stopped dead until PWA and WPA started. He did a tremendous amount of government work.

Bill laid out the first slum clearance and public housing in the country. It was in Atlanta, the University Homes. He also laid out airports in lots of different little towns around the South. We forget those good things that meant a lot to the state, a lot of that work was done in the Depression days. I can't remember just how it was connected, but it seems to me that some of the work that I did with preschoolers in the churches was with federal money. At one time, we had a nursery school, and Mrs. Roosevelt was going to be in town and visit our nursery school. I remember begging and borrowing and sewing and getting new clothes for all the children in the nursery school, so they would look nice when Mrs. Roosevelt came.

I was, of course, a great admirer of Roosevelt, as I still am. But, otherwise, I was only slightly aware of the larger political movements of the time, because actually looking after the family and looking after the things that were sort of at hand occupied my time.

The first thing I ever remember organizing was during the Depression. I was a member of the Junior Service League in Decatur that later became the Junior League, and we had a puppet committee that met at my house. We would spend all fall making the puppets and the spring showing them in the schools. Then, if the children wanted to make them, we would help them. I'd always been interested in dramatics, so I wrote a lot of the shows. My kids loved playing with puppets.

One year we decided we would have a booth at the county fair, but it wasn't successful because nobody had a nickel to come to it. The kids didn't have any money, and the place was packed with kids, none of them doing anything. They would stand around the hot dog stand and look so hungry and not be able to buy a hot dog. I just couldn't stand it, so I decided that something had to be done about it.

In the meantime, we had been working to establish a free health clinic. This was before the days of the Hospital Authority in DeKalb County. It disturbed me that people were sick and didn't have any way of getting medical attention, except begging it from some private doctor. The private doctors that were big-hearted were overrun. I thought, "Why can't we have a place where people can go and be treated?" The Department of Public Health did things like treat syphilis and give vaccinations, and did an excellent job. But they didn't do much, overall, in the way of treatment.

A couple of us ladies got together with the county's public health director and decided that we would try to set up a clinic. It wasn't any organization, just a group of people that I had known around Decatur who were interested, particularly in poor people. We rented an old building in Decatur, and that was the first clinic. Decatur already had a dental clinic, the churches had started that, so we put the dental clinic there. Some of the public health clinics, like the well-baby clinics, were already in existence, so they put them there. We added a general medical clinic. The doctors gave their time, but we had to pay for the nurses. Most of the people who helped there were church women, and of course all of us worked as volunteers. The women's auxiliary would help in getting up the baby clothes and things. It gave people a chance to give, and give a little bit or give a lot.

We got the county to give us some money, and we raised privately the money that the county didn't give us. Scott Candler was the county commissioner. We had a one-commissioner form of government, and he wouldn't ever give us the money unless I came and asked for it. So once a month, I had to go to his office and sit and wait for him, and sometimes it would be a lengthy wait. He wanted to hear about what the clinic was doing and ask questions about it, and then he would give me the check. That irritated me, because it seemed to me that the county could just send us the check and not take up a whole morning of my time. But that was Scott Candler. Still, I always had a real good relationship with him, mainly because my brother and father had an excellent relationship with him. My father was on the city council in Decatur at the same time Scott Candler was the commissioner. I never had respect for the way Scott Candler operated, because I basically believe in a more democratic form of government than Scott Candler would have ever allowed. I differed on that particular point with my father and brother, because they both thought Scott hung the moon.

Our intent was to reach poor people and people that needed it. We didn't differentiate between black and white. The white and the black came the same days, the same time. Some things, though, were segregated. They had a white syphilis day and a black syphilis day. Those were segregated clinics, and all the public health clinics had been segregated. We had a white well-baby day and a black well-baby day. But we didn't have any segregated waiting rooms, though usually the blacks sat down at one end and the whites up at the other end.

One day the Grand Jury came over and inspected us, and they got after us, said we were breaking the law because we were not segregated. They commanded that we be segregated. Well, this made us very angry. We just hadn't thought about it. We were thinking about treating sick people. But we put up a partition. Actually, the waiting room was a big, wide hallway,

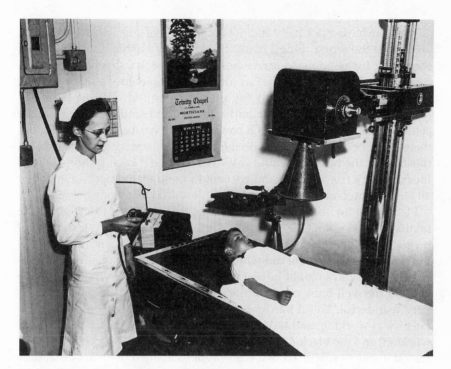

THE DEKALB CLINIC PROVIDED HEALTH CARE AND PREVENTIVE
MEDICINE TO THE POOR IN DEKALB COUNTY.
(Photograph courtesy of Frances Pauley.)

so we put up a partition about halfway down. It was sort of a natural line between where the blacks and whites had been sitting. We never put up any signs, and we never told the people they had to sit one way or the other. We were thinking about equality and justice, but weren't thinking about real desegregation and what that would require. But we still had the same doctors, the same clinics, the same attention for black as white.

I used to work on the baby days, because I could do the same things as a nurse's aide. I could undress the babies, and weigh them, and dress them again. The babies that came usually had on dirty clothes or worn-out clothes or raggedy clothes, and so we kept baby clothes. After the baby was examined, the baby was dressed back in dry, clean clothes and wrapped in a warm blanket. That took a lot of clothes, so we were constantly begging for clothes, old clothes or used clothes that we would give away.

To me, to have a sick baby and not be able to take it to a doctor would be just about the worst thing I could think of. My husband was sure that some day I was going to arrive home with a sick baby, just because I couldn't find any hospital that would take it. Sometimes a mother, if she found a place like a hospital, any place that would take the baby, the mother would just disappear and you couldn't find her, because she couldn't take care of the baby. Of course, she'd eventually come back. But there I was, or the clinic was, with the care. "What are we going to do with this baby?" the hospital would say. "We said we'd keep it three days or four days. It's free of fever, and we couldn't find its mother." I remember all kinds of problems that we had. But I never did bring one home.

I learned a lot about race in that clinic. I learned a lot that upset the myths I had known. One thing that I remember that impressed me very much in the clinic was that on well-baby days so many more blacks brought their babies than did whites. Just a great majority of the patients on well-baby days would be black, and often the father would bring the baby to the well-baby clinic, a black father. That, to me, was just really very wonderful. You'd hardly ever see a white father there. The white father was working, and the white mother wasn't. The black mother was working, and the black father wasn't. I think that was probably the basic reason. I was so surprised that there were so many more blacks that took advantage of the clinic. And they fed their babies better. They fed their babies pot liquor and vegetables, where poor whites, especially mill people, didn't feed their children well. They fed them soggy white bread, soggy white biscuit with greasy gravy.

One thing that I decided was that many of the black people had learned something about nutrition from working in Miss Anne's kitchen. The white people—we had many mill people, with Scottdale Mill right down the road—were worse off than any blacks I have ever seen anywhere. They were the most malnourished. We had a woman in the clinic in charge of nutrition, and the most malnutrition in the county was in the mill district. And most of them had lung problems because of the lint and so forth in the mills. In the schools, the children didn't get along as well, because they were malnourished, which meant a lot of times that they were low IQ. The blacks were lucky that they weren't white people.

The Scotts were very, so-called, "religious," and they were very active in the Presbyterian church. In fact, I guess they founded the Presbyterian church in Decatur. They had church service every day that the mill people were more or less required to go to. I don't know as they *said* they were required to, but let me tell you, they'd better go. They would have it between the shifts in the afternoon about three o'clock. They would let one shift off fifteen minutes early, then the other shift would have to come fifteen minutes early, so that they got the people from both shifts there for a prayer meeting. Often one of the bigwigs from the Scott family would come down and read the Bible and pray. I went to them once or twice to see what it was like. You know how you have certain pictures in your memory of how a room looked? I remember distinctly the emaciated, unhealthy look on the faces of those white people, with no expression on their faces, completely sad, completely out of it, standing there waiting while Mr. Bigwig gets up there and reads the Bible. I think that was the time when I began to hate the rich. To see what the Scotts did, this leading family in the community, what they did to those people who worked there. It was sinful, very, very sinful.

That was the clinic, and it was in existence for a long time. But we still didn't have any place to send people to the hospital, because back then we didn't have any tie-up with Grady Hospital in Atlanta. We would have to get them in some way or other, by hook or by crook, and maybe find a relative who lived in Atlanta or something, and get them in the hospital when they had to be hospitalized. So we worked through the Hospital Authority, which meant DeKalb County joined in with Fulton County in supporting Grady, and our patients were eligible for Grady. So that was a big, big, big, big day for health care in DeKalb County when we had free hospitalization and free clinics all the time. After that got going well, and people began to go to Grady, then we closed down the clinic.

I came to know the principal of a black school out at Scottdale, Maude Hamilton. I had been going around to tell the schools to go to the clinic. This was just a terrible shack of a school. It had a contaminated well and outdoor privies. But she was quite a woman, I want to tell you what! She knew exactly how to judge you and ask you for a nickel or a hundred dollars, or a sewing machine or a book. She would know exactly, if you came to visit her, what she could get out of you.

Well, one day I went out there, and I said, "I smell something. What are you doing, cooking?"

"We've got a hot lunch program," she said.

I said, "Now, tell me."

She had the first government hot lunch program in DeKalb County. She'd gotten an old stove, she had collected dishes, and the government gave her enough money for all the food and for somebody to prepare it.

"Why," I said, "this is the greatest thing I've ever seen. These kids are getting a meal. Why can't we have it in every school?"

She said, "All you have to do is ask for it, and here's the lady's name."

I said, "We'll call a meeting."

I asked her, if I called the other principals in the county together, would she tell them how she did it. She said she would. In my youth and innocence, I just simply got a list of all the principals in the county and called them to a meeting. I didn't check with the superintendent, just called a meeting. They all came and the room was crowded. I remember that although Mrs. Hamilton was superior to everybody there, in more ways than having a hot lunch program, she couldn't sit in the room with them. She had to sit in the hall while she was waiting for her turn to speak. Things were that segregated.

Mrs. Hamilton told them how she managed it, and all of them were just elated to think that there was something they could do. So we decided that we would ask the federal lady to come the next week to meet with the principals. They all came back, and she told them what they had to do to have free lunches. The schools had to furnish the kitchen.

But where were we going to get the equipment? None of them already had a kitchen. Mr. Kell, the president of the clinic, was there, and he worked for Coca-Cola Company. He stood up and said, "Don't anybody hold back because you don't have a kitchen. You just go down to Beck and Gregg Hardware and buy what you need for the kitchen, charge it to the clinic, and I will see that it's paid for." I just thought he had a gravy train because of Coca-Cola money, and I didn't worry.

It ended up that in six weeks we had hot lunches in every school in the county. Children were getting not only hot lunches but in many schools they were getting breakfast as well. The school attendance just rose enormously. Kids were fed, and everybody was happy.

Mr. Kell came in one day and said, "What are we going to do about paying these bills? We've got twenty-five thousand dollars, it seems to me."

I said, "I thought you had Coca-Cola money for that."

"I haven't got any Coca-Cola money," he said.

Well, I tell you, I spent some sleepless nights. I decided that if I got five thousand people in DeKalb County to give five dollars, we'd have it, and we'd even let them give it on time, like a dollar at a time. We got a little empty storefront up on Decatur square and put up a card table and two chairs, got some volunteers in, and we began to try to raise the money. Well, I learned one thing. If you've got to raise twenty-five thousand dollars, don't try to get five dollars from five thousand people. That ain't the way to raise money! But we started that way.

Then I called a meeting of the preachers to talk about the poor hungry people. Three came. One talked against it, said that we were just making people dependent. One said he was in favor of it. One didn't say much. They didn't go back and do anything in their churches about it, not any of them. So we called a luncheon at the Candler Hotel for the businessmen. They turned out for the free lunch. We asked the preacher that was on our side to come and say the blessing, and he didn't show. So I would say the help we got from the church on feeding the poor in DeKalb County was absolutely nil.

I was still very active in the church at this time. I made a speech at our church about it and got severe criticism, was called a communist, and so forth. After my mother's death, I used to go to church religiously. I thought I should, because she was interested. But I never really did get at all involved. My mother had been president of the Woman's Missionary Society, and they had given me a silver bowl when I got married. I used to hate to go to their meetings, because I thought it was such a waste of time. One day my neighborhood friends were all out nursing the babies in the front yard, and I said, "I have to go to the circle meeting."

They said, "Well, look, Frances, don't you really think that you've paid for that silver bowl?"

That just brought me to my senses, and I quit going.

Overall, the luncheon went over pretty well. The businessmen began to give some money, and we raised about half the money. One day the superintendent called me to come to his office. I knew him real well because he had been principal of the high school when I was in school. He said, "I just think this is such a wonderful thing. These children are coming to school. They are being fed. Their attendance is so much better. We are getting so much more money from the state." They got money from the state according to attendance. So the school system took over the other half of the indebtedness. And he offered me a job to boot! I couldn't imagine doing any more than I was doing, because I already had my husband and my father and my brother and my two children and two dogs and three cats. If I cooked and I sewed and I kept house for them, that was all I could do. So I didn't take the job.

That's how DeKalb County started its hot lunch program. I think the main thing about getting things done is—and I think I still have a tendency to do the same thing—if you see something that needs to be done, just go ahead and start. I think that's the first lesson in organizing. Don't sit around until you get everything on paper. Just go ahead and do it. But then be prepared to swim to shore.

My father and husband were supportive of me in all of this. I remember one time we were riding out in the country one Saturday afternoon. I said, "Look, none of these houses have screens." We had a lot more flies then, before DDT. And my father said, "Oh, my God, she's now deciding that everybody in DeKalb County's got to have screens!" But I didn't.

In terms of my family, I always had a few real guidelines. I was always home, unless it was something very unusual, when the kids came from school. I felt that when they opened the door and said, "Mama," Mama wanted to say, "Come in." I think that's so important. I used to have friends that would stay home all morning and clean up the house and do all that, and then about time for the kids to come home, they'd go out to a bridge game or something. The kids would come home to an empty house. It usually ended up that they'd be over in our yard. My father used to say I ran a free kindergarten. I more or less did; I was glad to be able to. We did have a big yard and lots of things for kids to play with. There wasn't anyplace else that they seemed to want to go.

I planned to spend the most time possible with my kids. I think it pays off. Children are home such a short time. I worry when people feel like they have to be away from their children. I regret it for their sake. Right now, I think a couple would have to have one car, and they'd have to have a lot less clothes, and they'd have to have a lot less things in the house, but they could just live on what the husband could make and take care of the babies as long as they are babies. Then they could start to do something outside.

When my daughters were babies, I would hire somebody to clean the house and I took care of the children. Most of my friends hired somebody to wheel the baby up and down the street. That was the thing to do in those days, to have a nursemaid for your child. Even during the Depression, it was always possible for me to have a little bit of help. You could get help so cheap, because somebody would be happy to work for you in order just to eat. Food was very, very cheap, so I never worried about how much food they had, or if they took home a bit of food. I was just glad that I could help them feed their family. I always worried that I wasn't paying enough, but I always paid as much as they possibly could get somewhere else. I was glad I could give them that much, because it was so hard for them to get any kind of a job. When I didn't have enough money to have hardly any hired help at all, I'd have somebody come in at four o'clock in the afternoon and cook dinner at night. That way I was free to take care of my babies, see that my babies were fed and bathed and put to bed. Then all of us could have a good adult meal.

The household was my entire responsibility. That was women's work. I'm still surprised when I see men cook and wash dishes and babysit. I would have felt funny to have Bill waiting on Papa. Papa wasn't his responsibility. Housework wasn't man's work, just like I never mowed the lawn or worked in the garden, except to grow a few flowers here or there. The whole society was regimented as far as what men did and women did.

When World War II came, it had an effect on everybody, just from the rationing of food. The children used to get a great kick out of the food rationing. One of them would go and get in the line early, the meat line, and then the other one would go and relieve her. Between the two children and me, we could maybe get some meat. When we were victorious and got any old piece of meat—it wouldn't matter much what kind, we certainly weren't picky about what piece of meat we got—everybody was happy.

We were always entertaining some of the soldiers. We started out with some that we knew, and then we'd get to know others and others. We used to save our sugar rationing so we'd have some sweet things to have when we would have some of the soldiers there on the weekend. All of the food rationing was difficult, but we certainly had enough.

We had Camp Gordon, a big camp nearby, and I volunteered with the Red Cross as a Gray Lady. In the war years, my primary activity was in the Red Cross. I was in the one of the first classes trained for this big army hospital. I remember in the Battle of the Bulge, they were shipping people directly from the battlefield by airplane right into our hospital. We got them that quickly from the front.

That was a very difficult job. I wrote many, many letters and made telephone calls to mothers and wives, saying that their son was back in the States. Maybe he had lost his leg or lost his arm, because I remember we had so many amputees. We'd have a whole ward with both legs off, a whole ward with one leg off. They'd even have them classified in the hospital that way. I certainly came to realize how terrible it was for a young, able-bodied man to lose a limb.

They had one ward where everybody was going to die. That was so terrible, because as soon as somebody got put on the ward, they knew they had no chance to live, because they knew that that was the ward where everybody died. I was assigned there for a long time. Boy, that was a hard ward to work on.

There was a guy in the hospital that everybody called Frenchie, a Cajun from south Louisiana, who had always made his living hunting and fishing. Now in the war he lost both legs. What a terrible thing, especially for a young man who had spent all of his time out in the woods. So I spent as much time as I could with Frenchie. One day he said, "I want to learn to read English."

I said, "Sure, sure, I can teach you to read." So I went down to the Red Cross and got some simple reading books.

When I went back to the ward, I had to wonder how I was going to do this, since I was only there one day a week. There were a couple of old sergeants who were as grumpy as any storybook sergeant, and I went to them and said, "We've got to teach Frenchie to read."

They said, "Yeah, yeah, Frenchie can learn to read."

So every week, I'd make the assignments and the sergeants would make sure Frenchie did his homework. You just can't imagine what it did for the ward. Everybody got interested in helping Frenchie learn to read, and of course Frenchie did learn to read. And Frenchie learned to write too.

Everything was going along just fine until one day I went to the hospital and somebody said, "The Colonel wants to see you." Now I had left home that morning in a real hurry and my uniform had a hole under the arm. I didn't have time to fix it, and there I was. So all I could think about was, "Will he notice this hole in my uniform under my arm?" So I thought to myself, "Keep your arm down, keep your arm down, and try to behave like a lady."

I went in and he said that everybody knew about Frenchie learning to read, and he wanted to know what method I had used to teach him to read. Well, I didn't know there *were* methods for teaching, and I had no idea what to say to him. I don't know how I got out of that meeting, but as far as I know, he never did find out that I had a hole in my uniform.

I think the reason that Frenchie learned to read was because we all believed that he could read. If we hadn't, I wouldn't have bothered to find the books and persuade the sergeants to help. Frenchie really didn't seem all that bright, and he could hardly speak English. But because we believed, he learned and he learned fast. He taught many of us a whole lot.

3 "I wasn't going to belong to anything that was all white": Democracy and Desegregation

After World War II, Frances's interest in politics grew, taking her into some of the hottest political battles of the 1940s and 1950s in Georgia. Through the League of Women Voters, one of the few ways for women to effect political change during this period, Frances worked to make Georgia politics more representative and democratic. Her first challenge was the county unit system. The state's unique and notoriously antidemocratic means of apportioning votes guaranteed that the votes of rural Georgians carried more weight than the votes of their urban counterparts. Under this regime, two Talmadge governors, father Eugene and son Herman, held sway in Georgia politics for many years, so much so that Georgians divided into Talmadge and anti-Talmadge factions within the Democratic party. Frances aligned herself with the anti-Talmadge forces, which included politically active African Americans, the more progressive elements of the labor movement, and white liberals. The onset of the National Association for the Advancement of Colored People's (NAACP) legal challenge to racial segregation, culminating in the Brown v. Board of Education *decision of 1954, which outlawed segregation in education, took Frances squarely into campaigns for racial justice.*

In the 1950s, as now, the politics of race were often divisive and heated. Candidates for public office hurled racist invective and vowed to resist desegregation to the bitter end. Governor Ernest Vandiver, who eventually oversaw the desegregation of Georgia's public schools, vowed that "not one" black child would sit next to a white child in a Georgia classroom. In such a charged climate, Frances counted her allies few and far between. "It took somebody with a lot of stamina to stand up in a little town where everybody knew you and nobody liked what you were doing." Yet that is precisely what Frances and her colleagues from the League of Women Voters tried to do—sway public opinion toward accepting change in the racial status quo. Desegregation also had a profoundly personal meaning, as Frances came to see that she "hadn't really known black people." Having grown up under segregation and white privilege, she found that lessons had to be learned, often painfully.

Bylaws of the League of Women Voters of DeKalb County,
adopted November 6, 1947
Purpose: The purpose of the League of Women Voters of DeKalb Co.
shall be to promote political responsibility through informed and active
participation of citizens in government.
Policy: The League of Women Voters of DeKalb Co. may take action on
local governmental measures and policies in the public interest in confor-
mity with the Platform of the League of Women Voters of the U.S. and the
League of Women Voters of Georgia. It shall not support or oppose any
political party or candidate.
Membership: Voting members shall be women citizens of voting age.

Around World War II, I became involved with the League of Women Voters. I was interested in politics, and the league was one of the few ways
that women could work. All the different things that we tried to do, like
the clinic and the school lunch program, so much really depended on the
government, and maybe the league could influence the government. But
we didn't have a League of Women Voters in DeKalb County, and it kept
bothering me that Atlanta had all of these things and DeKalb County
didn't. So two or three of the women who worked in the Atlanta league
and lived in DeKalb County decided to organize a separate league. I
joined and became the local president soon after the war. We grew real
fast and we had a real good league.

Josephine Heyman was the first president of the DeKalb league. She
was one of the better leaders, but she wanted to get out of it. She was
facing a lot of pressure, a lot of anti-Semitic feeling in Decatur. I remember her sitting and talking with me, trying to persuade me to take the
presidency. Finally she said, "It's going to be a real easy year. The election is over and there's not anything big coming up." And that was 1947,
the year that we had three governors, three people who claimed they
were governor.

Eugene Talmadge was elected, but there was also a bit of a write-in
vote, although we didn't know this until later. People had written in Herman Talmadge. Little did we know that Eugene Talmadge was dying.
And he died between the time he was elected and the time he was to
become governor. Then we had three people claim to be governor; the different ones who had run. One was Herman, from the write-in vote.
According to the law, the election was thrown into the House of Representatives, and the House had to decide. Needless to say, Herman was
elected by a great margin. I will never forget that day, when Herman and
his boys came winding into the capitol with much noise and confusion

and took the governor's office. It made us realize some of the bad things about our political system. But all the league could do was observe everything that was going on and report it. There wasn't any action that we could take.

One of the first things I did was to be a monitor at the legislature. We watched and recorded what happened at the capitol. At that time they didn't have electronic voting. You couldn't go down to the clerk's office and get a copy of the bill and the roll call votes. To get a roll call vote you would have to get permission to read the journal, and to get permission to read the journal was kind of like getting in Heaven. The only way you could do it was to hear it when it was read. We used to hang over the upstairs edge of the balcony to look and see how people voted and mark it down. We had to do a lot of the stuff that now you can just walk into a clerk's office and get. It was a lot more difficult. It was also a lot more important to the public for the league to work in the legislature, because things weren't made public as much.

One of the missions that we had in the league was to get the facts out—how was the government run, what was happening, just the plain nitty-gritty facts. Then, of course, as time proceeded, we tried to influence their way of thinking. We would put pressure on the right places and influence the leagues over the state to influence their men back home. At one time we got out a weekly newsletter during the legislative session, and we would tell the local leagues what had happened and what to say to their men. That had to be done very quickly, if it was going to be of any use.

I still think the league is one of the greatest training grounds for young people, because it teaches you, first, to do your homework and know what you're doing and be intelligent about it, and then it teaches you to go on and step out there and get it done. For the young women that come to the legislature as league observers, it's a good way to get started in the legislature, to really learn how the wheels go 'round.

I think we did a pretty good job for a bunch of volunteers. The leadership in the 1940s was very sophisticated leadership. They knew many of the legislators and they knew many of the people in power. I think they personally had influence through the power structure of the state and the business of the state. Their husbands could meet on the golf courses and in the Capital City Club with the people in power and really wield some influence. Some of it was through their husbands, but I think some of it was through the women.

The league now doesn't do anywhere near as much as we did. They can't now, because so much of the leadership works. The women who were the league leaders in my day would now have a good job for pay. I'm sure I would have had a career. Sometimes my volunteer work was as much as a full-time job, a forty-hour week. The league gave women a chance to do something that took a lot of intelligence and a lot of know-how, rather than just to be sure that they had the latest salad mixed up and the prettiest candles on the table for dinner. And these women had the very best education—the big eastern schools, Smith and Vassar—and they were very smart. Most of them were well-to-do, because they at least had enough money that they had good servants at home so that they could go to the league office and stay all day.

But the men didn't like us, called us the "Leg of Women Voters." They were making fun of us, as I imagine they did even more with the early suffragists. We took a lot of ridicule from men, mainly because we were women. They didn't like us meddling in their business. The League of Women Voters at that time was way out in Georgia, compared to other organizations. It wasn't way out nationally, but relative to Georgia, it was way out. But I think they respected us, and I would rather have that than most anything else. I think that was because we did always try to have our facts correct, and we knew we'd better. Still, they didn't admire us like some other women who visited the legislature. I was in the halls once and some women came—they weren't league women at all—and they had on little fancy aprons and they brought cookies. They were giving cookies to the men and acting so simpering. I finally said to one of them, "You make me ashamed to be a woman," and she said, "I'm not a woman, I'm a lady." That was in the halls of the legislature!

At that time, the league was very strong on a national level. You had a group of women on the national level who were extremely well educated, and they had a social consciousness. They were marvelous leaders. Anna Lord Strauss was one of the presidents that I thought so much of. She and I got to be very good friends, and we kept up our friendship until her death. During this time, the tendency on the national level was for the league to stretch out. Anna Lord Strauss had been elected from the floor in 1944. She was nominated from the floor because she thought that the league ought to open up to more people. When she was elected, the staff and a lot of the old board members walked out. Percy Maxim Lee followed her as president of the national league, but she also had the same idea that the league should be open. There they were, those two very wealthy women, and they were very different, in their philosophy, from the wealthy women who ran the Atlanta league.

That same feeling got into our state league. So we decided, some of us lower-echelon, just old common folk, that we would run somebody from outside of Atlanta. The Atlanta league women had always run the Georgia league and the Atlanta league out of the same office. We felt, as I remember it, that they were a little snooty. They thought they knew better than anybody else, particularly that they knew more than anybody out there in the state. They felt that everybody in the state was still barefoot, and they didn't realize that there were other people with just as much education living in other towns in the state. They just felt very superior, and Atlantans still do. Atlanta still thinks it's superior to the rest of us. But we were trying so hard to spread the league, to have the league encompass everyone, not just the elite.

So we ran Johnnie Hilbun from Augusta. Johnnie was just entirely a different kind of person from these highly educated, married women with a lot of time on their hands. Johnnie was a single woman, a businesswoman; she sold insurance. They didn't like that, but we ran Johnnie and Johnnie got elected. She became president in 1948. Then there was a problem, because here they had this high-powered office without any staff, except a secretary. Johnnie wasn't going to have the time to put into running it that these smart women had. So she said she was going to have two vice-chairmen. One was me and one was Louisa Gosnell. She called us her "two vices." Louisa and I were good friends; both of us were math majors at Agnes Scott. We did the day-to-day running of the league, but Johnnie was a very active president. That was kind of a breakthrough for the league, because the state league had always been the same leadership as the Atlanta league.

Louisa and I gave a lot of services to local leagues from the state level. Johnnie pushed organization, and Louisa and I liked to organize. We organized a bunch of local leagues during this time. I used to say that I'd get three people that wanted it, and then I'd go. I'd go down and sit down with them and let them find the rest, and then we'd get a group big enough together to organize. After they'd organize, we figured a way to meet with them and babysit them for a length of time. We had a manual on how to train the board and a manual about how to carry out the program.

I liked politics, and I really did want to run for the legislature. I just thought it would be more fun to be in the legislature than anything. So I decided if we could get twenty people to run for the legislature, ten of us could get elected—maybe. We could have joint fundraising, we could have our own smoke-filled room. Well, nobody but Johnnie ever said they'd run. Never could get twenty to run, never could get ten to run. The time just hadn't come when people were ready for a woman to run or to give them any money to run. Money was a big factor in it. The women that had money were not the women that wanted to run. We should have pushed on a little harder, taking more of a stand. But you had your life to live, and that was just your little extracurricular. You still got home in time to see that the family was looked after properly. Because it was not the day when a husband would go home to cook the dinner because the wife was busy that night.

As my daughters got older, I still had my rule to be home when they got back from school. Often that was the time of day nobody else was there, and that was the time that things spilled over, that they told me things that had happened. These were the most meaningful conversations. And as they went through high school this became even more important. When they were little ones, they would go outdoors and play. I don't think I mattered to them as much as in high school. Also both Joan and Marylin were interested in dancing, and they danced with the Atlanta Civic Ballet. Consequently, a lot of my time was taken up with chauffeuring, and I worked with the costumes, which was fun, because I liked theater.

It was during my time with the league that we integrated. We took "white"—the clause restricting membership to white women—out of the DeKalb County bylaws first, in 1947. I found "white" in the bylaws, which I didn't know had been in there, and I said, "Now at the next convention, it comes out. How shall we do it?" I was kind of underhanded in the way I did it. We decided we would rewrite the bylaws; they needed it badly. They were in bad shape, not just in that way, but other things too. So we sent the new bylaws out to the leagues and said, "You have your old bylaws. You can compare these." We didn't put them down side-by-side—saying, this is the old, this is the new, which was usually the way we did it—because it would call people's attention to the change. I don't mean that we hid it, but we didn't try to advertise it. Still, the majority of people knew what was happening, and the new bylaws were accepted.

Then we worked on the state level. We lost some people. One or two leagues that were weak folded. On the question of segregation, I think we lost the Thomasville group. One of the big shots in that league financed it heavily, and she was a real segregationist. That one folded. But new members came in, a growth of new people. A lot of people like to join something if it's doing something. So we got good people in the league. Years later, when I was in the Georgia Council on Human Relations, I went to Rome, Georgia, and went to a League of Women Voters meeting, and there were ten whites and five blacks there. It was the greatest thrill.

The real problem was in the Atlanta league. Atlanta had the biggest fight and they split in 1956. The original elitist group were the ones that were the segregationists. And we had upset them earlier by removing them from leadership on the state level. They just wanted to keep the league as their own private club. They were just as opposed to the labor unions and the working person as they were to somebody who was black. Really elitist, more I think than racist. That was one thing that we were fighting all along in the league, as well as fighting racism. It was really to make the league a democratic organization.

Political Circulars: League of Women Voters of Georgia

KEEP OUR GENERAL ELECTIONS FREE
VOTE AGAINST CONSTITUTIONAL AMENDMENT NO. 1 WHICH
WOULD EXTEND THE COUNTY UNIT SYTEM

For more than one hundred and twenty-five years election by straight popular vote of our Governor and other state officers has been part of our Constitution and part of our tradition. Don't destroy this tradition by replacing, in effect, the popular vote system with the county unit system!

GEORGIA VOTER
August, 1952

AN OPEN LETTER
AN URGENT PLEA
TO THE RESPONSIBLE LEADERSHIP OF GEORGIA

We call on political leaders and candidates for public office in the State of Georgia to see that their political campaigns are free from appeals to racial and religious prejudice.

We respectfully urge the newspaper editors and publishers of Georgia to decline any political advertisement which makes such an appeal to intolerance.

And further we ask the managers of radio and television stations of Georgia to do everything within their power to discourage any such violation of the basic principles of this State and this Nation.

League of Women Voters of Georgia
Mrs. William C. Pauley, President
1954

what's the price tag
on amendment no. 4?

$122,000,000⁰⁰

That is the Amount Spent in 1954 for the Public School System of Georgia.

DON'T GIVE IT AWAY TO PRIVATE HANDS!

vote *against*
amendment no. 4
nov. 2

georgia league of women voters

Informational leaflet produced by the Georgia League of Women Voters in its campaign against the private school amendment.
(Courtesy of Frances Freeborn Pauley Papers, Special Collections Department, Robert W. Woodruff Library, Emory University.)

THE PRIVATE SCHOOL AMENDMENT

On November 2 citizens of Georgia will vote on a proposed constitutional amendment which reads: "Notwithstanding any other provision of this Constitution, the General Assembly may by law provide for grants of State, county or municipal funds to citizens of the State for educational purposes, in discharge of all obligations of the State to provide adequate education for its citizens."

THE LEAGUE OF WOMEN VOTERS OF GEORGIA IS OPPOSED TO THIS AMENDMENT AND URGES ALL VOTERS TO VOTE AGAINST IT. IN ORDER TO MAINTAIN PUBLIC SCHOOLS, WE MUST DEFEAT AMENDMENT NUMBER 4!

GEORGIA VOTER
October, 1954

I became state president of the League of Women Voters at a very fascinating time in Georgia politics. I was always kind of lucky at being in certain places at the right time. This was the time we organized to fight the county unit amendment, and we won in 1952, defeated a constitutional amendment to put the county unit into the state constitution.[1]

Probably the county unit system was fair when it was first set up, because it was set up with so many votes for each county, like the electoral college. But then as the state became more urbanized, it meant that all the cities were losing their vote. One vote in Echols County would be like twenty votes in Fulton County, and it had gotten to be way too lopsided. Of course the legislature didn't want to change it, because those men from the rural areas were running the state. So Herman Talmadge, the governor, wanted to get it written into the constitution so it would be harder to get rid of. But to write it into the constitution demanded a popular vote. What we did was organize as much as we could in every single county in the state to influence the vote against it.

The league played a key role in the county unit fight. Our whole government was very undemocratic, which made it a real league item. The

---

[1] Editor's note: The county unit system was in essence an indirect system of election. Each of the state's 159 counties was assigned two, four, or six unit votes, depending on its population; the eight largest counties had six unit votes, the next thirty carried four, and the remaining counties had two votes each. Victory went to the candidate who amassed the most unit votes, rather than the largest popular vote. The practical impact of the system was to assign greater weight to the rural counties, relative to urban areas, in determining the outcome of an election.

county unit system was absolutely against the league's philosophy. Just counting "one man, one vote" was the appeal in defeating the county unit. And it was really in metropolitan areas where we had leagues and therefore people who were very much opposed to the county unit system. We didn't have leagues in towns where they had only two thousand people in the whole county. But we did in Columbus and Macon and Atlanta, the larger places.

We formed a coalition of organizations. Citizens Against the County Unit Amendment was the name of it. Our slogan was "Strike One" since it was amendment number one. We had a steering committee made up of various organizations and the league. It was interracial, but white dominated. Morris Abram, a young lawyer here in Atlanta at the time, was the most vocal leader. We had Judge Neil Andrews, a federal judge up in the northern part of the state, as chairman; Grace Hamilton from the Atlanta Urban League; Art Levin from the Anti-Defamation League; Ida Patterson from Churchwomen United; Harold Fleming from the Southern Regional Council; and someone from the political action committee of the Congress of Industrial Organizations. It was the first time in anybody's knowledge that we had blacks and whites, Jews and Gentiles, and church women and labor, all sitting down in one tight, close committee. John Greer worked with us from south Georgia. He had been in the legislature, and he knew the nuts and bolts. We used the League of Women Voters office as headquarters until we outgrew it. I learned how to work politically with a lot of organizations at that time.

We raised fifteen thousand dollars for the "Strike One" campaign. All of these groups involved couldn't decide what they were going to do about the money, because nobody trusted each other—and I mean nobody! Finally they decided that the only trustworthy group was the league. That's one thing, the league has always kept its skirts clean. So I ended up the treasurer. And I'm telling you, that's when I learned about how money is passed around. I remember one night I got a call, someone told me if I'd come down after dark on such and such a corner, they'd give me a packet. I went down and got back and opened up the envelope and there was two thousand dollars in it. I nearly dropped dead. I don't know who gave that, and I didn't want to know. It was much better that I not know.

Mayor Hartsfield, the mayor of Atlanta, helped us behind the scenes. I think that he helped us raise some of the fifteen thousand dollars, but I couldn't say that for sure. I don't have any way to prove that, except that he was always openly calling to do away with the county unit system. Any city of any size certainly wanted to have a larger voice in the legislature.

We never met twice in the same place, because the Talmadge group put so much pressure on us. Said we were the anti-segregation, pro–civil rights crowd who seek to destroy the county unit system. I used to say we had two parties in Georgia, and our parties were Talmadge and anti-Talmadge. Oh, the problems we had with the Talmadges. The Talmadge family didn't do this state any good. It was a nasty, nasty fight, because it turned into just being racial. They made you feel like you were going to lose your job or they would do you in some way. Nobody ever got hurt, but you had all these threats. Anybody that was a little bit scared would have left. That's why the money was given anonymously a lot of the time.

I remember the excitement and the pressure. It was the first time I had just worked day and night without making the bed, without doing anything, just putting my whole self into it. We just simply had to win, and we did, but by a hair. I always treasured this compliment: Governor Herman Talmadge said afterwards, "I could have won that thing, if it hadn't been for that god-damned Frances Pauley!"

All this racism about the county unit, and we had a terribly, terribly racist race for governor in 1954. That summer I believe that racism and bigotry was at its height politically. And in the league we thought, "What can we do?" We came up with a tolerance pledge, a pledge not to appeal to racism and religious prejudice in the campaign. We printed it up, blew it up 'til it was seven feet long or five feet long. Some of the leading, most acceptable League of Women Voters people took it to the governor, which of course made for a beautiful presentation. We fixed the telegram so that you could take really good pictures of it, and we got excellent publicity. Then we took that and sent it to everyone who was running for office that year and asked them to sign it. Then we published the names in the paper of people that had signed it. I don't know that it had any great impact at all, but we just felt like it was something we had to do. We did every trick we could think of to try to influence some of the positive factors.

Now, meanwhile, school desegregation also started heating up. In 1953, in November, Talmadge saw the handwriting on the wall. He got the legislature to pass a resolution for a constitutional amendment to do away with public schools and have the state give money for private schools. In fact, even a year before that they began to make state money available to build black schools. They saw what was coming, so they had really been putting money in, to do everything they could to keep segregation.

The league took a stand against this. In April 1954, the league had its convention, and after a very heated debate, we took a stand for public schools, which really meant integrated schools. The league was pretty consolidated on it, but I don't think many people really felt like desegregation was ever going to come. But some of us knew it would, eventually. On May the 17th came the *Brown* decision from the Supreme Court. After the decision, I visited every league in the state, and the leagues were with us. They weren't with us like they had been on the county unit—within the league there were people who didn't want to work on this—but the league stayed together and fought on.

We hadn't yet voted in Georgia on the private school amendment. We had to vote the following November. So then we tried to get various organizations together. I said, "This will be easy. We'll do it like we did county unit. It'll be fun to get together and fun to work on something else." I thought I had learned something from the county unit fight that would help me, and I thought a lot of the county unit people would be with us. But they weren't. There were certain people that felt one way about county unit and a different way about school desegregation. So it meant a new organization. I found out that's true of anything. A few people in it might move on, or you might pick up some new people that you know, but as far as the group as a whole, it doesn't move. I think that's why there's no use carrying grudges. This one's going to be with you this time and against you another time.

It was a whole different set of people that believed in public education. With the county unit, there was a lot of real personal political interest in it. The cities wanted more representation for their area. Also, the county unit was more governmental philosophy. It wasn't altogether a matter of black/white, because it was "one man, one vote." You didn't have that with the private school amendment. When it came down to that amendment, that was nothing but a race issue. This got down to who was going to sit next to my darling little child. People's deep prejudices, I guess, were beginning to come out. I think it was just a real basic black prejudice that some people had that maybe they'd been taught as children. I don't know why they had it, but I think it was just a matter of prejudice. There's not any rules and regulations about prejudice; it's not logical.

Much earlier, the first league meeting that I remember going to, a state meeting in the early 1940s, I was shocked because they thought they had done something in taking a stand against the white primary.[2] I just didn't think there was anybody living that wasn't against the white primary. But it *was* a big deal. I just didn't realize it at the time. I didn't realize the depth of the racism. I remember a lady from Statesboro saying to me, "I don't feel about Negroes like most people do." She said, "I think they're human." And I couldn't even answer.

---

[2] Editor's note: The white primary, as its name suggests, was a method of disfranchising black voters in the South by limiting participation in primary elections to white voters. As the South was heavily Democratic, the primary election was often the only election of any consequence. The white primary became a common practice across the South in the early twentieth century and was ruled unconstitutional by the U.S. Supreme Court in 1944.

Basically, a lot of people in Georgia didn't believe in public education. We didn't even have public education for a long time after everybody else in the United States did, because the South didn't believe in public education. The Minimum Education Foundation Program of the early 1950s was the first time that the state put a bunch of money in public schools. Before that, there'd been local control and local funding. Of course, the league had worked hard on that too.

But the league fought on. One time all the leaders—most of them were women—that were working on the fight against the private school amendment got telegrams from Governor Talmadge. He asked us to meet in the capitol and to give our plans for how we could keep segregated schools. That's what the telegram said. So we got together, heads of statewide organizations, like the league and also United Church Women, and decided to write one statement, that we were against the amendment and in favor of public schools, and we signed it.

Statement on the *Brown* decision
June 25, 1954

We come before the Georgia Education Commission at the suggestion of the Governor to present our views toward a sound and democratic course of action in response to the Supreme Court's recent decision on segregation in the public schools. We wish to propose a way of proceeding whereby a practical plan can be developed with the full participation of every community in the state . . .

Support of the public school system in Georgia is our objective.

Public education is a state responsibility under the Georgia Constitution (Art. VIII, Sec. I). However, the Georgia Constitution clearly states that the United States Constitution shall be supreme (Art. XII, Sec. I). All state officials are sworn to uphold the Constitutions of our nation and State, both of which declare the supremacy of the United States Constitution.

As law-abiding organizations, we will gladly take part in planning how Georgia may best meet its responsibilities consistent with the highest law of the land . . .

We do not underestimate the problems we face in Georgia in the light of the Supreme Court's decision. But there is every prospect that a generous amount of time will be allowed for adjustment. We have faith that the people of both races will find workable solutions within the framework of the United States Constitution and a public school system. It is the obligation of state leadership to make that possible.

We decided that Margaret MacDougall, of United Church Women, would give the statement at the meeting. We chose her because she's so sweet and such a lady. She gave the statement, and then they called each one of us presidents to answer questions. They did everything they could to frighten and intimidate us, asked us nasty questions and were insulting.

I was the last one to be questioned. It was a very hot day and the capitol was not air-conditioned at that time, and I was dressed in navy blue trimmed with white, and white gloves, white shoes, and white hat. I went forth very sedately. I was called, and Talmadge's lawyer, named Buck Murphy, started questioning me, and he questioned and questioned. One of his first questions was, "I suppose you want your daughter to marry a 'nigger'?" That was the tone of the interview. I was determined they weren't going to get the best of me. I stood there, and I can remember how hot I was, and I can remember how I felt the perspiration trickle down, and I was wondering if it was dropping on the floor, and I had this vision of a pool of water because I was that hot. The day was so hot and then the questions were so hot.

Talmadge picked up and asked meaner questions. He already knew me and hated me from the county unit fight. They would go back and forth, and finally they gave out of questions and I still stood there. Finally at the end I said, "And, gentlemen, are there any other questions?" That took all I had. That took everything I had to ask that. I was so scared they'd have another question, and I was just simply done in. But I was always so proud of myself for being able to just stand up there, because they had the church women and the different people that had been on our side, and they had just practically made them dissolve in tears, and sit down one after another. I just was determined they weren't going to do me that way, and they didn't. Oh, my, it took me days to get over that.

The Parent Teacher Association (PTA) was so frightened at that meeting that they dropped out. We lost PTA support, and we really had counted on having PTA support. As I remember, the league worked alone rather than as a wide coalition. We worked mainly to get good publicity through the papers. We didn't get as good as we had with the county unit fight, but we got some. In the end, we lost in November in the general election. But we lost by a very small, very small number. I still think if the votes had been counted right, we would have won.

There were so many things that were so hard at this time. The whole subject of welfare came up, and we adopted a welfare item in the league program. We had a big fight in the league about whether we should work on public welfare. There were just as many people opposed to welfare then as there are now. Because even then the black/white issue came in, whether or not they're going to give black people enough money to live on.

I went to see the head of welfare for the state, Alan Kemper, after I was president of the league, to tell him that we were going to work on welfare. The league's welfare chairman was with me. While we were sitting in the office waiting to see him, his secretary said to us, "I wish you all would do something about keeping the poor people from coming up here and asking us for help. Why don't you tell them where they're supposed to go. I just think maybe Hitler was right. We ought to make soap of them." When we left and got out in the hall we stood there and said, "Did that woman say that? Surely I heard wrong, she couldn't have said it." When we went into the office, Kemper didn't stand up. He stayed sitting behind his desk with his feet up on it. He said, "Ya'll think ya'll gonna get me fired, don't ya?"

We said, "No, Mr. Kemper, we don't."

He said, "I just want to tell you that Herman Talmadge is my best friend." That was welfare, that was the head of welfare.

Still, what we did on the state level on welfare was exceedingly important. I think we did a lot of basic education that needed to be done at that time. And I learned more organizational skills from the league than I would have ever had the chance to learn anywhere else. I was really plain lucky that I was president of the league at a time when so many interesting things were going on. A lot of times not that much is cooking.

When I finished my term as state president, many of the leagues nominated me for the national board, but I was not elected. That hurt me, because I felt like I had done an outstanding job. It had been a very difficult situation. I knew I had made a lot of mistakes, but I felt like the league had grown so much. Just in numbers, numbers of leagues and numbers of members and its recognition. It just kind of hurt me that they didn't elect me to the national board. But I've always been so glad, because I did get so involved in civil rights. I think that was much more meaningful to me.

Letter
Mid-1960s

Dearest Children,

You have met Mrs Mays--she has been a great help to me. She sees through me--and she says--you have to learn to laugh. I first thought--you are an actor--you were always the fool or the comic in your years with college and amateur theatricals--you can laugh. I did one night when she was present--she was glad--but she didn't know I hadn't learned to laugh. It was still an act. Then I began to learn--and I found laughter is the greatest relief in the whole wide world. Crying is a relief too. But then you have a head ache--and your eyes burn--and you have made people unhappy. Laughter gives the same relief and no one suffers--in fact they relax and maybe laugh too.

Isn't that funny? Because I thought this was true when I was leaving college--I thought this in a very stupid superficial way. And I went to see one of the highest--I guess liberal--anyway--he was the highest on my estimation--and I said, "I really want to enter a field of service--I can make people laugh. Here are my credentials--isn't there somewhere in the church where I could serve??" He told me no. That anything that was connected with the kinds of things I had done were evil in the eyes of the church. He then--very nearly wept with me--and told me I better seek to serve outside the church.

Oh well--I have always tried to be of service. But I am sensitive about this. Because the Negroes have shown me how awful paternalism is--so I hesitate to say--or think--that I want to be of service. But anyway I still do.

If it is paternalism--so be it. I hate it. I sure hate the people that look down on me--but can't you help with--and not for--I would like to work shoulder to shoulder. I know I am in a superior position because I am white. But that makes me feel inferior. I know I have hated my white skin many times. I could go--and maybe help work--if only I weren't white.

It is a fascinating world--and I am so thankful I can live in it and do a few things that I enjoy.

Love,
Mother

I had made a resolve within myself in 1954 that I was not going to belong to, give my efforts to, give my money to, or support in any way anything that was segregated. That's what I believed, and I decided that I'd better live up to it. I thought the only issue of importance in the state for the near future was desegregation. So we dropped our membership at Druid Hills Country Club, and that was bad because we lived across the street and it was easy to take guests over there to eat. It meant I'd have to cook more. But my cooking didn't improve much, I'm afraid! I already wasn't going to the Methodist church in Decatur anymore.

I also realized how little I knew. I had been on the board of the Atlanta Urban League. I had been on different committees with blacks in different health organizations. But I hadn't really known black people. All I knew was the cook and the yardman and what they told me. I didn't know much about poor black people; I didn't really know the problems. I decided that I had to learn, so every time I'd see in the paper that there was something over at Atlanta University, I'd go to it. And it didn't take long to make friends. If you're white in a black group, you stand out.

There's a funny story about my going to commencement at one of the colleges at Atlanta University. My husband Bill was parking the car, and I had gone up and was waiting for him to come. I was standing behind all the chairs and it was outdoors. Well, before Bill came, here came the procession. When they got to me, the president was leading the line, and he recognized me, so he bowed. I bowed back. The man behind him thought I was bowing to him, so he bowed, and I bowed. Mrs. Eleanor Roosevelt was the speaker that day, so she's coming along third in the line, and she thinks I'm bowing to her, so she bowed. I felt like two cents, bowing with everybody, but there never was a time I could stop.

So many pictures of Mrs. Roosevelt make her look ugly, but I want to tell you, when she smiled she had almost the most beautiful face I ever saw. I wouldn't take anything for having seen her that far away, bowing. It's a wonderful remembrance I have.

I think Mrs. Mays, Sadie Mays, taught me the most of anybody, because she was blunt about it, and liked me enough that she didn't mind telling me. She was the wife of the president of Morehouse College, Benjamin Mays. I remember that she was the one who first corrected me when I said, "Nigra." She said, "Now listen—Negro." That's when "Negro" was the word to use. Not many people would correct a white person, and that was wonderful to have a friend like that because it meant well for my education. She never minced words. Benjamin Mays and my husband also liked each other, so I remember a good many social occasions when we would gather. Mrs. Mays would worry about me. I remember one time, she said I was taking it all too seriously, that I had to laugh more. She called me out to her house to give me this little lecture. Then, not long after that, I saw a little motto that was framed, and I bought it and gave it to her. "Laughter is God's hand on the shoulder of a troubled world." She was so pleased with that.

Mrs. Mays invited me to join the Women's International League for Peace and Freedom (WILPF), which was an integrated group that talked about international issues. It was already well established at Atlanta University when I started going to it. Just a few whites were in it. It was black-run, and we were very much in the minority. It was wonderful because we learned so much. There was a WILPF convention and we decided to send two people, a white person and a black person. So we began to figure, how could we go? Wasn't any hotel, any motels where we could stop. Then we'd have to figure out, who did we know that we could stop with? Well, I know I never did go, because we never were able to work out that trip. That's when I was faced with the fact that you can't go into the hotel, because you can't take your friend with you.

To give another idea of the racism at that time: I was on the Tuberculosis Association board, and it was an all-white board. So I said, "Since tuberculosis is more of a disease among Negro people than it is among white, why don't we have a Negro on this board?" Finally they decided they would, and they asked Whitney Young, the head of the School of Social Work at Atlanta University. I had gotten to know him already. We had been working on some various integration things, race things, so I knew Whitney before he came to that board.

Before the meetings of the board, we always were in the habit of having coffee. As people assembled, we had coffee and then the meeting would start. But they gave Whitney the time a half an hour later for the meeting, so that he wouldn't be there for the coffee. They were nervous about blacks and whites eating together. So Whitney came in, and everybody was about half through, and some of them were already sitting down. I went over to greet him, as well as the director of the association, and she escorted him over to the table. I went over to the coffee table and got him some coffee and a piece of cake, or whatever it was we had, and took it over to him. It never even dawned on me that I was doing something that I shouldn't be doing, but I want to tell you, I was taken to task by some of the members of the board afterwards for having done that. After all, he could be on the board, but we still didn't have to eat with him.

The Hungry Club met every Wednesday, and I always went to the Hungry Club at the black Young Men's Christian Association (YMCA). It was a weekly lunchtime lecture series, and it was one of the few places, one of the very, very few places, where white people could go before the end of segregation to learn from black leadership. I was so glad that they let me come; I appreciated it. They always had good speakers. In fact, I wish we had it now. We still need to cross lines—class lines, more than racial lines, now.

Then I began to invite people to my house. Grace Hamilton, head of the Atlanta Urban League, came a lot, and Don Hollowell, a leading attorney in the civil rights movement. The neighbors gave a few threats, like they were going to blow up my house! I always had an answer that I still think was good. I always said, "Oh, I'm so sorry you feel that way. Now what did they do? Did they do something down on the street? Were they rowdy or noisy?"

Frances Pauley (center) at a banquet of the Atlanta
branch of the Urban League, 1961.
*(Photograph courtesy of Frances Freeborn Pauley Papers, Special Collections
Department, Robert W. Woodruff Library, Emory University.)*

"No, they weren't."

I said, "I wouldn't like it at all if they were. I just wish you could get to
know some of these people. They are so interesting." And I always talked
just like that to them, instead of arguing with them about not blowing up
my house. It would quiet them.

Things have really changed. You hate to say that sometimes, because it
sounds like you think that we don't need further change, but we're about
halfway there, maybe. At least we've come a long way when I think of
going into a restaurant and not even thinking about whether you're in an
integrated group or whether an integrated group is sitting at the next
table or not. I remember once when I went to Paschal's Restaurant with
Don Hollowell. We were sitting close to a window, and they came and
asked us to move to another table. They said if the police went by and saw
us, they could have come in and arrested us, because, see, it was illegal. So
that's a long way.

I realized more and more how wrong white people had been, and the
one thing that amazed me then, and still amazes me, is how black people
could be so kind to us. It seemed to me that it's been a tremendous effort

on their part to overcome the hatred that they should feel toward us when we had behaved in the manner that we had over the years. For black people to overcome that hatred was a personal achievement, it seems to me. I don't know whether I'd ever be able to do that or not.

I don't think I ever learned compassion until I met some black people, and particularly older black people. Some older black women taught me more about what real compassion is than I ever learned anywhere else. Just caring how somebody else feels, how they hurt, just understanding and putting yourself in their place. A bit later than this, in the sixties, when I was working in Albany, I knew Marion King. She was pregnant and had gone to take some food to her husband in jail. He had been jailed in the civil rights movement. The police beat her up and she lost her baby. She was in bed at home, and I went to see her. I was so angry; I was so furious with the police. I thought I just couldn't stand it, to sit by her bed and she had lost her baby that they had wanted so much, and her husband was in jail. She began to talk to me and told me that I simply must not hate, and that I must not be angry, that I wasn't hurting anybody but myself. I'll never forget that. That's what I say is real compassion. Here I was white, and it was a white cop who beat her up.

I still regret that occasionally I feel a little feeling of white superiority creep in, and it makes me angry when I feel it. Intellectually knowing that there's not any differences in the races, in any respect, really. Then, all of a sudden, within yourself to feel that because I'm white, I'm a little better. That feeling would creep in just because of the way society was at the time. It just makes you ashamed of yourself, ashamed of white people.

But, you know, you get in deeper and deeper, and if you think you can ever, ever get out, you're caught.

Press Release
January 19, 1959

HOPE, Inc. does not propose to argue the pros and cons of segregation vs. desegregation, or states rights vs. federal rights. It has one aim - to champion children's rights to an education within the state of Georgia.

School desegregation, of course, remained an issue for many years, and I continued to work on it for many years. In the late 1950s, it became a question of how were we going to get together to fight to keep the schools open. The legislature had passed laws that allowed the governor to close schools upon integration, and we had a desegregation suit for Atlanta that was going forward. We didn't know what to do; different people were struggling with what to do. Out of that came HOPE, "Help Our Public Education," the fight to get the legislature to desegregate public schools rather than abandon them. That was another very, very hot fight.

HOPE was mainly an organization of respectable, middle-class white people. I was contacted in the beginning by the organizers of HOPE, and I would not go with them because it was all white. I had said I wasn't going to belong to anything that was all white. When I went into it a bit later, we had a great discussion about whether it should be all white or not. By far the large majority thought we could do best by being all white. I was certainly of a divided opinion about it. I hated to break the promise I had made to myself. On the other hand, this was a political issue, and at that point it looked like maybe this would be the best way to go, tactically. Also it takes something to integrate. People weren't accustomed to it. So I had a lot of discussions with the black people I knew, and they agreed that what we wanted was to keep the schools open and that tactic seemed to be the best. And maybe it was, in the long term. A good many black people gave us money. So I threw in my towel and joined HOPE.

I did the legislative part, organized the people to work in the legislature, to observe and lobby the legislature. Then I worked on statewide organization. We formed HOPE chapters all around the state. I already had League of Women Voters contacts and other contacts that had fought both the county unit and the private school amendment, the very type of people that we needed in HOPE. I had a base of people out in the state, while most of the other people in the group just knew Atlanta. While I was out working in the state, people such as Fran Breedan and Muriel Lokey and Betty Harris were running the office in Atlanta and doing a wonderful job.

The leadership in the different towns was more women than men, simply because I was organizing it. I knew more women at that time. I can't remember any place where the men took the leadership in HOPE. We did have a good many men in HOPE, and they did so much, so that's unfair to say. But I also think that the women had the time to do it for free, and the men didn't. HOPE was also about children and education, and at that time, even more than now, women arranged for the children.

In Athens, with the university people, we had a strong HOPE chapter. Beverly Benson had a really good Athens group. She did as much as I did, probably more, in helping to organize out in the state. We had a good chapter in Savannah, little chapters in Brunswick and Valdosta and Columbus, and members in many other towns. If you just had enough people in different towns who could work on their legislators, it would help—and it did.

I have kept up a friendship with a woman that worked with us in Tifton and a woman in Columbus. Those two women I still consider friends.

Mrs. Glenn Burton in Tifton, she and her husband were very religious people. They believed it was wrong to treat blacks the way that blacks were treated. They had a moral feeling about it. Armine Dimon in Columbus came at it from a moral point of view as well. It took somebody with a lot of stamina to stand up in a little town, where everybody knew you and nobody liked what you were doing, because school desegregation was very controversial at that time. That's when I began to learn what it was like to get ugly phone calls. My father would answer the phone and keep a count of when they'd call. He would try to get the name, which he usually couldn't get, but he felt that was a great sport. I'm glad he thought it was a sport, and not something that should not be happening.

I remember a number of the "stagey" things that we did in HOPE. We had a meeting to "Fill the Tower with Hope" in March of 1959. The Tower Theater was a theater downtown. We thought we'd get the best people we could to be on the stage. Well, nobody wanted to be on the stage. Finally we managed to get Sylvan Meyer. He was the editor of a little newspaper in Gainesville, and he was way out on civil rights and race issues and any kind of discrimination. He said he'd preside, and then Ralph McGill, editor of the *Atlanta Constitution*, said he'd speak. It was so wonderful that McGill would stand up there and speak, but he was a very hesitant convert to our side. I don't want to belittle him, but he wasn't one that was clamoring for civil rights and hunting for people to join. But we had respectable presentations and we did fill the Tower. It was inspirational, because you felt like there were some other people with you.

Another time, our U.S. senators, Richard Russell and Herman Talmadge, were going to speak at the legislature, and we decided we'd try to get them to speak for open schools. We were interested in the future of our state, and we were interested in every child having an education. This was going to mean that we were just going back to prewar days when all you educated were the landowners. Were they really going to sell our state down the river? We asked them for appointments, and they both gave us appointments at some horrible time, like eight-thirty Sunday morning. A group went out to see Talmadge and another group went to see Russell, one in Winder, one down in Lovejoy. We represented different organizations, statewide organizations. I went with the group to see Russell. He was absolutely amazed to see who we were, the caliber of people, because he thought all the good people wanted segregated schools. The look on his face, that's the main thing I remember. He kept questioning, "And you say you're from the United Church Women? You say you're from the Rotary Clubs?" I think we shook him.

Then the day that they came to the legislature, we packed the gallery. We had people come real early, because we had tried to pack the gallery

WE WANT

PUBLIC

SCHOOLS

SIGN USED IN A DEMONSTRATION IN SUPPORT OF
PUBLIC SCHOOLS, 1954.
*(Courtesy of Frances Freeborn Pauley Papers, Special Collections Department,
Robert W. Woodruff Library, Emory University.)*

one time before. The word got out, and the secretaries and everybody else that worked around the place went over there, so there weren't any seats left. This time, we were there when the place opened, and we filled up every seat. We had little signs in support of public education, small enough that we could put them under our coats and not have them seen as we came in. We told everybody to dress very nicely and wear white gloves and told them not to say anything—not to boo, not to clap, not to do a thing. Because we didn't want to be put out.

I went down on the floor, so I could give a few signals. When the senators came in, these women didn't clap. There was silence, and the silence was so great. They sat, and they didn't stand up, and they didn't clap. Everybody stopped clapping down on the floor and turned around and looked at the gallery. And here were all the nice ladies with hats and gloves, sitting there so serious, not a smile on any face. I was just so tickled.

Then, as soon as one of the senators said something about schools, everybody took out their signs—"We Want Public Schools"—and held them up. Again everybody downstairs stood up and looked at them. It was dramatic. That was one of the most fun days, because everything you plan doesn't work out that well. I guess the Lord was with us that day.

We were also circulating petitions to save the public schools. They came in so well that we decided we wanted to do something with them. I never have liked things that you do and put on the shelf. If you don't plan some action, don't ask me to the meeting. We just wanted some way of publicizing the fact that many people wanted public schools. We pasted all of the petitions together, and we stood up on the top level of the capitol, at the railing, and dropped them. There were enough that they dropped down to the floor of the capitol. That was another nice sight. I always have said that my dramatic training has stood me in good stead. I've used it more than any other training that I got in college.

HOPE was dramatic but also did the nitty-gritty. We worked hard; we worked day and night. We were always trying to think of creative gimmicks to spread the word in public. All kinds of little things, like we'd say, "Now, when you get on an elevator, if somebody's on the elevator that you know, say something about it, like 'Well, the schools are going to be open, and isn't that going to be great,' and 'We've got to save the schools,' or 'I don't mind my kid going to a desegregated school.'" Our aim was to sell the community on the idea of open schools, so that's why we had all that publicity. We wanted to keep the schools open and have a good public school system. We believed in the public schools. I wish to hell we had somebody today that believed enough to have a strong organization in public schools.

I have a real fascinating story about HOPE and International Telephone and Telegraph (IT&T). When I went into HOPE, there were already three or four youngsters in there. They were from IT&T, although we didn't know this at the time. There were two boys and a girl, and it ended up that they took a lot of the initiative for fundraising. We raised money in lots of different ways, and they brought in a lot of it. They also volunteered to do all kinds of things that were time consuming. So we just latched upon them, of course. One of them was given to me to help on statewide organizing, and he was terrible. He didn't really believe in it. I quit working with him, because he didn't really believe in what he was doing. And I couldn't understand why he was in it if he didn't believe, because you don't do something like that when you don't believe in it.

There was another one, though, that really believed in it; he was gung-ho. He would do things like take charge of security. He did the security for "Fill the Tower with Hope." He said that he would contact the police and see that everything was guarded, and we didn't have any trouble at that event. One or two people had to be removed, but they were quietly removed. At another meeting we had at the Ansley Hotel, we found Mr. Ed Friend taping the meeting. Mr. Friend was Talmadge's photographer, and he took ugly pictures of people and spliced them together, black and white people together. That night he was taping the meeting, and we weren't allowing anybody to tape the meeting. We found him back in a little room where the speaker system was. Some of the IT&T boys had locked him up in the room, and I went back there and talked him into giving us the tape rather than be arrested.

I kept up with one of the IT&T workers for awhile. He came through here several years after that when he was no longer with the company. We went out to dinner and he said, "Did you every wonder why we were so interested in HOPE?" He said that IT&T gave several employees the order to work with HOPE and to spend any amount of money necessary. They simply poured money into it. They evidently believed that public schools were a good thing for business, which they certainly are. But they were also told by IT&T to keep an absolute record of the whole way it was organized and operated, to see how a community organization could work and be effective, and what ramifications there were. And he asked, "Did you ever think about how we got by with the huge mass meeting at the Tower Theater?" He had something like two hundred plainclothes guards there as security. And when I talked Ed Friend out of the tapes, this IT&T worker was right at my elbow, and he was sending out for help.

Now, I don't know whether the others in HOPE believed me when I told them the story, but it just adds up when I look back on it. It just really does add up. And we sure didn't have any trouble that night.

The Sibley Commission hearings in the spring of 1960 were a big part of school desegregation in Georgia. The governor appointed John Sibley, a banker and an attorney here in Atlanta, and a commission to go around the state and hear what the people had to say about integration. They were sure, and Sibley was definitely sure, that everybody was going to say they'd rather close the schools than desegregate them. They expected to bring in a report saying that nobody in the state wanted to integrate the schools. We realized that it was going to take a bunch of work to have that not happen. The commission's plan was to have one meeting in each of the ten congressional districts, and they were going to have them all in a short span of time. We were worried. How were we going to organize for all ten of them that fast?

In the first place, we didn't know how they were going to run it. The first hearing was in Americus, which was the worst place for us that they could have chosen. But we got a good many people on our side to go.

They got there and they were not told where to go. The commission didn't give out information about where you should sign up and how you could get in. We had a lot of people that went to Americus that never spoke. But Armine Dimon spoke at that first meeting. She was one of the most courageous people I have ever met. She really had the courage of her convictions. She was a real Christian in trying to see what was the right thing to do and doing it. It took a terrific amount of courage for a calm, everyday white person to walk up on that stage and say publicly, "I don't believe what it appears that the general public believes. I think that we should have desegregated schools, and it will not ruin our school system." It took people that had some inner strength to do it, because you were going against the authorities. You have to realize that people had been living with segregation as the law, which makes a difference. I think that maybe a few blacks spoke also for open schools, and they were scared. And you'd better be scared, or you'd get shot.

After Americus, two or three of us went to Sibley and said, "This can't go on. These people weren't allowed to speak. You've got to advertise that you've got to hear both sides. All we're asking for is justice." We had to keep on working and get all of the details in order to tell people to be sure and do this or that, in order to be able to speak. And it worked. Sibley was a fair-minded man, not a liberal man, but he was a fair man. I don't think he was on our side a bit, but I think he was honorable.

The next hearing was a different story; we did better. More people spoke for open schools, and at the next one, even more, until in the last five there were more people speaking for open schools than closed schools. I never did get to go to one of the hearings until the last one. I didn't even listen to them, because I was already working like crazy to get people lined up to go to the next one. I did every bit by phone, because that's all I could do. I didn't have time to get from one place to another. I never left the telephone during that time! That's when it pays to already know some folks and have some credibility. But it was hard getting people to have the courage to go down there and speak out before the cameras.

The Sibley hearings wouldn't have been anything if it hadn't been for the T.V. It got so when you saw somebody come up on the stage, you'd know whether they were segregationists. When you looked at the T.V., you could almost tell when a person came up to testify, which side they were on. Somehow the picture brought it through. I guess it's because they weren't actors, they were real. The people on our side were just so nice and so good and so right in comparison with the others who were filled with hatred. I remember talking with the camera people that did it, because it made such an impression on me. They said that the camera brings out the truth.

In the end, Sibley just couldn't believe what he had heard around the state. The report that the commission gave said that the public schools in Georgia should be preserved. And that, I think, did more to turn Governor Vandiver than anything else. You ought not ever give up, you know it? Because a lot of times you win in the most unlikely times.

What made the breakthrough in school desegregation, though, was the University of Georgia. The NAACP won that case, and Charlayne Hunter and Hamilton Holmes entered the University in 1961. The NAACP was so smart in picking the University of Georgia. Because all of those people over there in the legislature, practically nine-tenths of them, graduated from the University of Georgia. They weren't about to see their alma mater close. I remember the day that Ernest Vandiver, we always called him "Little Ernie," finally gave in. I was in the gallery and heard his speech. He was talking out of both sides of his mouth, and I just couldn't stand it. I left disgusted, instead of happy, that he had given in. Somebody came up to me and said, "We've got to go and send him a telegram from the League of Women Voters, congratulating him. He has given in."

I said, "I will not."

But they said, "Oh, if he's got to eat crow, he might as well have a little molasses on it."

So I went and sent him a telegram.

World Politics Brochure, American Foundation for Political Education Late 1950s

JOIN THE WORLD POLITICS DISCUSSION GROUP IN YOUR COMMUNITY! Basic Aim: This program is designed to help participants develop sound and independent opinions on world affairs. In this way it serves not only *you*, but our country as well, since democracy draws its strength from the wisdom and character of its citizens.

As hard as I worked on school desegregation, I wasn't giving all of my time to HOPE or all of my time to any one thing. That's one of the nice things about being a volunteer; you can do several things at once. In the late fifties, I worked with Harry Boardman of the American Foundation for Political Education in New York and Paul Rilling of the YMCA to organize discussion groups on world politics on an integrated basis. We would have two series of discussion groups, fall and spring of each year, and they would meet weekly for ten weeks. It was a little bit like the Great

Books idea, in that each discussion session was based on selected readings. We continued these programs for four or five years.

What we tried to do was to get pairs of discussion leaders, one black and one white, to work together. We drew our leadership in the black community the same way as we did in the white community, primarily from academics and professionals. We got mailing lists from Atlanta University professors and we used a lot of university professors over there as discussion leaders. Harry Boardman, the Eastern Regional Director of the World Politics Program, would come down from New York to train the leaders and help organize the program. That worked very, very well. It made for a very exciting and interesting group. It was a little different from some of the other things that people had been doing.

To find places for the meetings was difficult. I really walked my feet off in this city trying to find places, and tried to see what churches we could get into. The black churches were used to having meetings with some white people there, but what was very unusual was for a white church to have any black person there. So we tried to have meetings in white churches or white institutions. There were always, in every church, some people that didn't want us there. The objections were that we were communists, we didn't belong in the church, we weren't religious.

I remember one instance in particular. Paul and I went to an Episcopal church, and they said, yes, we could meet there. We had one meeting. I think one lone professor from Atlanta University came, so it was an integrated meeting. The next thing we knew, the minister called up and said that he had some complaints from his congregation, and he thought we had better not meet. So Harry and I ventured forth to talk to him to see if we couldn't get him to change this mind. But, no, he wasn't about to change his mind. We had quite a conversation, and Harry and I were both trying to behave, and had behaved, I think, very well, in spite of the way we felt. We got about half way down the walk going out, and the preacher was still standing in the door. He called after us, "Don't you understand, I have to save my church."

Harry turned and looked at him and said, "Save your church for what?"

But we usually were able to iron things out very successfully. Still, every single little thing that we did took all kinds of time, simply because it hadn't ever been done before. Also it wasn't that unusual for blacks and whites to meet together and talk about racial issues, but to talk about communism or the state of the individual, that just did not take place. Because when you were talking about racial things, you were still keeping this separateness, and what we needed to have was real integration, which is not easy. It's much easier to do things separate. "Separate but equal" was easier, even if it wasn't equal.

This was a new experience for the participants. If you'd never been in an interracial meeting, if you'd never sat around the table with blacks and whites, to discover that you're there on an equal basis was new. You weren't there in a paternalistic way at all. That was what was so valuable, to try to get away from this superiority/inferiority racial kind of feeling that whites and blacks had. There was a little sense of superiority among the whites vis-à-vis the blacks in a discussion group. But it didn't take long to move away from that, and maybe the South was ahead of the North in a way. Because we already had a lot of associations with blacks, and certain types of friendships with blacks, and a feeling and a liking for blacks. You had something substantial to build on, to go to the next step of equality. For the first time in your life, maybe you realize that we all hurt the same way, love the same way, and we all are alike.

You hate to say something that was as small a program as that was influential, but I think it was. It was so early, and those early things were sometimes the most difficult. But here you had something that went beautifully, that perhaps softened the way to do the bigger things. It was unique in the late fifties.

Letter

January, 1963
Dearest Children,

Old Vandiver says in his news conference that the most important thing he did was to keep the schools open. That he was the brain! Such a world!

Love,
Mother

4 "Trying to make a bridge": The Civil Rights Movement

For all that had been done to lay the groundwork for racial change in the 1940s and 1950s, a "new movement"—as Frances characterized it—emerged in the 1960s as the NAACP's legal strategy against segregation expanded into a mass movement. In Georgia, as across the South, thousands of protesters took to the streets for marches, pickets, and boycotts. Action bred reaction. As civil rights activists demanded equality and justice, many others, including local, state, and national leaders, defended the racial status quo.

Frances carved out a role for herself in this movement as executive director of the Georgia Council on Human Relations, the state arm of the Atlanta-based Southern Regional Council, a regional planning agency devoted largely to research and policy analysis. Frances put a more activist stamp on the council's program, and she extended it into every corner of the state. In the process, she forged alliances with major civil rights organizations. "I felt my major job was to try to form this bridge," she recalls, "to try to get blacks and whites together."

Like many movement activists, Frances has dramatic stories of threats and arrest, but organizing for the movement typically involved more prosaic work— endless rounds of meetings, hours of discussion, long drives from one end of the state to the other. Frances logged some seventeen thousand miles in her first year with the council. In short, she was more negotiator than protester.

Letter to the white citizens of Albany, Georgia

July 30, 1962

Dear Friend:

Now in the extremity of misunderstanding and danger in Albany, when racial unrest disturbs the streets, threatens the prosperity and embarrasses Georgia before the country and the world, let us consider what Albany citizens of good will can do to permanently resolve the troubles.

The experience of other Georgia cities—Savannah, Macon and Columbus, to name a few where white and colored neighbors have come to some agreement on Negro demands for their public rights—suggests several fruitful and reconciling steps which can be taken to help the city out of the impasse.

First, it seems clear that no Georgia community has come to any racial agreement without meetings, sympathetic talk and new understanding between whites and Negroes. Mistakes have been made by the Negro citizens—mistakes have been made by various inter-racial organizations yet the underlying principles are still there. Truth can be found through knowledge and understanding. Albanians can as individuals and as groups seek this truth.

Second, it is equally clear that Albany's present crisis hinges on the refusal of City Commissioners to meet with and discuss grievances of Negro citizens. These, the elected officials are responsible for the just conduct of public affairs—Mayor Asa D. Kelley Jr., Buford Collins, L. W. Mott, C. B. Pritchett, Allen Davis, W. C. Holman Jr., and T. H. McCollum, members of the city commission, who seem to have delegated delicate and vital policy decisions to salaried officials whom they control—need to know their constituents [*sic*] feelings about this disasterous [*sic*] situation. Elected officials are notably responsive to the pressure of such expressions, a salutary change of mind can be brought about at city hall.

Third, it is also clear that the fastest growing town in Georgia is in grave danger of economic loss and stagnation which afflicted Little Rock. Business and political leaders in Albany who value their prosperity can save it by opposing the recalcitrance of city hall and by demanding reasonable agreements to restore peace, healthy business and continued economic advance.

Ask yourself this question "What can I do?"

a. Talk to and write your city commissioners, asking them to settle this disorder now.
b. Write your Chamber of Commerce—They want it settled. Tell them they have your endorsement.
c. Call or see your minister, discuss the situation with him; pledge your support.

Let us open our minds, let us listen to reason and seek the truth. And let us act for a just and happy end to this dangerous, damaging and senseless struggle.

Sincerely,
Mrs. Frances Pauley, Director
Georgia Council on Human Relations

To me, the movement means pretty much the sixties. The one thing that I think is so important about the movement is that it was a *movement*. It was not an organized effort of one person or a few people or a board's decision. It wasn't any high-powered organization. It wasn't Madison Avenue. It seemed to be a grassroots movement that was coming up all over the United States, and particularly all over the South. Now, certain leaders emerged, like James Farmer and Martin Luther King and so forth, but there were a tremendous number of heroes and heroines on a local level that really were the movement. In fact, I wish that we could get a grant, and let's just take Georgia and see if we couldn't get a list and a little account of what different people did in different towns. Because if we don't do it soon, it's going to be forgotten.

Now, my association was never in any leadership capacity. I headed up the Georgia Council on Human Relations in this period, beginning in 1961. The council was a group of black and white people together, and we were trying to help the leadership. We were not saying to the leadership, "We think you should do this, or you should not do this." We were saying, "Here we are. What can we do to help you do what you're planning?" I would stick my head or body on the line, but I wasn't going to stick somebody else's. So that was the secondary role that the council played, and sometimes we didn't even get into being a secondary role. But we did what we could; we would do what the leadership requested.

The Georgia council was part of the Southern Regional Council, an interracial group which was set up in 1944 to work on race relations. The Southern Regional Council tried to organize in each southern state. There was already a similar human relations group in Georgia, and the lady that had been in charge of it for a good many years was Mrs. Dorothy Tilly, a leader among women in the Methodist church, who I had met as a little bitty girl. She was a very good organizer and worker, but she had gotten old. Mrs. Tilly and many of her people worked under the existing circumstances of the day. They were really working for "separate but equal." They were not caught on fire with anything new, with the new movement. Then a retired white minister headed the Georgia council, and it had sort of died down, was kind of dormant. I was asked to take over the directorship and I did. But I said it was going to be different, that we were going to get out of the church basement and also widen our membership. Since we grew out of Mrs. Tilly's work, we had a whole bunch more women, but over time we became pretty evenly divided, men and women. I began to gather together younger people, and we were talking about equality. I found out that if I went into a place to reorganize or organize, I'd get new blood and new people, and then after we had the meeting set up, I'd be sure and invite all those older people. Because it wasn't that I didn't respect them, but they were going to be so damn cautious. I would never have gotten off the ground.

The Georgia council job was the first time I ever got paid for working. Paul Rilling, who worked with me on the world politics discussions, talked me into taking it. At that time, he was with the Southern Regional Council, as head of the fieldwork part of the council. The only two jobs I had in my life, Paul talked me into, but I really did want a job. My kids were gone from home and I wanted something more to do. I could then do something on a regular basis. Still, I didn't know whether to take the job or not, because I didn't really feel like I was qualified. I hadn't worked with black and white, men and women. I didn't think that I had the background or training or experience to do it. But I guess nobody did. So I asked Dr. King, because he had moved to Atlanta by then and I had gotten to know Coretta, and he encouraged me to take it. He said, "I'll help you. I'll help you with a fundraiser right away." The Southern Regional Council had said they'd pay my salary of six thousand dollars, give me space for an office, and I would have use of a part-time secretary. For anything else I'd have to raise the money.

King got Carl Rowan, a well-known black journalist, to speak, and the Jewish Progressive Club let us meet in their building, a real nice place. So that was very much out of the church basement. We worked hard on it, and we had a big crowd, and it was perfectly beautiful. We had equal black and white, and the seating was so that you looked out over the audience and it was integrated seating. It wasn't all the blacks over here, all the whites over there.

We had some students from the black colleges who taught the group to sing "We Shall Overcome." I remember that so distinctly, because a lot of people didn't already know "We Shall Overcome." And I remember Carl Rowan singing on that platform, with tears streaming down his face. King introduced Carl Rowan, and Rowan made a beautiful speech. It was just a perfectly marvelous evening. I was just so thrilled.

Then I got called in by a couple members of my board—initially I had the same old board that had been there before—and I thought they were going to say, "thank you," "here's a bonus," or something like that, because this meeting was such a wonderful success. Instead, they reprimanded me and threatened to fire me, because we had a cocktail party and served alcoholic beverages. If you had paid an extra amount, you got to come to the cocktail party ahead of time and meet Carl Rowan, and that helped raise a bunch of money. I've always remembered how absolutely astonished I was when I went in thinking I was going to be complimented and then to go in and have to defend myself. Well, they didn't fire me, and I don't think they stopped me from having meetings and serving alcohol, although we certainly didn't do that very often. We didn't have that much time and energy. But we weren't a temperance group.

FRANCES PAULEY, AT HER DESK AT THE OFFICE OF THE GEORGIA
COUNCIL ON HUMAN RELATIONS.
(Photograph courtesy of Frances Pauley.)

That was the beginning of how we raised some of our first money. We
also had dues for membership, and some members would pay more to
support the council. Then I found out that the easiest way to raise money
was to go to New York, because at that time the people in the North
thought that prejudice was only in the South. It eased their conscience to
give money to help save the poor South. So I would go up to New York
twice a year while I was with the council and visit foundations and raise
enough money for us to operate on. You can't plan a program and carry it
out and raise money all at the same time, not one person. If I raised
enough to hire some more help, I'd hire some more help, and if not, we
would just simply live within the money I raised until I went back again.
None of us took any kind of a sizable salary. I used to say I took enough to
pay the housekeeper to keep the house, because my father was living with

us. I passed my money on very quickly. The Field Foundation gave us the most, it seemed to me, but there were a lot of family foundations helping out. Raising money from foundations is a lot easier than having fundraisers. Anna Lord Strauss, from my League of Women Voters days, helped me. She would usually invite a few people over to have me explain to them what was happening in the South. I ended up with a seventy-five thousand–dollar budget and had seven people working in the office.

One time I was talking with a man connected with the Field Foundation, and he asked me what would I like to have in the council if I had money. I said, "Well, the first thing I'd like to have is enough to hire a black man on the staff."

Next day, he said, "If you'll write me a letter and ask me, you can have the money."

So I contacted Oliver Wendell Holmes in Savannah; he was my first choice. Mr. Holmes was originally an Atlanta man from a very prominent and wonderful family. It's the same family as Hamilton Holmes, who integrated the University of Georgia. Mr. Holmes had a perfectly adorable church, a little picturesque black Congregationalist church in Savannah. I went over to Savannah, because I didn't want to write him or call him. I wanted to face him, so I made the appointment with him. I got about halfway through my sales pitch, and he said, "When do you want me to go to work? I can start Monday." It was the most wonderful thing that had ever happened to me, because he was such a great man. I learned so much from him. He was quiet but had such good creative ideas.

When I took the job as head of the Georgia council, our main job was to organize groups, interracial groups, around the state to promote racial harmony. We were all trying to make sense out of this thing called *racism* or *prejudice*. Once, in 1962, I was asked if I would come to the Dorchester Center and help with the citizenship school that Septima Clark was running. She was a great woman with a great program in adult education. I eagerly went and worked like a dog on a speech about taking part in the making of political policy. The audience was absolutely quiet and attentive. At the end I asked for questions. A little lady with a broad Mississippi dialect asked, "How come when Miss Anne go out of town she lets me tend her house and her chillun, even let me sleep in her bed. But if we get on the bus she ain't gonna sit by me?" One question after another. I spent the night in Dorchester, sleeping dormitory style. The next morning when I opened my eyes, there were two rows of black faces watching me. They were sitting on the edges of the adjacent cots. As soon as they saw a sign of life, the questions started again. Did you ever try to explain the nature of prejudice? When something is as illogical and unrealistic as racial hatred, there simply is no reasonable and logical answer.

I felt my major job was to try to form this bridge, to try to get blacks and whites together, and no matter where I went that was the first thing I did. I would not start if it was all black or all white. By this time, with both the League of Women Voters and HOPE, I really had a network of contacts in the state. But the Georgia council was still more a middle-class group, because we didn't have poor people in it. We'd get a little broader representation in the local councils than we had in the state council, maybe from lower middle-class to upper middle-class. But we wouldn't really get poor people.

My contacts were white, so I had to make black contacts. I often worked with Vernon Jordan, who was doing statewide organizing for the NAACP at this time. Sometimes Vernon and I would go into a place at the same time, he on the black side and I on the white side. He'd tell the blacks that it would be safe if they worked with the whites that I got together, and I'd tell the whites it would be safe if they worked with the blacks that Vernon got together. So Vernon would help me learn from black leadership.

It's hard to get that confidence from blacks. They try you, and I don't blame them! Nobody trusts you the first time they see you, if you're a stranger. And certainly if you're a black person, you're going to be more cautious of a white person before you really tell them what you're thinking, and they don't do that very much.

I had this happen even before I was in the council. After Dr. King and Coretta moved back to Atlanta from Montgomery, Coretta asked me, "Will you help do something for me?"

"Coretta, you know I would do anything in my power for you."

"Would you come and work at our summer Bible school?"

"Coretta, I've never been to a Bible school. My children didn't go to Bible school. I don't know what a Bible school does. Isn't there something else I could do?"

"No, I want the children in this church to know there is one white person who loves them, and I want you to come."

So I said, "All right, I will."

That was one of the worst summers of my life! I didn't have any coaching. On the first day, I got down there at quarter to eight o'clock and was the first one there. Everything was locked up, so I stood there on the sidewalk 'til somebody went in. I said, "I'm Frances Pauley and I'm here." As different people would come up, I'd introduce myself, and I got acquainted with some of the adults. The children came, and then we all marched into the church to have the opening exercises.

Then they assigned people, and thankfully I was assigned to someone I remembered meeting. It ended up that we were on the top floor, which was the hottest of all, with about fifty kids. She tells me, would I please start out by telling the story of Zacchaeus. And I looked at her. I remembered something about a sycamore tree, maybe, but I wasn't real sure, and that was as far as I could remember. I said, "I'm sorry, you'll have to do that." So I spent the day doing things like picking up the pencil when she dropped it. She told me at the end of the day, "Tomorrow we're going to start on our crafts, and so would you please bring twenty-five ice cream cartons, those big cartons, to make trash baskets out of, and bring colored pictures that the children can paste on them."

I got home and I called a friend. She told me how you're supposed to do it. I learned how to paste and shellac them. Then I went out and tried to collect twenty-five of these things. I went to every damn ice cream place in town, and I ended up with twelve. Night came and there wasn't anyplace else for me to go, and all I had was twelve. She said twenty-five. I spent the rest of the night cutting colored pictures out of magazines. The next day I had my car full of stuff and she was very surprised. So I had done good!

On the last day of the session, this lady was praying, and she said, "Thank you for this session. Everything has gone real well, even Mrs. Pauley." I had made it. I had passed.

And I said to God, "God, I'll do anything, if you just don't make me come back next summer." I don't think I ever did a harder task in my life!

I started organizing for the Georgia council and, of course, you had added reason to organize because the movement was starting. The main thing was to get blacks and whites together to work on whatever desegregation problem they had in their town. My job was to set up an interracial council but also to plan a program of desegregation activity. Every one was a plan for action.

I remember going into Rome, and I visited with the white people, I visited with the black people. I got some leadership. By the time I got enough leadership on both sides, both black and white, we'd have a meeting. I remember the first meeting there was in the Episcopal church, and at this meeting I started out by saying, "What is it that bothers you the most about segregation?"

One guy says, "The signs in the washateria—'white only'." I remember this because the meeting was tense; they weren't used to having interracial meetings.

So here a white lady speaks up. She hadn't lived in Rome long, and she spoke up, "Oh, I thought that meant white clothes."

Well, of course, everybody laughed. So we decided we would desegregate the laundromat. Wherever the local group wanted to start, that's where we would start. I wouldn't dare go in and tell somebody else what to do.

Then they decided that it bothered them that blacks couldn't get any books at the library in Rome. So we decided to take the library on. We'd go and visit them and ask them if they didn't want to desegregate, if they wouldn't allow blacks to use it, and so forth. I remember Mr. Capus White, he was a cook at Shorter College, and he went to the desk and asked for a cookbook. They very kindly took him over and showed him the shelves where the cookbooks were. That was how the library was desegregated in Rome. A lot of places, the libraries were the first we attempted to desegregate, because people felt safer about that.

I remember a bright kid who was really a sight. It was in Moultrie, I believe. The people were having marches and the kids were very much a part of things, demonstrating and singing freedom songs. We had a meeting, and I said, "Let's think about what we want to accomplish."

They said, "There are those signs downtown at the courthouse for white and colored water fountains, and we want those signs down."

So we sat there thinking and talking, "What can we do about this? How will we make a change?"

First thing you know, this gangly kid named Inman left the room. Next thing we know, they called and said Inman was in jail. He and another kid had quickly left the meeting and had gone down and yanked the colored water fountain out of the wall by the roots, which, of course, left the water spewing all over the courthouse. Needless to say, I loved it. We got Inman and his friends out of jail and went on. That was *real* direct action!

Sometimes it was a racial incident that got us going. A little riot, or a little altercation, maybe a bunch of whites going into the black section of town and having a fight or something. People would be saying, "Let's get together, we've got to work this out." Then they would call me to come in, to help them work on an issue like that. I'd then say, "Now, wouldn't you like to have a council?" That was after I was known enough that somebody would call me in. Before that, when I was just getting started with the Georgia council, I would just have to get my own contacts and go.

I'd keep going back repeatedly to work with the groups. I'd go back if they called me back, and they would if they were having some problems. Practically everything you did was a fight because no place was used to this. Time after time, town after town, that I went into, it would be the first interracial meeting that they had ever had. In some cases, this was before the Civil Rights Act of 1964, and this made it much more difficult. Anytime you had anything that was interracial, you really were breaking the law. Unless you decide you are going to break the law and have civil disobedience, which I highly approve of, you have to plan it very carefully. It's not just a matter of casually asking a few people in for tea.

A SMALL-TOWN CIVIL RIGHTS DEMONSTRATION IN
CRAWFORDVILLE, GEORGIA.
(Photograph courtesy of Frances Pauley.)

In Rome, the White Citizens Council, which was a group of whites who were hostile to the movement and desegregation, came and took pictures of our people as they were leaving meetings, and then found out who they were and where they worked. Then they began working on trying to get their bosses to fire them. Really put the pressure on. They had a meeting of their own, showed the pictures and talked about the different people that were there. I thought they'd scare our people off, but our president went to the citizens council meeting and sat in the back. When they got to his name, they said, "This is a funny name."

He stood up and said, "The name is Max Schiable, and I am Max Schiable. Anything that you would like to ask me, I'm here."

Our group decided to stick. They planned another meeting but couldn't find a place to have it. Every place was scared. Finally a white Episcopal church at the edge of town, real isolated—which scared the hell out of me when I looked at it, because it was too far away from everything—they said we could meet there. When we got there, every single person whose picture had been taken was there and had brought a group with them of new members.

And the White Citizens Council showed up! Franziska Boas was our chairman. She's the daughter of Franz Boas, the great anthropologist. She was very interested in the council because she said her father had given his life to proving that there was no difference in the races. We got to be really good friends; I'd stay with her when I went to Rome. Anyway, Franziska and I stood at the door. Franziska went out and invited the citizens council in, and they didn't know what to do. So they came in and sat at the back of the church. It was a little bitty church. Franziska opened the meeting and said, "Come on. We want you to join us. Come right up here." She insisted until they came! Nothing happened; everything went off all right. We went right ahead with the meeting. But that was scary. And if anybody had gotten hurt or killed, you know it would have been my fault.

Franziska was an accomplished dancer. She danced in New York about the same time as Martha Graham, and when she got too old for that circuit, she came down to teach dance at Shorter College in Rome. Mr. Holmes and I used to stay at Franziska's home when we would go to Rome on business. Once Mr. Holmes went up and there was a black yardman out raking the front yard. Mr. Holmes went to the front door and rang the bell. Well, the yardman thought this was pretty strange, a black man going to the front door. So he stopped raking and was leaning on his rake when Franziska came to the door, greeted Mr. Holmes, threw her arms around him, and gave him a big hug. The yardman was so astounded that the rake fell out from under his arm. He completely lost his balance and fell flat on the ground.

Franziska had several big dogs, and they seemed to always stay under the dining room table. One night when Mr. Holmes was there, he sat down with Franziska at the table and started eating. But the cook hadn't been in the dining room, so she hadn't seen who was in there. Well, she came in the door with a plate of hot biscuits, and she saw Mr. Holmes sitting at the table. That was not exactly customary in Rome in those years, to see a black man sitting at a white lady's table. It surprised her so much that she dropped the biscuits on the floor, and the dogs rushed out from under the table and ate them all up. Mr. Holmes said that was one of the times they missed having good biscuits on account of him being black.

Often in south Georgia I got help from Episcopal ministers, because the Episcopal bishop, Bishop Stuart in Savannah, was so marvelous. He was the biggest help I had of anyone who wasn't actually in the organization. He called me in and told me whenever I went into a town to go to the Episcopal church and ask them to help me. "Pressure, pressure my men," he said, "Ask to meet in their churches. And tell me if they refuse." I don't think I ever let him know anything, except that they did help me, because the truth of the matter is they did. We had our first council meeting in the Episcopal church in Rome, and we almost always met at the Episcopal church in Macon. The church in a lot of places really did help us get on our feet.

I did work with Bishop Stuart when people needed help. He and I had a lot of conversations about the minister of this darling little Episcopal church in Terrell County that was having a hard time. The church had been built by a very wealthy landowner who owned a huge acreage of land in that county, but he was a great segregationist. The parishioners were giving the minister such a hard time, because he insisted on an open church. The final thing that they got so mad at him about was that he shook hands with a black man on the street in the town, and the church called him to task for that, told him he was not to do anything like that. He said he couldn't stop with shaking hands; he would have to do even more. So they pulled their support away from him, boycotting him really, and he had just a terrible time. I remember that I went to Ash Wednesday service there, and his wife and I were his audience, and he preached the sermon to the two of us. I kept telling Bishop Stuart about this, and he moved the man into a good place somewhere else, and he closed the church. The Bishop would not allow them to have another minister. I don't know for how long, but at that time that church was closed.

We had some interesting things happen on the other side too. There was a black woman who came to the Episcopal church in Rome and said she wanted to be a member. She came to church every Sunday and she sat kind of off by herself. She didn't try to take Communion. Finally, one Sunday, this southern colonel–type guy said that he worried because she didn't take Communion. He asked the minister if it would be all right if he asked her to take Communion. And he did, so that broke that. But then she didn't come to any of the church suppers because, after all, you know you can't eat together. Well, once the young people were sending out their invitations for Shrove Tuesday, a pancake breakfast or something, and they forgot and sent her an invitation like everybody else. She came and after that it was all right.

I was working in Burke County once. I had met a good many of the blacks and we had talked, but I was having a hard time getting any of the whites. So I started visiting the white ministers and finally I got enough white ministers for a meeting. We had our first meeting, and the blacks did not say one word. They just sat there. It was the first time there had ever been an interracial meeting in that town. So we went back to Herman Lodge's home. Later, in the 1980s, Herman Lodge became a big-shot in the political scene down in that area. We went back to his home. I talked with them, and I said, "Now look, we can't have this. The next time, you've just got to talk. Go home and you think about what you're going to say. Think of a question you can ask, so that you'll be prepared."

We went to the next meeting and the whites started talking, as usual, and the blacks were still silent, and so I looked over at one of the men, and I said, "Now, Reverend So-and-so, what do you think about that?"

He stood up, and I'll always remember how he looked. He was very, very dark, just almost black, and he had on a stiff, stiff starched white shirt, and he had a Bible in his hand. He stood up, and he said, "I have a question that I want to ask you. We read this book. And it says love your enemy and love your neighbor as yourself. And I want to know what book do y'all use?" I'll never forget that as long as I live. And I bet you those men didn't forget it. I don't think anything that anybody ever did had any greater effect on that community than that man asking that one question. A lot of times people just have to be jarred. I'll never forget how that group looked. I see their faces, I see the table, I see where they sat, and I see this old black man and this white shirt. I can see it just as plain as if I were there yesterday. That was the most beautiful, beautiful occasion.

People are born into a certain way of living. It takes a jolt to get out of it. It doesn't really mean that they're all that mean and bad, but it takes a jolt to make them see that maybe they could make a change. It's not easy to change things.

Diary, Georgia Council on Human Relations: Savannah

<u>March 26, 1961</u>: Savannah was so interesting. I talked and visited all sorts of people, black and white. I got there in a time of tension. The children (Negro) were boycotting the school--of all asinine things. There is violence there every whip stitch between the teenage white and blacks. I got the first steps of organization done. I have a steering committee with 6 Negroes and 6

whites. (I didn't realize the equal division until I
got home).

March 28-April 3, 1962: Conferences with chairman and
co-chairman and meeting on Job opportunities with
group--conference with Education Chairman.

March 27-29, 1963: Savannah needs something???
Probably new leadership. Hope the trip helped. We had
2 meetings, outlined some programs, etc.

June 5-6, 1963: Went particularly to work with the
Mayor and Chairman of the school board in starting
preparations for fall desegregation. The theater
opening had been a fiasco. The Mayor was very upset.
Anyway, I did a little good, maybe. Then I met with our
executive committee to make plans that they could carry
through. There is a great possibility of real riot--
gangs of whites and Negroes on the streets looking for
trouble. Sit-ins in restaurants. Just real jolly! But
it is nice to have the Mayor's respect. Holmes will go
down also next week.

June 11-14, 1963: Purpose: To work with Savannah
Council and other local leaders to break through with
gains. Demonstration (enormous) twice a day. Police
behavior very fine. Split in Negro community. Hosea
Williams under SCLC--NAACP under W. W. Law. Negotiations
under way--question whether they will be successful.
Susan Waters house shot into night of 12th.

June 27-July 1, 1963: Worked with new committee of
organizations. 20 organizations (34 people) present.
B'nai Brith, PTA, League of Women Voters, own Council,
the "Savannah Group" an interracial etc. group. Very
good meeting. Worked with Mayor, City Manager, our
Council, Hosea Williams group. Did what I could.

July 22-24, 1963: Worked with: 1- Business men's
group. "Committee of 100"--They asked for advice etc.;
2- Worked with "Optics" (Operation peaceful transition
in Chatham Schools); 3- Met with council membership;
4- Visited police and FBI re continued shooting at
Susan Waters home; 5- Met new school superintendent--
found him cooperative; 6- Advised League of Women Voters President on difficulties re-admission of 7 Negro
members to LWV. Successful trip. Good white people.

Worked very little with Negroes since Mr. H. will be
back.

March 2-5, 1964: Collected $100 donation. Met with
leaders. (Hosea Williams, W.W. Law and Lee Adler (head
of businessman's committee)), to work out plans for
preparations to see that Savannah is able to be ready
for passage of the Civil Rights Bill--to have
facilities open and not have resistance etc. Good
cooperation. Meeting planned--to have at Adler's home
with Mayor, Negro leaders, and white leaders--Good
prospects.

March 25-26, 1964: To begin work on "Operation
Opportunity." To work for peaceful compliance with
Civil Rights Act. Lee Adler had called together a very
fine group of men to start the program. We had an
exceedingly good meeting. Making plans for substantial
effort. The effort to be led by the Committee of 100,
businessmen organized last summer--All in all--good.

April 23-24, 1964: Worked with official from Washington
Civil Rights Commission. I made his appointments and
got him started on his survey. (He stayed a week). My
expenses will be totally reimbursed. Met with our
chairman--made plans for a return trip. Also planned
for Mr. Holmes to go down to work with recruiting for
school transfers. Maybe he can help unite the two major
Negro factions in working on this one project. No one
is working now. Our council there is not strong. But
the people really listen to Mr. Holmes and me.

October 27-29, 1965: To attend Civil Rights Committee
and Work with our Council. This was a successful trip.
Mr. Holmes went also. We pulled together a good
meeting of new Savannah folks. The group must be
completely reorganized. It has gotten too apathetic
with leaders having moved etc.

April 9-13, 1967: Savannah student group. Marvelous
young people have a good tutorial going. Savannah
Chapter--There are problems but maybe they will still
do a good job. Savannah, Burke, Augusta. Home and
tired--Too much in one trip--I don't seem to learn!

My first experiences with the Georgia council were in Savannah. Savannah
had very little publicity about its civil rights movement, but it was

absolutely wonderful. It had a well-organized black community, having a mass meeting once a week, sit-ins, marches—long before some of the other places in Georgia. They had one of the most perfect movements, because a lot was accomplished with very few people being hurt. Mr. W. W. Law was head of the NAACP in Savannah, and they decided to work to open public accommodations. This was before 1964. Mr. Law used to save things for me to do that he needed a white person to do, like buy tickets for bus rides because they wouldn't sell them to a black person. I'd go buy ten tickets, or whatever else he requested.

I never saw anybody who could work as hard as Mr. Law. He'd say, "Well, we'll have a meeting on that tonight." And I thought, "Have a meeting tonight?" Nobody knew about it. He'd sit down, write the throw-away, and have the girl warming up the old mimeograph. He'd have another boy out there getting up some cars to deliver them. So by the time he got done, the girl was standing at the machine, and as they ran off the mimeograph, the boys took them and got in the cars and went out and gave them out. And that night I thought, "They're not going to have anybody." But I went and they were hanging out the windows. He was something else.

Now, Hosea Williams is also from Savannah, and Hosea was working there as a chemist. He was ambitious politically and interested in the movement. He sought to be a leader. He eventually left Savannah and came over to Atlanta. Hosea is a strange person, because a lot of the things he's done have been good and a lot of the things he's done haven't been good.

Some real thugs came into Savannah and infiltrated the movement, and they were really doing violent things. They began burning. One night we had a whole bunch of fire alarms, some of them false and some of them real. The black leadership, Mr. Law and Mr. Holmes and others, were very, very upset about this. Finally they decided what they were going to do, and they came and told me. I told them it would never work. But this is what they did, and it did work: They made up a bunch of posters, and then they called this group together. They said, "Now, listen. It's really not the people here that are the trouble. It's Wall Street. What we need to do is to picket Wall Street. Here are some tickets to go to New York. We believe we can make them come through." They literally had bought tickets and got the thugs out of town, which I thought was so creative. It got some of those people setting the fires out of town and got the business community to give in. The business community got worried with the fires, and rightfully so, because nobody was in control of those thugs. They weren't under the movement.

Savannah always has loved its city so. When Sherman's march came to Savannah, the leaders came to the edge of the city and surrendered so Sherman wouldn't burn Savannah. The leadership there always has treasured their historical city and preserved it. Also there's quite a big Jewish population there, and they were excellent members of our council and worked very hard to have better race relations in Savannah. Lee Adler, a local man, was big business and old Savannah and all that, and he was on our side. The Manger Hotel chain was on our side, and they took an active part. So between the chains and the businesses, they decided to call a meeting and said something has got to be done. They said, "We'll give in and open the restaurants and hotels." They wrote the copy for the newspaper, decided where on the newspaper they wanted it, and the next morning, they had given in.

I don't know why the bigger newspapers never picked it up. There never seemed to be the photographers or the press around in the movement, and yet it was bigger and better organized than Albany. Yet Albany got all the publicity.

The first marches were in Savannah, and they were very frightening to me, because they would march at night, awful late at night. The black people would get off from work, and they would have supper somewhere, and then they would march to the squares. Of course, in Savannah, with all those squares, you have wonderful places for meetings. My part—and a part I played a lot of times in lots of places—was listening to what all the white people were saying and keeping in touch with the marchers. I remember standing by the sideline and listening to what the white people would be saying, and it frightened me very, very much, because they were sounding so terribly violent. Talking about who they were going to shoot up and what they were going to do. Then I would go and warn Mr. Law. But he knew this. Somehow to me it was kind of new.

I had a new experience in Savannah that I'd never had before. I was standing on a corner of one of the squares, it was the opposite side of the square from Morrison's Cafeteria, and I was standing there waiting for somebody to pick me up. The blacks started to enter Morrison's, and quick as a flash—I often wondered where the people came from—quick as a flash, there were really two mobs, a white group and a black group, and they headed for each other. Well, I never remembered moving; I never remembered deciding to move. All I remember—and this made me see how mob psychology can really overcome you—because the next thing I knew, I was standing in the middle of the square and I had gone across, joined the black group. The fire engine had come with the hoses and separated the two groups, and I was standing in the park, all of a sudden catching my breath and wondering what was going on.

Your emotions can so often get ahead of your thinking. That was a good experience for me, because you so often say, "Well, I wouldn't do a thing like that." But once you've had one or two experiences like that, you realize you're not real sure what you would do. I was so glad afterwards that I just had instinctively gone to the right side.

I really got my feet wet in Savannah.

Diary, Georgia Council on Human Relations: Albany

<u>January 2-3, 1962</u>: Met with Albany Movement at their request to map out strategy for meeting with City Commission. Also met with group of white women and continued making white and Negro contacts toward creating a Council. A most successful trip. Sorry the expenses were high.

<u>April 19-21, 1962</u>: Tried to get negotiations started again. No luck. Good luck with white community. But Negro community in chaos. Charles Jones conducted mass meetings Thursday and Friday night--persuading people to "go to jail and be free." Visited widow of man who was killed by Police. Made plans for meeting on May 4th. Hope for success then. What an unholy mess!

DEMONSTRATORS AT A MASS MEETING IN ALBANY, GEORGIA, CHANT "FREEDOM!"
(Photograph used by permission of AP/Wide World Photos.)

<u>May 3-4, 1962</u>: SNCC is awful in Albany. They are doing
more harm than good. They have one absolute fanatic--
Charles Jones. Crazy mixed up kid. Sensitive, sweet,
bitter, full of hate, talking love your white brother.
Meaner than sin--all wrapped together. I did a few good
things I think. Went to see the grieving widow. This
seemed to make the biggest impression on the community
of anything. Got a few more whites in conversation.
They are really waking up--but just about 3 months
late. The damage is done to their town. But the city
commission still doesn't give one inch. It was a fine
meeting--The Negroes came from all the different
factions. I had invited all those who hated each other
the worst. Then I had 5 ministers. This was a real
achievement. A Quaker couple came. The chairman of the
Church Women. In all 13 whites and 16 Negroes. I could
have had two hundred Negroes. But I had been selective.
I was afraid they would keep the whites away. We had a
fair meeting. The Negroes kept saying sharp remarks to
each other and the white people did get the
significance. I really felt like Mr. in-between.
<u>July 9-10, 1962</u>: Attended mass meeting of the
movement. Strategy meeting of steering committee of
movement. Court--verdict of King and Abernathy. Visits
with local Council--white and Negroes.
<u>July 27-August 1, 1962</u>: To help in crisis to attempt
negotiations. Decided to mail letter to occupant mailing. Spoke at mass meeting Friday night. Had a
<u>horrible</u> Saturday struggling at jail, city hall, etc.
trying to find how badly the SNCC people were hurt. All
too much for too few people of good will to handle.
<u>September 1-8, 1962</u>: Attend meeting of Council. 30
present. SNCC sent delegation of 5 or 6, which
presented a problem since they were not in accord with
the purposes of the Council. A very difficult group--
many factions--each knifing the other.
<u>September 20-25, 1962</u>: Decided to make education
survey and work on employment at Turner.
<u>November 7-9, 1962</u>: Talked with Dr. Hamilton and
Slater King about program. Went to Turner Air Force

Base. No consideration, information obtained. I almost lost my temper. Wrote complaint to Pres. Committee.

January 15-17, 1963: Answered call of Col. at Turner Air Force Base who was investigating the complaint I made concerning discrimination in employment. Good session, hope it worked. Worked out some possible solutions with the Civil Personnel man. Worked with High School Principal on some new ideas to try to combat juvenile delinquency. Negro community still torn with jealousy and bitterness. Worked with Father Shipps on plans for white people who are not members of the Council.

May 30-June 1, 1963: Meet with our group to see why it is not moving. Particularly to meet with Negro ministers (at their request). Dr. Anderson (leader of the movement) is leaving town. The ministers are going to try to step in and get something accomplished. I don't know what will happen. Bill went with me. He visited the grounds of the burned churches to see if he could help them get started. Something is holding up the works??? Bill has offered to do the site planning (for free, of course). Albany is a sick, sick, sad, sad town.

November 1-2, 1963: Stopped in Griffin to check on KKK activities.

December 12-14, 1963: Our Council has lost its white members almost entirely. A very sad sight. The old stalwarts came to the meeting but they were not discouraged. They told me that I should take hope. Albany is awful. But we will not stop trying. We will help with the hospital survey and help with a Christmas letter from the Albany Movement.

June 21-23, 1964: To speak at the annual meeting of the Colored Federation of Womens Clubs--Interesting group--A very few of these women will ever use--or at least not in the near future--use any open facilities. Got a few good names--(Hot!!!--no air conditioning--as usual in Albany).

October 8, 1964: Work to get help for 4 kids in High School. One girl makes A's, others not doing so well.

Talked with Fortson about local problems plus Mrs.
Barnum, Mrs. Hiers and Jimmy Carter. Slow, slow. But
maybe we are making some headway. Some encouragement
from the whites.
<u>October 12-14, 1964</u>: Checked with Hamilton and Mrs.
Blythe. The last white person has chickened out. We
will continue to work--but on employment with Negroes.
C. B. King made a good race. His appearance on TV with
local whites was very educational. He is optimistic.
I'm not--Albany sickens me. But if we work in
Thomasville and Americus and maybe some other places
things may improve everywhere.
<u>November 8-11, 1964</u>: Made survey for Civil Rights on
compliance with Civil Rights Act. Gave me a chance to
talk with several people about the local situation.
Still harsh coldness on the white side.
<u>June 16-19, 1965</u>: To find witnesses for Civil Rights
hearing. To contact new members for Council. Hectic
three days. Hearing was fairly good. Council is dead.
Must have new leadership. Negroes continue to be very
split. No good cooperation from anyone. Great need in
Albany for hard work. We have been away too long.

I can't remember the first time I went to Albany, but I went at the request
of the movement. When the movement started in southwest Georgia, I
practically lived down there.

Dr. Anderson was chairman of the movement at that time, and there
was a black section of town, a subdivision that some of the blacks that had
a little money had opened up. There were quite a few professionals, black
business leaders, and black officials at the military base close by. The city
had promised them sewers and city services, and then they reneged on it.
That caused them to organize. This was not yet civil rights. It was just a
matter of justice, getting what the white people were getting since they
were paying taxes. That kind of started the movement.

Then the Student Nonviolent Coordinating Committee (SNCC) came
down there, and they had a real good, strong group, with Charles Jones,
Charles Sherrod, and Cordell Reagon. So it turned more and more into
civil rights activity, what you really call the movement. They started having mass meetings, and getting the people out for marches, and many of
the people that marched were very young people, almost children. The
Albany mass meetings were something that you would never forget.

I've wondered since what part music played in it. That singing was so tremendous that now I get quite emotional sometimes when I hear some of the songs. I don't think that there's any way of ever reading or seeing on television or ever getting a real feeling of what some of those mass meetings were like, and some of that singing was like. Sometimes when I hear those songs again, they're almost hollow in comparison with the way they were when those audiences sang them. It was something about that, the movement and the feeling of the movement, that was just so compelling. I suppose that's the reason that you always stick with it and keep on trying to do something about it.

They had a real strong NAACP there, and Dr. Hamilton, who was a dentist, was the chairman of that, and Mamie Reese, who was later up here in Atlanta on the Pardon and Parole Board, was in that. The NAACP was real strong, active, but they weren't for getting out in the street. The NAACP in Albany was middle class, older, and they were working for change but in a very slow and methodical way. But they would pay the bail money to get marchers out of jail. They might not agree on all the tactics, but they certainly agreed on justice for all. It wasn't as separate as people thought, the older ones and the kids.

I'll tell you how Martin Luther King and the Southern Christian Leadership Conference (SCLC) got to Albany. Bill and I were over in Brunswick, vacationing with our kids and grandchildren at the beach, at St. Simons, and I got a call from SNCC, this was Albany SNCC, asking me to come over. SNCC would call me whenever they needed me. I would do whatever they said. I was never in on planning what they were going to do, but I would do what I could to help them. So Bill and I raced over there, drove from Brunswick over to Albany, getting there at about two o'clock in the morning. I went to the Holiday Inn where we usually stayed and called Claude Sitton of *The New York Times* and asked where the SNCC meeting was.

He gave me a telephone number. I called it, and they said, "Come out such-and-such a street, and at such-and-such corner, somebody will flag you down." They weren't going to say over the phone where the meeting was, for fear somebody would hear them. So Bill and I rode down the road, stopped the car, and the SNCC kid got in the car. We got to this house, and all the shades were pulled down so you couldn't see in at all. It was dark as pitch. And there sat these bedraggled, tired-out, worn-out SNCCs, trying to decide what the hell to do next.

Half of the SNCC kids were in jail, and the other half were trying to decide what to do. Bill and I sat there. I never felt like giving my advice, because I didn't know what advice to give. All I wanted them to know was, whatever they decided, I'd help them. So they began to talk about whether or not they should ask King to come and help them. You know, there's a lot of controversy about whether King just went or whether SNCC asked him to come to Albany. Well, I'll have you know SNCC asked him. I heard it. They got on the phone and called him. He said he'd consider and let them know, and he called back and said he'd come. There were not any difficulties that I saw, in the beginning, between SNCC and SCLC. Andy Young came and Wyatt T. Walker came. It seems to me that Wyatt T. was more a leader than anyone else. I thought he was one of the best people King ever had with him.

I used to work with them all, all the groups in Albany. Dr. Hamilton and I were good friends; the head of the movement and I were good friends. What we tried to do was get an interracial negotiating committee set up. We got set up with a number of people appointed by the city council and a number by blacks. We didn't have a local council on human relations set up by this time; we hadn't gotten that far yet. We were trying to work out some negotiations with officials—the police chief, the Mayor, city fathers—concerning demands, particularly for city services. The committee drew up an agreement, and the blacks in the movement went along with it. The committee took it to the white city council, but the council wouldn't agree and sent back the most insulting telegram I have ever heard in my life.

When the news came, we were in the little back room in the church where the meetings went on. King was there, Wyatt T. Walker was there, Dr. Anderson was there. I can't remember who else from the movement was there. And I cried. I don't often cry, but I was so disappointed. I hadn't had any sleep and I was just fatigued. The weather was terrible, cold and raining, and I was chilled to the bone. Wyatt T. Walker looked at me and said, "My God, it's the first time I ever saw a white woman cry. I didn't know they could." I was the only white person in there, and I just wanted to bury my white skin.

Also I had gotten arrested that day. I always did try to avoid going to jail, and I never did, though I got pretty close. The closest I ever got was in Albany. I was down at the black church where the headquarters were. This real smart woman was working in the movement; she was a college professor at Albany State, and she and I were going somewhere. We left together from the church, got in the car, and started to wherever we were going. The first thing you know, the police stopped us. I said, "Get out! Get out fast! Let me take care of this. If they arrest me, I don't want you arrested." She was pregnant, too, real pregnant. She got out the other side of the car and disappeared. The police took me in, and I thought, "Oh, God, now Papa will find out about it, and Bill will find out." That was one thing that was worrying me, because I didn't always tell them about some of the narrow escapes I had. I also knew the jails were full, and they were taking people out to the neighboring little towns. I was afraid I was going to get put in a jail and forgotten.

They couldn't decide what to charge me with, because I hadn't broken any law. About that time, Pat Watters, the newsman with the *Atlanta Journal*, came up. Those newspapermen were great to me down there. They used to make me have a room in the motel with some of them in rooms on both sides. I said to Pat, "Please call Southern Regional Council and tell them to get me a lawyer and a good one, fast. And for goodness sake, don't tell Bill or Papa."

About that time, down comes a policeman who said, "The Mayor says to charge Mrs. Pauley with a traffic violation and let her go." And they were glad, too, I think. They just didn't really know what to do. So they charged me with not stopping at a stop sign, and I paid ten dollars.

Do you know what that little woman who had been riding with me did? She went to the mayor and told him that I had been arrested, but that I hadn't done anything. That's why the mayor sent the word down. That took a lot of courage, for her to go to the mayor.

I went back to the motel. I sat down, and I thought, "What am I going to do now?" The police had advised me to leave town. Am I going to go or what? Am I going to chicken out or what? I couldn't decide. I didn't know what would happen if I didn't leave town, but if I left town how could I come back? I sure wasn't through. So finally I decided that I better go back down there and tell the chief of police, Laurie Pritchett, that I wasn't quite ready to go. I went down there but I was scared. So I went to a little gift shop next door and did practically all my Christmas shopping. Then I looked up the steps, and the steps kept getting longer and longer and longer. I didn't think I would ever make it up to the top. But finally I went in, and I said, "Sir, I just wanted to tell you I have a few other things that I want to do before I leave town, and so I won't be leaving quite yet." Then my conscience was clear and I went on about my business.

That was the same day that the answer came from the city council about our negotiations. When the telegram came and the white city council didn't agree to the plan, the movement people felt it was a defeat, a complete defeat. And Pritchett was breaking the movement; he was arresting people. People that had jobs, they were losing them. The "jail, not bail" strategy was just a fizzle. They didn't have anybody else that was going to go to jail. People were getting too scared. So King pulled out and left. I tried to meet with King. I wanted very much for them to stay and to work on something else to try to heal some of the wounds. The black community was just so split. I was unable to get to King, because Andy Young was so protective. I wasn't telling him what to do; I just didn't think they ought to pull out like that and leave them down there. When King left, there was deep depression, and various factions blaming each other that they hadn't succeeded, rather than blaming the damn white people. That was the tragic thing about King coming in, no matter where it was. When he left it was always deflating. But I don't think that means he shouldn't have gone in.

The thing that people don't realize is that King played such a small part. He came in and he didn't really stay so very long. It wasn't such a big part that he played. The whole Albany Movement was the people there, and the same thing was true of the whole movement. It was a grassroots movement. It's overrated, King's influence, just because he spoke so beautifully and wrote so beautifully.

I'm glad I stuck it out. We kept going, even after the movement stopped. I wouldn't have given up for anything because people felt so hopeless. We had organized a council and it was struggling. One thing the council did was to send out a letter—"occupant mail"—to the white people of Albany, asking them to be reasonable and negotiate. I got some people in Atlanta to help me write it, and we worked and worked and worked on this letter. I tried to get somebody to sign it whose name would mean something, but nobody would sign it. We ended up deciding that rather than just not do it at all, I would just sign it myself. I got 278 answers that told me to go to hell, in no uncertain terms. One of them was a card, and it said, "We know why God made snakes and rats and roaches, but why he made you, we'll never know."

I think I got one positive response from somebody who didn't live there. I was surprised. I thought there'd be some decent people. There was one lady, one white lady, in Albany who invited me to come to supper at her house when her husband was out of town. He worked at the air base; they weren't really natives. That was the only time any white person ever asked me to have a cup of coffee with them in that city, much less come to their house.

But I had complete support from my husband, though I was very careful what I didn't tell him. I wouldn't tell him the riskiest things. I was very lucky with my husband, because he thought that people ought to do what they wanted to do. He was proud of the things that I did. I remember once, when they'd had a lot of church burnings in South Georgia, Bill said that he'd like to go down and see if he could help them in planning how they might rebuild. It ended up that he helped some of the churches rebuild. He was always interested in what I was doing and always supportive, or I couldn't have done it. My brother, though, he tried to stop me. He was worried about it, and there was some danger connected to it. I appreciated him worrying about it, but it wasn't about to stop me. I think he was honest in just being afraid that I was doing something that was dangerous, because he wasn't what you'd call a prejudiced person.

As for my friends, a lot of them just dropped me like a hotcake. One of my best friends was having a party during this time, and my husband and I were helping her with it. She took me aside and said, "Now, during the party, Frances, would you just do me a favor and not talk about civil rights and your job." Well, I wasn't in the habit of making people uncomfortable if I was in a social gathering. It hurts. She was one of my best and closest friends.

We kept trying to make a bridge some way in Albany. We organized a prayer group, some black women and white women in town, and that didn't work. That petered out. We got some black and white businessmen together who were worried about business. They met secretly at night, out at the Episcopal church at the edge of town. We had to make sure there wouldn't be a majority of blacks. The white businessmen said they would meet with the blacks, but didn't want to have too many blacks. They were so scared a hundred would come. They didn't know that I'd have a hard time getting ten blacks that would have courage enough to go up there and meet with them. They didn't know that part, and little did I tell them. That group did last longer than some of the others. We tried prayer groups, we tried business groups, we tried ministerial associations. The council eventually failed.

We also had hangers-on, wide-eyed liberals that liked to talk about having been to Albany. They'd come down to see what was going on. Dr. Anderson, who was the head of the movement, had a house that was very nice, a new house. It was headquarters for the movement in Albany, and everybody from out of town came there. They expected to be bedded down and fed. Those people would come from all over the United States and eat the food, and do you think they would do anything about bringing any food or anything? All the Negroes in the community would cook up stuff and bring it over.

One time, one of these liberals asked Mrs. Anderson where to spend the night. She said, "There's not a place except our bed."

And he said, "Well, we hate to take your bed, but if you don't have any other . . ." And he took it! He took Dr. Anderson's bed.

One time I went down there and ate, but I took a stack of pies from the motel, nice warm apple pies. They told me it was the first time anybody from out of town had ever brought anything to eat.

We decided one thing that we could work on would be jobs. That was something we could unite on. This brought some of the older NAACP blacks together with the movement people. Dr. Hamilton, the dentist, was a leader in our employment efforts. Then we got some of the federal people to help open up jobs at the bases; they had all these bases there—army, air force, marine, a lot of government installations in Albany. They had officers that were supposed to see that the hiring was done in a nondiscriminatory way. So we started in with them, and then began to work with some of the businesses, and that's how we helped to bring the community together, because it was awful for everybody to hate each other so bad.

Diary, Georgia Council on Human Relations: Southwest Georgia

<u>July 19-22, 1965 - Brunswick, Baker County</u>: Went to Brunswick to meet with council to work on School desegregation and Housing. Left before I was quite ready because of emergency call from SNCC in Baker County. The mass meeting in Baker was unbelievable. The Negroes so very great--quiet--determined. I was run out of town by the whites on the following day. Took a poor sick beat up kid to the hospital. He was unconscious. What a night!! Tried in every way to get help from Sanders. It was all very terrible. But I was very, very glad to have been there.

<u>October 24-26, 1965 - Albany</u>: I was a witness in the Federal Court Case concerning civil rights workers in Baker County--On Monday I waited from 9 til 5:45 to be called--in a room with 20 people and five chairs. It was better than several field trips. I feel I really know those friends!! Judge Elliott is awful! I did a little better but still am scared on the witness stand. The Negroes were so appreciative that I felt terrible--They have done so much! I talked with Al Henry at Koinonia about the possibility of forming a Southwest Georgia Chapter since we can't get a group in any town. Actually this part of Georgia is ahead of the Eastern counties--all because of Negro activity plus others like us!

<u>December 6-8, 1965 - Albany</u>: Organizational meeting of Southwest Georgia Council. Everything went <u>very</u> well. Good trip--<u>76</u> present, 8 whites--But at least we have tokenism.

<u>December 29-30, 1965 - Tifton</u>: 2nd meeting of Southwest Ga. Chapter--It was great--101 present--good

program on voting--a _few_ more whites--Maybe it really
will work. We'll see! The young preacher Barbour was a
dear! He'll get killed!

March 21-24, 1966 - Albany: Had _good_ meeting in Albany
in the Court House. A real wonderful occasion--over
100 present. Good visits re: employment with our
chairman and also head of breadbasket. Visited the
integrated nursery--17 Negroes, 14 whites--_Unbelievable_
in Albany. Went by Koinonia to "restore my soul" after
the filth of Dawson. The children from there are still
being ostracized in Americus. What will become of that
town? The question that bothers me very much is the
steady increase of hatred both by Negroes and whites.
What will be the result? Why can't white people wake
up before it's too late?

May 22-26, 1966 - Albany: Met with S.W. Ga. Council.
Excellent meeting. _But_ Father Wright our best white is
being kicked out. Albany is hopeless!!

July 27-28, 1966 - Sylvester: Met with S.W. Ga.
Council. At least 100 present. Many owned their own
farms. This group is progressing but we need a strong
leader. Mr. Thomas & I are carrying too much of the
load. However, it is well worth it. Checked with Atty.
C. B. King's office on Welfare cases. "Welfare Rights
Committee" active in Albany.

August 20-22, 1966 - Tifton: Stopped to see our
contact Barbour in Tifton. _Yes_, he has been run out of
town. We have _no_ whites left. They leave faster than
we can find them.

August 30-September 1, 1966 - Cordele: Went at the
request of Bramlett, Supt. of Schools. He was frantic--
afraid of HEW and terrified of the Negro Movement--He
listened--Poor Man!! Met with Negro leadership. There
will probably be more demonstrations. I hope not until
the kids are more settled in school. The kids are
doing all right at the moment. It's a rough town! We
_do_ have some friends--the Chamber of Commerce man etc.
One good thing about the more violent SNCC--makes
folks like us!

November 9-11, 1966 - Albany-Baker County: We had a
meeting of the S.W. Ga. Council. Showed the Know Your
Rights Film. Talked with county attorney for 2 hours.

THE HILL FAMILY, THOMAS COUNTY, GEORGIA. THE TWO SONS
INTEGRATED THE SCHOOL IN THEIR COMMUNITY IN 1965.
(Photograph courtesy of Frances Pauley.)

Established some rapport. Each trip I take on one more
enemy to talk to. I can't stand but one. Spent at
least an hour with Charles Sherrod. I believe we can
work with that sad, disillusioned young man. In all a
good trip.
January 22-24, 1967 - Baker County and Albany: Baker:
Investigate various problems. Surplus Foods. Set up
OEO, etc. Attended mass meeting. Very pitiful. The
lack of experience in really taking part in the commu-

nity activities. It will take practice. Albany:
Meeting with steering committee of the S.W. Ga.
Chapter. An excellent meeting--all came. Here again
local leaders are having an opportunity to learn democratic processes within an organization. Again, at
times it is painful.
August 4-5, 1967 - Albany - Baker County: Baker: Met
with people to talk about how things are progressing
in the government programs. Sounds very good. I don't
know of anything that can be done in Baker except provide jobs--There simply aren't any. Albany: Had
welfare training for some 25 summer workers--(as well
as a few of the regular under Sherrod). Sherrod
continually disrupts. He is getting worse. As a whole
the meeting was good. I'd really like to have a Sunday
off. This weekend travel is something else.

SNCC asked me to come into Baker County as an observer when they
went in to try to get a local organization started. Charles Sherrod was the
leader, and he picked some of his most experienced SNCC people to go
with him. I said, "Oh, Charles," because Baker is so mean. "Do you have
to?" I don't mean I actually thought I could or even tried to stop them, but
I did at least tell them how bad I thought it was. Well, they knew how bad
it was far more than I did.

One night I was over in Brunswick and they called me and asked me to
come. They said, "We've had some bad trouble today. We went down to
the courthouse to try to register, and they beat up Charles Sherrod and
several other people. Do you think you could come?" They gave me directions to this little church out in the country. I rented a car, but the only one
I could get was a red convertible. I didn't want a red convertible; I wanted
to be as inconspicuous as possible.

I got there and they had everything blacked out at the church so nobody
could see in, and it was hot as Hades in that church. That was the time I
realized what it meant that it was good to perspire because it cooled you
off. I got completely soaking wet, as if I'd had a hose turned on me. Then
I began to cool off a little bit. The church was packed solid, and they were
so glad when I came in. I just went in and sat down; I didn't say anything.
Charles Sherrod had a towel around his neck that was bloody, and he kept
dabbing places that were still bleeding, where he'd been beat up. He made
a speech on why you were a bigger man if you didn't fight back. It was the
most wonderful speech on nonviolence I ever heard in all my life. I'd just
give anything in the whole wide world if I had a recording of it. A couple

of men in the audience argued with him about it, saying, "I don't think we should take it. We should fight back." Quite an argument on nonviolence.

In the meantime, one kid keeled over and fainted. I just thought it was from the heat. People took him out, and I thought as soon as he got outdoors in the air he'd come to. Well, the meeting was shortly over, and they said, "So-and-so is still unconscious. Would you take him to the hospital?" So they put him in the car, it was late at night. I started out, and I was scared to go fast, because I was scared a cop might come out of the bushes somewhere. Yet I was scared not to go fast; I was wondering if he was dying. Once he sort of came to and said he was cold. It was hot as hell, but probably he was soaking wet. There wasn't anything I could do about him being cold. I had that damned convertible.

So I thought, "I'll go by the SNCC office and I'll get somebody to come out and look at him, because if I take him to the hospital, the first thing they'll do is ask his name." So I went by the SNCC office when I got to Albany.

A couple of kids came out and looked at him and said, "Oh, that's so-and-so." They got in the car and went with us to the hospital.

But the hospital wouldn't take him. They said there wasn't any doctor on duty. And I said, "Oh, but you're going to take him, and we'll get a doctor."

They had one doctor on staff, and they said, "Well, you can call him if you want to."

I said, "What doctor are you supposed to call for emergency tonight?"

And they said, "Doctor so-and-so, but he won't come."

I called the black doctor, and he said he'd come. We waited and he didn't come. They had brought the boy into the emergency room, and he was still unconscious. So I called again and begged him to come. He didn't want to, but he finally came.

He gave the SNCC worker a shot that brought him around to consciousness. After he'd been conscious for a few minutes, he said, "You can take him home."

I said, "Take him home? In the first place, I don't even know where he lives. In the second place, he needs medical attention. You just put him in this hospital."

Well, he said, "Who's going to pay for it?"

I said, "I'm going to pay for it." Of course the council couldn't pay for it. We didn't have money to pay for anything like that. I paid for it out of my pocket, $150, before they would take him.

I'll tell you, that does something to you. You begin to see what it means when you can't get medical treatment when the medical treatment is right there. They wouldn't have taken him if I hadn't been white and paid the

$150. Then I saw a black orderly that looked friendly. I tipped him heavily and told him to see that nothing happened to that kid. He had internal bleeding from being beaten. They kept him for a few days, and we arranged medical treatment in Atlanta. That was an awful night. I lived a long time that night.

I went back down to Baker County the next day, because they were going to march again. I was scared to death. What was going to happen? I didn't march with them, because I didn't know whether it was a good idea or bad, or whether it was just that I was a coward. But I didn't. I figured that wasn't my role, that my role was something different. If I was on the sidelines, there were certain things I could do and certain ways that I could be a witness.

When I arrived, I went to a little cafe to get some coffee and chatted with the people. We got along fine. They didn't know me. Being fat and old, you can get by with a lot! Then I went to the stores; there was just one little row of stores. This was in Newton. I went into each of the stores. I would chat with people, all of them just as friendly as they could be. I very easily passed for a very nice white southern lady.

Then I went over to where the marchers were going to meet. I brought a load of them in my car over to picket. I let them out of my car on the courthouse lawn, and of course some of the white people in the stores saw me. I didn't try to hide. The white people were down here on one corner of the square, and the black people were up on the next corner, and the picket line was on the sidewalk next to the courthouse. There were no more than twenty pickets, mostly women and a couple of kids.

In the meantime, I had called the state capitol and asked for protection. But the state patrol wouldn't come. I called the Federal Bureau of Investigation (FBI). At that time, there was a man that was head of the Atlanta office who later was demoted, a marvelous man, just a marvelous man. I never did meet him face to face, but we had dozens of conversations. And he told me that I never did tell him anything that was a bad lead. So he was always cooperative. But the people that he would send would be horrible. At times he would pull out the local FBI and send some others who did not work regularly with the local police. But he sent some local FBI into Newton.

As the march started, the whites began to say ugly things to me. I was by myself, in between the group of whites on one corner and the blacks on the next corner. I didn't want to go over to the blacks, because I didn't want to get them in trouble by being with them. There was a kind of white mob, if you could call it that. Baker is real little, so it was a big crowd for Baker. A lady came up to me and cussed me out. I'm telling you, I never hope to get such a cussing out as that lady gave me. She used the foulest language I ever heard in all my life. Then the whites got in a huddle over on the corner, and they said, "Let's tar and feather her." Well, that didn't bother me because I didn't see any tar or feathers. But they kept on saying what they were going to do to me and to the "niggers."

The owners of the store told me not to stand there. They didn't want me in front of their store. So I'd move away, and the next man said, "Go away. We don't want you in front of our store." Then I'd move over again. I ran out of places to stand. Finally I went across the street to the courthouse. A white man came up to me and he had a gun. He said, "I'm going to kill you. You leave or I will kill you."

I went to the local police and the FBI. I said, "You see that man right over there? He's got a gun and he just said he was going to kill me. He told me to leave."

The FBI said, "Well, why don't you leave?"

So I went to the local police and I said, "See that man over there? He's got a gun and he said he was going to kill me."

And they said, "Well, why don't you leave town?"

I didn't know what else to do except to leave, but I didn't want to leave. I just felt like it was cowardly to go, but I didn't know where to go. I didn't have a motel room, a friend's house, anyplace. There wasn't anyplace I had to go.

So I got in my car and I rode up the road to the first filling station, got out and went in. I called the state capitol and I said, "I want to speak to Governor Sanders." I had talked and worked with Mr. Sanders in Augusta when there was trouble there. He had promised me that he would give me support in my work. He told me that although he wouldn't help me, he would always give me protection. On the phone I reminded him that he had promised protection. I told him a white man was threatening to kill me. I told him I was afraid they were going to kill those SNCC kids down there. I said, "If one of those kids gets killed, I'm telling you, it's going to be your fault. I've warned you. I asked for help in this place." I said it just as strong as I could. They did send the state patrol, and nobody was hurt that day.

It took a lot of nerve for me to go back. But I went back many times, and the Southwest Georgia Council on Human Relations did a real good job. The first time I went back, we had an integrated council meeting at the courthouse. We took the whites from out of town, just a few, all that would go. Plus the blacks that lived here. We decided we'd have the meeting on a noncontroversial subject. I believe it was something like how to establish a credit union. It was some economic thing. The room that we met in was upstairs in the courthouse. The only way up was a little single stairway, and everybody in there was scared to death. They were really

HUBERT THOMAS, SPEAKING AT FREEDOM DAY, MAY 17, 1966, IN
THOMASVILLE, GEORGIA. FRANCES PAULEY IS SEATED AT THE FAR LEFT.
(Photograph courtesy of Frances Pauley.)

scared. I thought we'd all have our tires slashed, and we wouldn't be able
to get away. That was the only thing I was afraid of. Father Austin Ford
was presiding. Father Ford was an Episcopal priest from Atlanta and a
board member for the Georgia council. He said, "What shall we sing?"

The audience said, "We Shall Overcome." We always ended meetings
with "We Shall Overcome." And they sang "We Shall Overcome," starting
with the verse, "we are not afraid." And there we were all just scared to
death.

The man that had threatened me came in with other local whites and sat
up in the front in the jury section. Mr. Hubert Thomas, who was working on
my staff—a great, huge black man—was the one that made the talk about
credit unions. The white people got so interested in what he had to say that
they asked him questions! Mr. Thomas worked practically full time in Baker

for a long time. He was from South Georgia, really an interesting person because he had been a follower of Marcus Garvey. He was a black militant, as his father was, and he hated white people. He never did get to the point where he would eat with me, but we got to be very good friends. I had the most tremendous admiration for him, and I think he did for me. Yet here he was working for not only a white person, but a white woman.

I used to stay at the Holiday Inn in Albany—Albany was always my base when I was in southwest Georgia—and I'd get a room at the back. The back of it backed up on the black area of the city. I always tried to get a room in the back, so I could come and go easily without having to pass through the front lobby. Also the black people that worked in the Holiday Inn knew me, and I remember one man particularly. He would always be there to carry my bags to my room. We'd get back to my room and then he'd come in, and shut the door, and sit down, and tell me everything that had happened since I'd been there last. And he'd tell it to me straight too. This was a great protection for me. They wouldn't have let anything happen to me.

The Southwest Georgia Council on Human Relations had about three whites and about three hundred blacks. The three is exaggerated; we probably had twenty-five. We started out with a bunch of whites. We started out with five preachers that really were great, but all of them either got run out or they left town. There was a Presbyterian minister and he left town; two Episcopal ministers and both of them left; a Baptist minister and he left; and the Methodist minister, he left. There were five ministers that left. They didn't leave because they were in the council, they left because they had taken a stand in the community.

One of the great things about being in and around Americus was going out to Koinonia to visit with Clarence Jordan. Koinonia was an interracial farm near Americus, and Clarence Jordan was one of its founders. Sometimes when I would get really down and so discouraged that I just couldn't see any way that we could make any changes, I'd go out and see Clarence. I don't remember anything he said in particular. It was just the way that he was. He had a way of making you feel that you had the strength and you could do it. I would always leave there knowing I could keep on, always.

I went to see Jimmy Carter who was also in that area. This was before he was governor, way before he was governor. I went because he was a leading peanut farmer, and also because they had been so active in the Democratic party. Carter was in his office, and his office was just a pigpen. It looked like it never had been dusted; it was just about as bad a little country office as you ever did go into. He was very nice and very lovely. We had a long talk about Americus, a long talk about everything. He said,

"I think it's absolutely wonderful what you're doing. But I'm sorry, I'm not going to help you. I believe in it, but I'm not going to help you, and I don't know anybody that's going to." That's just the way he is. But I must say this for him: He told his cook to send her children to the white school and he would see that they were protected. And she did, and he did. Then when they really integrated the schools in Plains, all the white kids went to private school, practically. Amy Carter was assigned to what had been a black school, so you can imagine how few whites went to it. But Amy went to that school, and I admire them for that. When he ran for governor, he was very careful what he said. He made like he was a racist. Still, they were extremely liberal for that section.

I still think Americus was one of the worst towns I ever worked in. Segregation came first; money came second. Most places put money first, and you could talk to them. But in Americus the bankers didn't move, and consequently Americus didn't move. I was powerless. I did well to get out with my own neck, looking back on it.

But we kept on working. Each time we met, we'd meet in a different county. We got a lot of really good government programs going in Baker. Some of them were large amounts of money. The council never took the grants and operated the programs. We always had the local group organized to take leadership and handle the programs. We tried to develop the local black leadership.

One educational program was particularly good: half of the day the adults did basic education, and the other half of the day they did job training that would prepare them to take some kind of job in the community. It was useful and successful. There was a sewing factory in Baker County, and we'd train blacks for that. The program in Baker was integrated. The whites and blacks came and worked together. We had the most beautiful graduation exercises in the same horrible courthouse where we had such a frightening time. Blacks and whites graduating together; black and white staff sitting together up there in the jury seats. That was a beautiful program but an expensive one. The people got paid for a long time. And Mr. Thomas worked in Baker County for many months.

Carol King, attorney C. B. King's wife, started the first integrated day care in Albany, which turned into one of the first Head Start groups in the country. She went on to be on the national board of Head Start. One day I was riding down a white street in Albany and noticed both black and white mothers and children going into the front door of a very attractive, well-kept house. I saw one lady let a little white boy out of her car, and she said to him, "Be good, son, and don't play with those nigras." But this was an integrated group of kids with an integrated committee of mothers, in Albany, Georgia, in the sixties.

We also got interested in welfare rights, and we organized welfare rights groups. A lot of places where you couldn't get any whites for a council, you could get blacks in welfare rights. We had about forty different groups in the state. Some places had councils and welfare rights groups, but the councils generally weren't interested in the very poor. And council work got harder and harder. We expanded our program until it was just about killing us, and yet we didn't have enough money to hire any more people. Organizing costs money, and lots of members means a lot more money. If you get a strong local council, the local council wants to do things locally, and they need money locally. The kind of people we had in the council didn't have any money. And we certainly weren't popular in the South to get any money from southerners.

Fundraising was always difficult. I knew of a couple of instances when I asked for money for welfare rights, and the Southern Regional Council didn't back me up. In fact, once or twice, the Southern Regional Council told me that I was going too far, that I had to be more careful, tread more gently. I just felt like they were being too chicken about it. If you're ever going to do it, you have to do it. Put your foot in the road, take a step. I was more activist than the Southern Regional Council, trying to organize community action rather than to be a study group. But we relied on the Southern Regional Council for information, just the actual facts. We could depend on them for that, and that takes a lot of time. But it seems to me that if they had encouraged and helped the state councils more, they would have been better off.

Then there were some people that were beginning to say that the organization should have a black head, that white people shouldn't be telling blacks what to do, and so on. I did think it was time we had black leadership. So I finally decided that it had just gotten to be too much of a hassle over the money with the Southern Regional Council. I decided I'd quit and turn it over to somebody else. This was in 1967.

My successor was John McCown, a black man who had been with Office of Equal Opportunity in Athens, Georgia, and we had worked together on some joint projects. After he had been hired, I wanted to introduce him to the different foundations that I knew in New York. So we went up, and Father Austin Ford went too. We got there in the middle of the night, and the clerk at the hotel where I'd made the reservations took a look at white Austin and black John and me and said there wasn't any such reservation.

I said, "I believe if you look, you could find it."

So he said, "Well, now, I have one big room. How about that?"

I didn't crack a smile. I turned around and said, "Well, sons, what do you think? Can we sleep in one room?"

They didn't crack a smile, neither one of them. And Austin said, "No, Mom. I've had my own room since I was twelve, and I want my own room tonight."

The man was so flabbergasted that he did not know what to do and quickly found us three rooms.

That was the end of my days with the Georgia council. After I left, I went into the Department of Health, Education, and Welfare (HEW) in the Civil Rights Division, and that was a whole new life.

5 "An equal chance for education": The Federal Government and School Desegregation

After leaving the Georgia Council on Human Relations, Frances embarked, at age sixty-two, on a new career with the federal government. In the Atlanta regional office of the Office of Civil Rights of the Department of Health, Education, and Welfare, Frances joined a team of southerners working to implement school desegregation, some fifteen years after the Brown decision. She encouraged, negotiated, cajoled, and ultimately threatened school districts with loss of federal funds if they did not comply. Frances often chafed under the regulations of the federal bureaucracy but took pleasure in having the power of the federal government behind her. "We had the law, and if you discriminated you did not get federal funds. That was what the law said and what the government meant."

The bulk of Frances's assignments were in Mississippi, but her work took her to a number of southern states, including Georgia. There she continued to support many of the families she had worked with so closely during her Georgia council years as they struggled to make equal education a reality in their communities.

Civil Rights Act of 1964

An act to enforce the constitutional right to vote, to confer jurisdiction upon the district courts of the United States to provide injunctive relief against discrimination in public accommodations, to authorize the Attorney General to institute suits to protect constitutional rights in public facilities and public education, to extend the Commission on Civil Rights, to prevent discrimination in federally assisted programs, to establish a Commission on Equal Employment Opportunity, and for other purposes. Title VI, Sec. 601: No person in the United States shall, on the ground of race, color, or national origin, be excluded from participation in, be denied the benefits of, or be subjected to discrimination under any program or activity receiving Federal financial assistance.

Letters to family

December 14, 1969
Dearest Cousins:

I am working for the U.S. Dept. of HEW Office for Civil Rights. I make school boards sad in Mississippi. I am state coordinator for Miss--hold a G.S. 14--of which I am proud since my family likes their comfort. I am usually in Miss. three or four days a week. Bobby keeps house for me. I do little else. I hurry home to get things lined up, shopping done, things planned etc. and leave again. I like the work but get tired of airports. As you can imagine for the last year the work has been very frustrating not knowing where we are going to go with the new administration--and still don't know. However I got a raise which astonished me no end. Since I'm not given to keeping my mouth shut about some things. I wish there was some way of really having a holiday--but there isn't. I see my old friends and hear of their aches and pains and Drs etc and I am glad I have to forget mine and hit the road . . .

I have walked through so many horrible schools in Miss. that I think children would be better running wild. Then once in a while you hit a good one where children are happy and learning . . .

I guess you read of our exciting victory over City Hall and the Chamber of Commerce and the Newspapers in Atlanta election. We have a Jew Mayor and a Negro Vice Mayor! How about that! At a time when the country is getting more conservative! . . .

I went to Washington on a quick assignment and Bill fell down the front steps and landed on his head! Well he has always been hard headed as you know--and he is fine now--but he had a week or so in the hospital--and I came home scared to death. Papa was upset--wandering around and not eating. But now all is well. Bill is home and around the house. He is feeling pretty good. Papa is getting back to normal . . . He has shaved--because I told him I liked hippies and hoped he would grow a beard . . .

Needless to say we are all old and feeble. I worry about getting feeble minded. But I watch them youngsters in my office and I do better than they!

Love,
Frances

March 2, 1969
Dearest Children:
   The four days I spent in Ripley Tenn. was unlike any in my life. I never was insulted so many times and I never felt so much hostility. They know we as Feds have to behave properly and we aren't free to tell them off. Did they ever make life miserable. They asked me if I slept with Mr. Bo--and other such things. We left one motel because they put Mr. Bo. on the back and us on the front. (Joe Wilson, a young white man, and me.) All that was bad enough--but after we left they reported us. They wrote to their Congressmen, their Senators, Finch, Ruby, Paul and the whole works . . . We came home pretty much whipped . . .
   I was pleased to find that I was not grounded after Tenn. I was made the captain of the team to go to do another in depth study this week . . . Then I later found out that they wanted me out of the way because they were going to have a meeting with the Fulton officials. I know they will let them off the hook. So I didn't feel so good after all.
   Austin was going down to march in the Worth County march so we decided to fly to Albany and rent cars--he to go to Worth and me to Cordele . . . I had been forbidden by my office to go to Worth.
   We got to Albany and some one told us that the Youngs were in town. (Their daughter is the one that was still in jail for an undetermined sentence because she cursed on a school bus.) Well, I was afraid to see them because I had not seen them or helped them in any way--but we went over to where they were. They saw me coming and rushed with open arms. What compassion!

Well, we went to a motel and got a drink and sat
around talking about everything--and there was a phone
call and it was C. B. King in Atlanta saying that
Dorothy was out and he had a chartered plane arranged
to take them to Atlanta and sign the papers. Well, we
rushed to the airport--some other Negroes joined us
and there we stood in a circle singing Freedom!! as
the plane warmed up and took off . . .

Saturday was the worst cold rain you ever saw. I
wanted to go to Worth--but I went on to Cordele to my
meeting . . . The march was to be at noon. Well I left
Cordele at 4:30 and got to Worth in the middle of the
march. It was most impressive but I was sick not to be
in it. I watched and listened to the white threats and
saw the white guns and the white clubs and got more
and more afraid. But nothing happened--It was only
some supernatural power which prevented it. I'm sure
of that. When the march returned to the church--I was
there--and honestly I was simply overcome--the people
all came and hugged and hugged me--like I had done
something . . .

Well, it seems that the word was out that I had
defied the Federal establishment and went to the march.
Abernathy now thinks I am just a bit below God--such
carrying on--Isn't it funny the things that people
like and the things they don't even notice . . .

Must be off to the kitchen--I'm doing extra cooking
for a change.

Love,
Mother

I went to work for the federal government in 1968. Some of my friends
had been hired by the government in the new Office for Civil Rights in
HEW. This was established under the Civil Rights Act, which had
been passed in 1964. Ruby Martin was the head in Washington, followed by Leon Panetta, and Paul Rilling was the regional director of
the office in Atlanta. I didn't particularly want to work for the federal
government; I would rather have worked in some private agency in
civil rights where you had a lot more freedom than with the government. But Paul finally persuaded me to sign on. I needed a job, and

the government paid twice as much as I'd been making. So I took it and worked for five years.

I was very glad to go in when I did. In the first place, it was very unusual to be hired as a sixty-two-year-old, and they hired me as a GS-13 even though I had never worked for the federal government. That was just unheard of. And I got several promotions when I was working for them. They couldn't find people that had experience in civil rights. There weren't very many people with real, real experience in civil rights who wanted to work for the federal government. The federal government was entirely separate from civil rights organizations.

We were crazy about Leon Panetta. I had a couple of people between Leon and me, and I would just meet him when he'd come here on a field trip. But I admired him tremendously, just tremendously. There were some good people, great people in HEW from Washington. All of us were of the same mind. We had the law, and if you discriminated you did not get federal funds. That was what the law said and what the government meant. It was a lot of fun, because you had some power behind you, which I had not ever had before.

In my first few months with HEW, I worked on welfare compliance. This was difficult, because the problem with welfare was that the money came to the state. You couldn't take federal welfare funds away from a city or a county without removing the whole state. Well, we weren't about to take welfare money away from the whole state. So we would try to persuade people in welfare agencies to do better, but we never actually took the money away.

Now in the school districts it was quite different, because, in the first place, the schools weren't dependent entirely on federal funds and also they worked district by district. You could take the federal funds away from, say, DeKalb County, and it wouldn't affect the rest of Georgia. But that would make DeKalb County sit up and take notice. So within a few months of joining HEW, I worked in the education division on desegregation of schools.

In the early days we had a real mission. It was a matter of giving everybody an equal chance for education, no matter what the color of their skin. We were working our tails off to put that into effect. I think we had just a deep desire to see integration take place, because we really did believe that what had happened had been terribly unfair, and what could we do in our work to overcome some of that. It wasn't just a job for a paycheck at the end of the month; it was a whole lot more than just a regular nine-to-five job. But that isn't the way the government operates. The government operates from nine to five, brother, and that's it. That was hard for me to get used to. In fact, I don't think I ever did, particularly when I was out in the field.

I was the coordinator for the state of Mississippi, although I did work in some other states too. We had one office in Atlanta for the seven southern states. I would spend three or four days a week in the field, in Mississippi. I would usually be in Atlanta on Monday and Friday. Tuesday, Wednesday, and Thursday, I'd be in Mississippi. I had six or seven people that were under me, usually young men. This created a problem, because some of the men under me had worked for the feds and felt they knew a lot more than I did—and they did, about bureaucracy. And here a good-for-nothing old woman had been brought in over them. That gave me a problem for a short time, but it didn't last long. I think I really had a good working relationship with the staff in a fairly short time.

It was a fascinating job to go in, review a school district, and work out a way that they could be desegregated with the least effort and be the most productive. Before I went in, I would do my homework—see what the school district was like, have all the maps with where the schools were, know what the population in the schools was. All of this before I went there, because time was so limited and we had so few people working. I had to learn to work rapidly.

I had a schedule given to me by my boss—in this town today, another town day after tomorrow. That was quite different from my job with the Georgia council, where I'd go back and back and back if they were having some problems. In HEW, I never had as much time in a place as I needed to really do the job as I felt it needed to be done. That's why I would make arrangements to go in the night before to meet with the local people. Of course, a lot of the things that I did weren't exactly on the agenda that they handed me to do. HEW didn't emphasize any work with the community people. But with my nature, I wanted to know what the people wanted, what the people thought, and particularly the black people. After all, we were working on school desegregation.

I remember one terrible time in the Mississippi Delta. My boss decided that he wanted to go, and he advertised that we were going to have a meeting the night before. I told him that wasn't the way to do it, but that was his way of doing it. Hundreds of people came to make complaints— irate, all of them mad at the federal government. And no place would there have been any greater discrimination against blacks than there in the Delta. The black school would be nothing, and most of the white people— the top population—sent their children to private schools. The poor whites had it just as bad as the blacks, just about. Well, my boss got up, looked at the crowd, and turned it over to me! I said, "I'm going to hear every complaint here, I will listen to every complaint, if it takes all night." Which we did. During the complaints, I showed my sympathies, and people went away feeling better. I came home just feeling like I had really done something. I had kept order. The place was very angry, but I kept perfect order. I just thought I had been magnificent; I was so self-satisfied.

The out-of-state newspapers were there and picked it up. The papers criticized the feds for being in town and reported a white fed criticizing the white folks. One thing I had done was say "whitey" and some other terrible things like that. We came home and caught hell, because they had gotten the newspapers. We got called on the carpet for that good—that we shouldn't have had that publicity, we shouldn't have had that number of people, and why did we have the meeting in the first place.

When I made my own plans, I would always get into a town the night before and go to see the local blacks, because after my Georgia council work I was used to working with black people more than whites, certainly more than with school superintendents. I would find out who the local black leaders were, and I would go see them the night before. I'd say, "Tell me the dirt. I'm going down to see the superintendent tomorrow." They would tell me all, pour it out, so I would know a lot when I went in the next day to see the superintendent or the school board.

The next day I went to see the superintendent, which was supposed to be my first call in town. I would go in with a few rules. First, I would always compliment the superintendent, no matter how bad he was. You could always find something—maybe it was just how nice his tie was—that you could compliment. Next, I'd sympathize with him. I'd say, "I just really understand. You are in a mess here. You have people who are pushing you from both sides. People want you to desegregate, and other people want you to fight desegregation. You really are in a jam. I want to help you in every way I can." With that then, he would open up and tell me all about it. A lot of these men were in terrible situations, and some of them weren't so prejudiced, really deep down in their hearts, as they appeared to be.

One of the main things I learned was how you could be sympathetic with people and not dislike a person just because they believed differently from the way you believe. That was one of the secrets of success, to approach a person with understanding. It was good to be old and fat. I wasn't young then, and I got by with murder! I wouldn't take anything for that. It was really a wonderful experience for what it taught me, particularly about negotiating.

So the superintendent and I would talk about it, and I would feel him out. He would take me to visit the schools, and then if there was any sort of an intention toward moving in the direction of voluntary desegregation, I was there to get them to do it voluntarily. If the school district wanted it, it went fine. The whole question was if they wanted to do it. We'd try to persuade people to go ahead and integrate without a court case. And sometimes we were able to. What we had to do was to try to help them as much as we could, and pressure and pressure and pressure them. But if they didn't want to desegregate voluntarily, I would say, "Of course, if you do not desegregate, you'll lose your federal funds." Some schools had quite a lot of federal funds and that would mean a great loss to the school system. That helped tremendously in getting them to straighten up and fly right.

Then we met with the school board, plus their lawyers. We sat down with maps of the school district, and I would say, "Now this really is not going to be as hard as you think. There are a lot of different ways you could do it." In the meantime, I had stayed up all night, the night before, on how the hell could they do it. I would tell them they could pair certain schools, repair others, change these district lines, redistrict. The times I felt I was most successful was when I could really sit down with the authorities and work out what might be the best plan. It got down to where I really had a system and I really knew it. But in the end I would say, "Now it's up to you. I don't know your school district, you know it. I know you want to avoid trouble above all things, because of what that will mean to your town, so we want you to send us your plan of how you want to desegregate." And then I'd bid them farewell.

I'd get back home and write it all up: "We find that you discriminated in the following ways: one, two, three, four, five, ten. So, consequently, if you do not straighten up and fly right, we'll report you to the legal division of HEW for an administrative hearing, and you will have to." Which was true back then. I would write the letter, and my boss, Paul Rilling, would sign it. I remember one man wrote back, "I cannot understand you writing me such a letter. Why don't you talk to that nice Mrs. Pauley who came down here?" Paul got the biggest kick out of that.

We started out with the school districts that had the fewest blacks, because it was a lot easier to have a success story there. In those cases, it would really be economically sound for the school district to integrate. It was easier, for example, for them not to run two bus lines over the same area. That would help us on the next level, because we could point to success in this district. Then finally we headed on down to work in the Mississippi Delta, which was more heavily black.

The first desegregation was usually on a voluntary basis, and a lot of times it would be somebody like the black school principal sending his kids to the white school. Most often you had the best-prepared, the brighter, and more educated blacks that tried to go to the white school, kind of the upper crust of the blacks who had some education themselves and were certainly better fixed financially than other people. And they got along fine.

I found that if I got the football coach and the football team on my side, then I would win. The first day that the blacks were going to come into the white school, I'd have the football team on special duty to keep order in the halls. They were a big help because they were always popular. I think it was very helpful for me to have had my Georgia council experience, because it made me see how HEW could use a volunteer organization and how a volunteer organization could use HEW, which I hadn't understood before I worked with both. You have to have both. HEW had to go in and open the door, but then after the door was opened, somebody had to come in to help work out how we were going to do this. The little things helped, like having the coach bring the football team in.

A story I love to remember is the day in one town that the school buses were to be integrated. Everybody was scared and expecting chaos, and all the parents were wondering if somebody was going to be hurt. So on the first day the black and white kids were going to ride the buses together, some of the mothers went down to the bus stop to wait with the children and at least make sure they got on the buses safely. While they were waiting, one little white fella walked over to a little black fella and said, "I wish my face was brown like yours."

The black boy looked at him real surprised and said, "Well, why in the world would you wish that?"

The white boy said, "Then I wouldn't have to feel so bad when people are mean to you." I love that story, because I know how many times I just hated being white.

I didn't like the idea of one black child being picked out and chosen to go to a white school. As hard as we knew it would be, I thought there should at least be a group that could suffer together and support each other. I always tried to work hard to get up a whole group. But that wasn't true of one family that I worked with, the Hunter family.

Roy Lee Hunter was the first student to integrate the high school in Unadilla, Georgia. When it came time for graduation in 1968, the school officials tried to talk him out of coming to the ceremony. When that didn't work, they told him somebody would kill him if he came. Roy Lee said that he would be there anyway. So the Reverend Austin Ford and I went down for the occasion. We had notified the FBI and the state police. We picked up Roy Lee at his family's little shack, and we walked in together, keeping him in between us the whole time. They put him at the very end of the procession and made him walk several feel behind the last person. When the graduates were seated, he had a vacant chair by him and nobody on the other side. But he got his diploma and nothing happened. Nobody got hurt, but he had a hard time in that school.

The family ended up moving here to Atlanta. He's still here, I hear from him every once in a while. His mother now lives in California. I've kept up with them, with the whole family. Roy Lee had several brothers and sisters

ROY LEE HUNTER'S HIGH SCHOOL GRADUATION. HE IS STANDING AT
THE TOP, FAR RIGHT.
(Photograph courtesy of Frances Pauley.)

and they all graduated from the white school. That mother had a lot of guts. She had all kinds of pressures put on her, and the father lost his job. Sometimes the parents were very civil rights–minded, and they wanted the kids to go to the white school and the kids didn't want to go, and sometimes the kids wanted real bad to go and the parents were afraid. It was interesting. But you'd get to know them and know them well.

I remember another real bad case when I was down in Albany. It was very early in the desegregation efforts, and a couple of black girls had tried to go to the white school. The authorities trumped up some charge and had them arrested. C. B. King, a black lawyer who was so important in the struggle, worked a lot of legal maneuvers and finally got them out of jail. They ended up in court in Atlanta, and C. B. got a special plane to fly them home. We all gathered at the little airport in Albany, and when the plane landed, we circled it and sang "We Shall Overcome." There we were in the middle of the night, in a circle, singing. You never forget memories like that.

We would work with the school to set up some remedial courses that they'd have after school for the black kids that were coming in. Because often they just simply hadn't had what the white kids had had. The great difference in the education that blacks had received made it very difficult to integrate the schools. You didn't have compulsory education for the blacks; only the ones that wanted to go to school went to school. The only books they had were the old leftover hand-me-downs from the white school. They didn't have decent books, didn't have decent libraries. Sometimes the teachers were magnificent and sometimes they weren't. It really just depended on the school system itself, and each was a little different.

I always used to say they had three Mississippis. They had one Mississippi in the Delta, and they had another Mississippi on the coast, and another Mississippi around Jackson. You can't summarize something as being typically Mississippi, and I had cases throughout the state. There were various kinds of superintendents and various kinds of school boards. The coast was always the easiest place. They were the most tolerant of each other, and you'd find real desegregation. You'd find some places where blacks and whites would really be living on the same street. It seemed to me that the southern part of the state was much less rigid and much less prejudiced than the Delta. The Jackson area was a lot more like Georgia; it was pretty much the same as integration in Georgia—some powerfully mean segregationists, and also some other people that were trying really hard to have the situation smooth and that weren't really prejudiced. I found Mississippi better than Georgia, by the way. Usually they didn't want conflict; they wanted everything to be smooth. It wasn't that they were dedicated to integration or segregation; they just wanted a good school system and they wanted it to move smoothly. In Mississippi I found fewer of what I call the armchair liberals. Very liberal in their talk, but they weren't going to get out of their chair and do anything. In Mississippi it seems to me that more people, if they felt that way, were apt to try to put it into motion. It was easier to work with white people in Mississippi, because you knew what side they were on.

I remember one man who was on a school board who helped us work out a plan for his district. He had sent his children to some kind of integrated summer program with black and white teachers. His son had some words, got into some trouble, and came back. This man took his son back to find out what happened. He found out his son had been rude to a black teacher. He went back home, and he said, "We're teaching our children to lie, and we're not teaching our children the truth. My child is going to apologize to that teacher and my child is going to the integrated school." This man's whole sense of values was good and honest. Lots of people were like that, and some of them were brave enough to stand up, like he did, and work for it. And his community desegregated schools smoothly.

You see, everybody had been brought up under "separate but equal," and that was the law. If you were a law-abiding citizen, you'd been taught that the blacks eat here, and sit there, and drink out of this fountain. You didn't think about it in any moral, or immoral, way. At least I didn't as I came up. You just hunt for the restroom that says, "White Women," just like you hunt for something that says, "Restroom." It doesn't have any moral effect on you until you begin to think about it and work on it. And then you see how crushing it was. The man who was just a good citizen obeying the law, going along, and then all of a sudden he saw, with a flash maybe, that segregation was wrong. A lot of them helped to change it.

We were very successful. I think we had about the most successful team in the country. I remember going back and visiting schools that we had desegregated, and particularly one school that was majority black. I got out of my car and I stood there. The kids were outside and the band was marching over in one place, and the kids were doing several outside activities. I stood there and I watched, and in every instance the groups were integrated and beautifully integrated. The first thing I knew, I had tears coming down my face. I was just so thrilled. It really did work. If it could work in Mississippi, it seemed to me, it could work anywhere.

This one little girl came up to me, and she said, "Before you leave, would you please talk to Susie's mother? She took her out and put her in the private school, and we have so much more fun here. We've learned their songs and they've learned our songs, and we've learned their games and they've learned our games, and we're having such a good time."

The private schools in Mississippi were a great issue, because so many times it took the leadership in the town away from the public school. What worried me was what was going to become of the public school. The main thing was to help build the public school, so it really would be superior to the private. In a way, that wasn't always too hard, because they found out in the private schools that it took money to have a good school. You couldn't have all the laboratories and all the things that you would like to have without paying for it in the private school. So it seemed to me that if we worked for the very best public schools, we could work for what would be the best way to influence people back into the public schools.

I'm a firm believer in public education, and this led me into an interesting conversation with Margaret Mead, the famous anthropologist. Margaret Mead often came to Atlanta and visited my friend Austin Ford. One night I was there for dinner, and we got into a great discussion about school desegregation. She made the statement that anybody who cared

INTEGRATION OF THE SCHOOLS IN ALMA, GEORGIA.
(Photograph courtesy of Frances Pauley.)

about their children at all would never send their children to public schools; they would always send their children to private schools. We got into a great argument about private versus public and what it meant to kids. The next morning at breakfast she said to my friend, "That fat lady that sat right over there and believed in public schools, now, she's not really white, is she?" I just loved that—from Margaret Mead!

Mr. Nixon came into office in 1968, and Mr. Nixon had different ideas because he didn't care about civil rights. It took awhile before it got down to our level, but not too long unfortunately, and then the damper was put on: "Accept these plans. This superintendent says he'll do this much. This is enough."

I remember one meeting in Mississippi in 1970 when John Dean was there. The Republicans had called a meeting of the superintendents of the schools in Mississippi that weren't yet desegregated. At this meeting, Dean took me out into the hall and read me the riot act, because I wasn't letting people get by. He told me that I should accept the desegregation plan even if they didn't desegregate. I told him I was very sorry, but I was hired to do this certain thing and I would do it. We went back into the meeting and I continued.

The chairman of the Mississippi Republican party wrote to Washington, D.C., asking for my dismissal. Shortly thereafter, I was removed from Mississippi. There was a hue and cry from many civil rights workers, but the decision was not changed. From that point on, I was gradually given more administrative work and less fieldwork. I had responsibility for Georgia, Alabama, and Tennessee. I'd always been a field representative, and sitting behind a desk was something that I didn't care to do. However, I did have a slightly enlarged staff under me, and we worked with great intensity toward finding the necessary facts to document the discrimination that we were continually facing. We brought some school boards to hearings and won some cases. Our success in this area was frowned on by my superiors, which stopped or severely hampered our work.

That was about the end of my career in school desegregation. I decided I'd finish out my five years so that I could get my pension, which is very nice today, because I still get a pension. But it was difficult because my friends, my best friends, were leaving because they couldn't stand what the Republicans were doing—or not doing. It wasn't a matter of what they were doing; they were doing nothing. They simply wanted to keep the status quo.

Finally the restrictions became intolerable, and my health was progressively deteriorating. It was strange that through many of the real dangers of the civil rights movement, I had been physically okay, but now I had a problem with such things as hypertension. So I quit and went back to my family. At that time, my husband was not well and he had a stroke. My father had died during this time, in 1972, so my household was very complicated. I was busy taking care of my home, but it also gave me a chance to get back into volunteer work that I had always done before. It had been an interesting five years. I had some feeling of accomplishment both from my voice within the department and from the work in the field.

After all these years—I left the federal government in 1973—I certainly still think that integrated education should be the goal. I completely agree with the blacks who say you don't have to sit next to a white child to get a good education. That wasn't at all the way I thought of it. But I do think that all kids need to have good books, good teachers, a good building. It just needs to be equal in that way. Still, I really think that children are so fortunate if they are able to go to school with people who are different. I think it's terrible if they just go to school with people of the same economic background, the same racial background, the same class as they are, because their education has really been terribly neglected. It's not just a matter of how far you get in mathematics, or how many books you've read—at least that's not the total answer to your education. Your education is you've got to learn to get along with people in this world. You certainly find that out if you get into business or any activities. Everybody's not the same, and it makes everything so much more pleasant and so much more interesting to have different people with different backgrounds. It makes life a lot more fun.

I've always believed that it means so much to a child to be acquainted with other children. With my two kids, in the neighborhood school that they went to, everybody in it was just about of the same class. All the fathers made just about the same amount of money. Then that school got too crowded, and since we lived kind of on the edge, Marylin was sent to another school. I was so thrilled, because in that school there was really a cross-section, some poor, some very poor. She had kids in her class who couldn't read, and yet she had some very bright kids in the class. It meant so much, I think, for her to see that in her education. I remember her coming home and how thrilled she was when one little boy had learned to read. She came home telling about it. She was so pleased.

I still think we should have integrated education. The goal was right and still is right and still should be.

6 "Everybody's Grandmother and Nobody's Fool": Advocate for the Poor

Julian Bond, a longtime friend and colleague, dubbed Frances, in an often-repeated phrase, "everybody's grandmother and nobody's fool." His description dates from the years when Frances founded and ran the Georgia Poverty Rights Organization (GPRO), a statewide group to organize and lobby on behalf of Georgia's poor and disenfranchised. The context for the GPRO's advocacy was the economically troubled 1970s and 1980s. Although parts of Georgia experienced a "sunbelt" boom during these decades, Georgia's poor saw high inflation cut into meager wages and diminish welfare benefits. With the GPRO, Frances made poverty—long a constituent part of her activism—the focus of her attention. Poverty rights organizing was a natural extension of Frances's civil rights activity. "Much of the racism of the forties and fifties," she observed in 1979, "has been transferred to discrimination against welfare and poverty in the seventies."

Many of Frances's closest friends joined her in the GPRO's advocacy with and for the poor, and several joined in recording the remembrances on which this chapter is based. Its conversational form is a departure from the first-person narrative of earlier chapters. Joining Frances to discuss the poverty rights years were Muriel Lokey, a friend from the HOPE days, and Betsey Stone, who, like Frances, brought skills and interests from the League of Women Voters into poverty rights organizing.

Letter to Anna Lord Strauss

January 15, 1974
Dear Anna,
    It is a joy to fall back into the old volunteer habits. I have accepted a position on the ACLU board and have been working with our lawyer on the Atlanta school case. I work in the Poverty Rights Office at Emmaus House. (A settlement type house in one of Atlanta's ghettoes.) I worked on the campaign and helped elect one of our Emmaus House mothers to the Atlanta school board. She says that I used to be her old broken down campaign manager and now I am her old broken down secretary. So

life goes on. But after the excitement of the 60s the
present takes a bit of adjusting.

Love,
Frances

FRANCES: I had felt for many years a great need for poor people to have
their voices heard. They were important, their voices were important.
They were the ones that hadn't had a chance to have their voices heard. So
it just seemed logical to try to get poor people together and have them
realize that they did have strength and power.

I began working on poverty rights even before I went to work for the
federal government. Father Austin Ford had been on my board at the
Georgia Council on Human Relations, and he kept asking the bishop to
put more money and more effort into poor people in the city. So the
bishop said, "O.K., I'm going to buy a house and you can live in it." At
that time, Father Ford was the minister at St. Bartholomew, in northeast
Atlanta, a well-to-do area.

We looked around, and we decided that an area near the center of the
city would be a good section of the city to have it in, because it was going
to be a Model Cities area where the federal government was going to com-
mit a lot of resources. We thought we could have an influence. So the Episcopal church decided to buy that property. They bought one house there,
the original house, and then it grew. It became known as Emmaus House.
They bought more houses on either side and then built a new center for
young people, for after-school training and so forth. They also had a
group of old people who met there with their problems. Emmaus House
has entered into a lot of community activities in the city and called attention to the fact that there are poor people and homeless people in Atlanta,
right here.

MURIEL: When Emmaus House was first set up, it was set up without
programs. Austin Ford went there not with any program that was
planned, but that he would see what the people in the neighborhood
wanted. A few months after he'd been visiting in the neighborhood, he
started women on welfare meeting and talking about their situation and
what they wanted to do. This was about October of 1967.

I was between volunteer activities. I didn't have one that absorbed me,
and I heard about his going down there. I went to see him and asked what
I could do. The first Tuesday I was there, a neighbor came to the door with
this little yellow card entitling him to surplus food, but he had no way to
go to the warehouse. There was a young man with Volunteers in Service

to America (VISTA) who knew where to go, and I had the car, and we took the neighbor and got him his surplus food. And that grew into the Surplus Food Delivery Program, which I coordinated. Ultimately we took food to five hundred families and had two hundred and fifty volunteers.

This brought a flood of volunteers over two or three years to the house. After they'd been visiting homes for a while, they would bring back information about things that were happening to people—being evicted without knowing what their legal rights were, or the check was lost and the caseworker hadn't replaced it, or they had no food in the house and what were they going to do—that sort of thing. These volunteers were learning about these families, and the neighbors were coming to the house bringing various problems. The volunteers were talking among each other and decided that we needed a special place for people to come where people are trained to look after this, because the front desk at Emmaus House could not look after it. The person who answered the phone was not trained. And, of course, it was in the late sixties when welfare rights was a national issue. There was a movement; there was something in the air. Welfare rights was popping up.

FRANCES: And the word "rights," I suppose, we felt gave them an incentive, a feeling that they had a right to be doing what they were doing. To give people a sense of the power that they had when they feel completely powerless, and are, in a way, because money does bring power. Poor people do have rights, but few of them realize it, and certainly people with money are not about to tell them. Everybody needs to know what their rights are in this world. I suppose it goes back to inalienable rights. There are certain rights that we are just simply born with and that we need to practice, and if we don't practice those, our life isn't as complete as it should be. Certainly a lot of poor people's lives are not now anywhere near as complete as they might be.

MURIEL: Along about 1970, there was a weekend retreat and a number of volunteers were there. At that retreat we dealt with the question, "What are we going to do? We need to do something. We need to set up an advocacy office for poor people where they'll have a phone number and know where to come." So we set aside a room in a building right near Emmaus House, and we had our headquarters there.

But how were they going to get the word out? Father Austin Ford talked to the person who was head of the welfare department in Fulton County, and that person agreed to include in the next welfare check a return postcard. The card offered the opportunity to receive information about rights and services by subscribing to what became "The Poor People's Newsletter," which we used to give people information that they would need to conduct their lives in terms of dealing with agencies. And they got seven thousand back.

FRANCES: I remember how aghast we were at the number of replies that we had to that card.

MURIEL: That was the beginning of the Poverty Rights Office at Emmaus House.

FRANCES: As I remember, we had two people on duty. We had two desks so we could handle two people visiting the office at the same time. You had people with all kinds of problems. They could have been health, they could have been housing, they could have been police. So it meant that you got a real cross-section of the needs in the city and how to handle them. We always tried to do something.

MURIEL: Utility problems, evictions, emergency food. You have to look at the total picture of income, housing, education, employment, health— all the systems people are connected to, to see if there's anything that could be improved.

FRANCES: The Poverty Rights Office required some efficient help, and these were all volunteers, friends of people that were already at Emmaus House working on other programs, like with old people. You had to really have a little training there to know all of the agencies and resources and so forth that were available for people, or else you wouldn't be any good on the phone or if somebody came in. That also, I think, was good for the agencies, too, to know that there were laymen and church people out there that were really interested in what the organizations were doing and if they were carrying out their agendas. So I think the Poverty Rights Office did a lot of good, and it certainly did train me in putting together all of the various agencies and how they fit in with poor people.

MURIEL: In the good years, I would have maybe a total of seven good workers. Of course, we had all kinds of social changes over those years. When we first started, the volunteers who started delivering surplus food and then worked into the Poverty Rights Office were not quite yet of the generation of women who were going to work or going back to school. So we could find volunteers.

FRANCES: Today is so different. A lot of the women that used to help with social work, volunteer work, are working now.

MURIEL: It was a different time. Then gradually, they began to leave us to go law school, or leave us to go to Georgia State to study counseling or gerontology, or to leave us to go to work because their kids were going to college and Mama needed to go to work to provide that. The availability of the kind of volunteers that we had, which were predominantly women, became less.

We tried terribly hard to have black volunteers there, too, and usually did have a couple as we went along. We were always trying to get neighborhood people to come in and work with us, but there were problems with that. People who live in the neighborhood often had some priority they'd have to see about, like the gas bill or something, rather than keep an appointment at the Poverty Rights Office. Our record-keeping system might have been a little intimidating for some people too.

I gradually set them up with systems, where a list of phone numbers were, how to keep the records. We have different volunteers every day, but a client coming in for help on a problem Monday and Wednesday and Thursday, the volunteer on that day has got to know where a file is, pick it up, find out what happened on Monday, and not reinvent the wheel. I described my job as keeping the chaos level down to manageable proportions!

FRANCES: Isn't that wonderful!

MURIEL: It was always that way. We always had chaos, lost files, everything. I remember at one time we opened twenty new cases in a week, something like that. Each case would be different. There were cases that went on for years. A woman who had trouble with a boy in prison and the way he was treated, that went on for years and years. Or it could be just finding the right person at the Housing Authority to get something straightened out and then the case was closed. Whatever it takes. We listened to the client and found out what they wanted and helped them walk through it. If they didn't understand the rule and the rule was to their disadvantage, we explained it to them to help them understand it.

FRANCES: The client doesn't know what's offered down at the agency, and the agency doesn't have as much outreach as it needs.

MURIEL: We let the client set the agenda; we were there to help out. We would help the client investigate if there were any possible way to improve it. Because we were about social change. We kept saying this and saying this and saying this, "We're not going to just put on Band-Aids." We even in those days talked about empowerment, trying to get people enough power and enough information, and working with them to get them to speak up for themselves.

We were occupied a lot of the time with trying to straighten out some agencies. If we found consistent reports that people were rudely treated, unfairly treated, not treated according to the law, not treated according to what the agency, public or private, holds itself out to be, then we felt it was our business to confront them in some way and go to the top. We were the only ones that I know of for a long time who confronted case-workers, such as the manager at an Atlanta housing project who demanded sex from a woman to get an apartment. We were there to somehow make a difference beyond one on one. But there were some days when we could never get our heads above it.

Georgia Poverty Rights Organization
Statement of Purpose
mid-1970s

Georgia Poverty Rights Organization (hereinafter GPRO) is a non-profit, unincorporated associat[ion] of poor people and people committed to furthering the interests of poor people. The goal of GPRO is to foster and protect the economic and social well-being of the poor. To this end, GPRO advocates on behalf of the poor in all available forums. GPRO strives to encourage and facilitate the participation of the poor in the public policy decisions that affect them. GPRO also works to educate the public regarding the issues that particularly affect poor people. GPRO is affiliated with Emmaus House, a neighborhood center operated under the auspices of the Atlanta Diocese of the Episcopal Church.

Georgia Poverty Rights Organization
Position Paper
mid-1970s

We believe that Georgia has the financial means to provide 100% of a realistic budget covering basic needs for eligible welfare recipients. We believe that Georgia has the heart to care for people unable to care for themselves.

FRANCES: I was working with the Poverty Rights Office while I was still with HEW. Then, after I retired from the government in 1973, I saw that the only way that you could make any changes, any radical changes, was really on a statewide basis. So we organized the GPRO, so that we would have poor people in various places in the state try to influence the legislature, tell the legislature that we have poor people. The GPRO, like the Poverty Rights Office, was run out of Emmaus House.

MURIEL: The two organizations were intimately related in our goals and our beliefs and our thrust. We weren't structurally related, just informally. I remember that Frances came to see me, and I knew that she'd been thinking about organizing. She said she wanted a name for the organization, and how would I feel about its being called the GPRO. In other words, would there be confusion? I immediately knew that it was an absolutely super idea. If people associated us together, I'd be very happy, it was an extension.

FRANCES: It wasn't just the name, we were actually doing the same thing.

MURIEL: So Frances just took that on, and you were coming in and out of the office. And you continued to, you've always done, one-on-one advocacy, Frances. In the middle of all of this, you always had two or three families you're carrying along, talking to on the phone, going to see the new babies, making sure there's a layette, straightening out the problems with the welfare department, calling up and giving sunshine. You've always done that.

FRANCES: Of course, we had a board, and the board was scattered around the state. They were all pretty active; they weren't just a name on a list. These were people that were really interested in welfare in whatever location they were in. I always felt the least structure you had, the better, because you can get so tied down and buried in the structure that you don't get the job done. A lot of times you can do something if you just go and do it, instead of waiting to organize to do it. By the time you get a committee and get the committee informed, why, then everybody's worn out, and you never get the job done. But if you just started out to do the job and maybe took somebody along with you, you might end up by accomplishing something. I guess it's keeping your eye on the goal, isn't it? Know what you want to do and keep at it and not let things sidetrack you.

We'd just go find one person in the community that would start in that community. In one town it might be the church, in another town it might be the NAACP. They might pick up on welfare and have somebody that was really interested in it. So it varied from town to town what organizations the Poverty Rights Organization worked with or influenced. Good old organizational patterns, I guess. Of course, I'd organized so many things in Georgia that I got so I knew people that were interested in different things.

MURIEL: Community organizing was something that you had done for years. You did it with HOPE, with the League, with the Georgia Council on Human Relations. And this was in that mode.

FRANCES: We began to have statewide meetings in 1975. People knew what their little community was, but they didn't see the picture as a whole. By coming together, they could see, and share with each other, that they weren't the only ones that had this kind of problem. As I used to say, "I'll get the only ones together," because everybody felt like they were the only one that had that kind of problem in their community. Here they could swap stories and really move ahead.

ANNUAL MEETING OF THE GPRO, 1985. JIM MARTIN, GPRO MEMBER
AND GEORGIA LEGISLATOR, IS AT THE CHALKBOARD; FRANCES IS AT
THE FAR RIGHT.
(Photograph courtesy of Frances Pauley.)

The legislative process was what we were really interested in, influencing our elected officials and learning more about government. We'd have a little course that we'd do about how a bill becomes law, about the setup of the legislature. It was really just a lesson in government for people that didn't know anything about government and weren't taught anything in school about it, if they'd even been to school, and many hadn't. Because the actual membership in the Poverty Rights Organization was poor people.

Then we'd bring a group from a town to the capitol to talk to their own legislators, to tell them what their need was. If you can't live on AFDC (Aid to Families with Dependent Children) and you've got to have more, but the only way you can get it is to get it through the legislature, well, then, it was just necessary for people to understand where that money came from and how to get it increased. We wanted them to come and help us work on it. It doesn't do any good just to have a lobbyist. The people themselves meant so much more to the legislator, because here was his constituent, the person who he wanted to vote for him next time.

MURIEL: That marvelous Central Presbyterian Church, right across from the capitol, had its doors open out on the capitol, and it was a wonderful refuge for people. They'd give you a room, a place to fix lunch and use the bathrooms, and let you go and see your legislator in these various issues of human rights and poverty.

FRANCES: A lot of times we could get the churches to help us, and the church women maybe would supply some of the automobiles that would bring them up, which would be another way of getting church people to know more about poor people too. If you got a woman with a car to bring a load up, you were really doing two things at the same time, or three, when it came to lobbying, because the church woman was learning to lobby too.

And funny things would happen. The first thing they do at the capitol, of course, is to look in your pocketbook. One day, one of the poor ladies there opened her pocketbook, and here was her gun! I hadn't thought to tell them not to bring their guns along, these being poor old people. And of course I would be with the one that hadn't turned her gun in. Well, I got tickled, but so did the man at the door, I think he was sort of tickled too. Anyway, he took her gun and we got it when we came back out.

Then we had our first statewide Poor People's Day at the capitol in 1980. Poor People's Day began with another organization, Christians Against Hunger. They decided to pick a week during the 1980 session of the legislature and invite people from various towns to come to visit their representatives. Members of the GPRO in many towns were enthusiastic. Lawyers and paralegals with Georgia Legal Services volunteered to train the visitors. We fed luncheons to the various groups who were encouraged to stay for a full day's meetings, having discussions and talking with their representatives. The experiment was a huge success. People came from many places, received good solid information, and to some extent were made to feel welcome at the capitol. In later years, it was agreed to have only a one-day effort, but Poor People's Day at the capitol continues even today.

BETSEY: Another thing was accomplished through that. The voice of the legislator changed from the home front to the capitol. One of the things that this organization allowed to happen was for that information to be taken back home. The Poverty Rights Organization could come in and say, "Your legislator is an obstacle to getting this particular piece of legislation"—an increase in AFDC or whatever it was at the time we were working on—whereas what the legislator was telling the home people was that he was doing the best he could.

FRANCES: One of the best things we did was to get the voting records out, get the home people really acquainted with how their representative was operating.

Narrative of Efforts to Increase AFDC Benefits

January 1, 1986

I first gathered together a group of agency heads who should have been interested in poor people. They weren't interested in anything but eating lunch and chit chatting.

I wrote to 80 people with whom I had worked over the years in the state. League of Women Voters, Georgia Council, HOPE, OCR, etc. Just good people. No titles. Asked them for lunch at Emmaus House. Many were interested in the idea, 45 came to the meeting . . .

AFDC had a $32 ceiling. The average grant in the state could not exceed $32 per month. In 1970 the average was $28.14 per month per person. There were about 53,000 households served.

In the 1974 session of the Legislature we won an increase to $32.55 per person. The rolls had doubled in size.

In 1975 we got rid of the $32 limit.

This was a major victory but also a defeat. Good, that it meant the state went to a new Federal formula where the state paid a larger proportion of the cost. But then Governor Busbee, to cut back both AFDC and Medicaid expenditures, had the department set a new eligibility standard. The rolls were cut from 350,000 individuals to 280,000 individuals, cutting off the working women, mainly.

You can imagine our dismay. In 1977 there was a surplus in the allocated AFDC funds. The Legislature wrote into law that the department could not pay over a stated maximum grant based on a stated standard of need. This has been said to be illegal. But it has never been challenged. Everyone was afraid to make the legislators so angry that they would further cut the appropriation for AFDC. The details continue to be written in the law.

We had marches and sit ins. We had visits to the Governor. We appeared at every board meeting of the

department. We had hand outs etc. We won some hearts
on the board. The Governor removed them from the
board . . .

In spite of added organizational efforts and more
people working we were not successful. Busbee was too
powerful for us. In 1977 there were more cuts in the
overall funding and the number of recipients. In 1978
the state funds increased slightly and the per person
average rose to $37.16. (National average was $78.92.)

Records told some of the story. The squeeze was
still on to keep people off the rolls thereby keeping
down the increasing cost of Medicaid. But the AFDC
payments were rising slightly. The greatest increase
in Medicaid was because of the old and nursing homes
and hospitals. Not with children. But cut the kids--
they don't vote.

The 1981 Omnibus Reconciliation bill did one good
turn. Hundreds of people would have been eliminated
from AFDC under the new Fed regs. Through the able
work of Attorney Frank Samford the powers saw that the
state could increase the standard of need to 190% of
former figure, decrease the % of maximum payments to
50% and the benefits would not be changed and we could
continue getting the same amount of money from the
feds, and not further decrease the rolls.

In the mean time GPRO, PAC, Christians, had been
working hard to get a new updated standard of need.
We had succeeded within the department but failed to
get the new standard of need in the Legislation. The
Department, afraid of the legislature, accepted their
word . . .

The 1983 legislature appropriated enough money to go
to an average of $64.82, per person. A long way from
$32 but a long way from meeting the need with
inflation. The rolls were still 50,000 short of 1974.
The poverty among children in the state was growing
while the economic picture of the state was improving.

1985 was well organized but how could advocates fight
money for public education? No way. We simply had to
accept a slight raise and grin and bear it. Our kids
needed good schools. It wasn't either/or. Brick and
mortar still was supreme . . .

We have many followers in the Legislators but none
of the big leaders . . .
Volunteer workers cannot be surpassed. Even if you
had a million dollars.
I have known of more people knowing more facts about
government. I have seen the dirty dog eared sheets
with GPRO voting records being used by poor people.
Our calendar of when to act is used more each year. We
have encouraged poor people to participate. If we ever
got a Governor who didn't hate poor people we might
have a chance . . .
Timing is something to learn. It is a year round job.
When the legislature starts the major work is over . . .
Good staff is terrific. Poor staff is worse than none.
Communications are essential. I spent much time just
keeping this one knowing what that one is doing . . .
Work like hell and hunt people to give the credit
to . . .
If we had done better the children of Georgia wouldn't
be so bad off today.

FRANCES: I was the GPRO's principal lobbyist. I got there when the session
opened and stayed until it closed. The only way you can lobby is to do
that, to really be there all the day, every day. Go early and stay late; you
never know when you're going to have that little chance. A lot of boring
hours had to be spent observing to be there at the moment when something important happened. If you weren't there for those boring hours,
you missed that.

BETSEY: I began working with Frances in the early 1980s. I had been
working with the League of Women Voters for about ten years. I knew
process, but I didn't know the Georgia legislature in any specific fashion.
Jim Martin, our friend in the legislature, told me that I didn't need to
worry, that Frances would teach me everything I needed to know. We
would observe at the legislature, at the committee meetings, especially the
budget committee meetings. We went to the DHR (Department of Human
Resources) board meetings, and Frances often spoke at those meetings.
The "conscience" of the board, they called her.

FRANCES: The welfare department would decide what a family needed
to live on, what a person needed to live on, and that was the standard of
need. That was one of the worst things; the standard of need was so low
that nobody could possibly live on the standard. If you could raise the

standard of need, that would really raise the living of many, many poor people. You couldn't increase the AFDC grant level, unless you raised the standard of need.

As an organization, we worked to get the officials on the state level to raise that standard of need. It should never have been a legislative matter. It's not for legislators to decide what the cost of living is. The cost of living is the cost of living. It's not what the legislature decides it's going to be. But they decided what the cost of living was for welfare recipients, and it's so short-sighted. I don't think the legislators understood the real problems and certainly didn't respect poor people. There's not much respect for poor people.

We had a few friends in the legislature. Jim Martin worked the most closely with me in the Poverty Rights Organization. Julian Bond was an ally. I met Julian during the civil rights movement, but I never did work with him during the movement. I got to know Julian Bond more when he went into politics and was in the legislature. He used to say, "Let's have a meeting of all of us liberals. I'll meet you in the phone booth." We were few and far between; it just wasn't popular.

BETSEY: That's because there wasn't a basic understanding of the welfare system, how AFDC worked, who the people were who were on it. There was a lot of prejudice and misunderstanding, a lot of assumptions. There was the assumption that everybody on welfare was black.

FRANCES: And also that people went on welfare just to get welfare.

BETSEY: The legislators didn't understand some of the finer points of the system. For example, once you turn eighteen, the welfare is gone. A lot of welfare families, the kid didn't graduate until he was nineteen or she was nineteen, because she may have missed a year in school. So that person got cut off and then had to go to work and didn't get a high school degree. The system was punitive. One thing they knew about Frances: they may not like what she said, but they always knew what she said was accurate.

FRANCES: And believe you me, I was careful. I always told them the truth. If I told them so many people were on welfare, that number was right, and I had checked it and double-checked it. I always tried to be accurate. You'd sure better be right, particularly if you're doing something that is unpopular, because if they catch you in just a little error, then they'll throw it all out.

BETSEY: That was one of the strengths that you had, Frances. Frances had a mathematical mind, and so the budget and the numbers were not off-putting for Frances. I think that was one of your real skills. The legislature was predominantly male—and that's an understatement—it was male.

That's one of the camouflages that they used, throwing those numbers and budgets at females, thinking they couldn't really understand. Frances just cut right through that. Frances would not only understand what the talk was, but when they would get up and move out to have their secret pow-wows, Frances would not tolerate that. She knew how to manage the process so they couldn't get away with that.

FRANCES: We were interested in open government, where the people that govern didn't just decide things, and the public maybe find out, or maybe not. It was very unusual for them to have anybody sit in on a meeting, and I don't know how many, many, times I went to meetings very much not wanted, and just opened the door and went in. Because it was supposedly a public meeting. I'd ride around the capitol off hours and see where the light was at and then go in, just open the door and go in. That took a lot of nerve. I wasn't wanted, because then they'd have to watch what they said. They weren't supposed to be having a secret meeting, and by law they couldn't make me leave. The public was supposed to be there, and in that I would be sure I was right. Again, you'd sure better be legally right. But if the public was supposed to be in a meeting, I didn't mind opening the door and walking in, even though I certainly wasn't welcome.

BETSEY: And then we sued them, over exactly this issue: the public's right to have access to these meetings. We lost the suit, but my sense is we won the larger issue about publicity. We exposed what was going on. We had the editor of the paper, the *Atlanta Constitution*, behind us. He gave us exposure. He kept the suit in the public eye.

FRANCES: The wonderful thing that we had—which we had not had for years—was the cooperation of the press. The newspaper coverage was great. It certainly kept the case in the minds of the legislators. We were always, always fighting for openness, because the government was our government, the people's government. They tried to be as secretive as they could, but we did get our foot in the door.

And all of these activities amounted to at least a full-time job. I spent much more than any forty hours a week. What I did would just depend on what was happening. When the legislature was in session, the focus was on the legislature, and I wasn't trying to organize during that time. That was the time when people who were already organized were having a chance to act. But it seems to me that more of my time overall was spent in actually organizing community groups. As I said, getting the "only ones" together. Just basic organizing. And the job got larger. The more you organized, the more groups you had. The more groups you had, the more problems you would have. There weren't enough hours in the day.

MURIEL: And you were taking care of Bill, having to see that someone was home with him and got him his meals.

FRANCES: I always had a household, because my father lived with me until he died at ninety-six. He was always healthy, he was never sick, but he was there. And Bill suffered from a paralysis and a stroke. I cared for him at home for a number of years, and after he went to the nursing home in 1982, I was at the nursing home five or six hours a day. I'd go at lunchtime and feed him. We'd wheel around and do whatever. Then I'd put him back to bed for his afternoon nap. I'd leave and have a couple of hours before I'd go back at five o'clock and feed him his supper.

Notes for Speech on the Development of Heating Energy Assistance Team (HEAT)

November 7, 1986

I have been asked to tell you a bit about the methods used in obtaining gasoline overcharge money for the use of the poorest people in Georgia.

The first effort was in organizing a coalition of government, business and advocates, all a bit suspicious of each other, but all with the common goal of finding at least an immediate solution to help people unable to pay the high utility costs and prevent any more deaths in Georgia from freezing.

HEAT was born and with it the state's Emergency Fuel Fund.

The second effort was one of just plain lobbying for a sizable portion of the overcharge monies to go into the Emergency Fund.

I play several roles in my present life as a volunteer. There are a few advantages in being over 80. Sometimes I am the sweet grandmother, sometimes the irate half crazy old fool. At times maybe the voice of reason. The DHR Board says I am their conscience.

To me the wonderful thing about this program is that it truly was and is a team effort. Business, Government, and advocates for the poor struggled together to plan and execute a program to attempt to meet the needs of the poor. We hope this winter no one will freeze to death.

My story begins in 1981. In our local GPRO office we had so many calls for help with utility bills that it was interfering with my sleep. I had to do something, even if it was wrong . . .

We found no enthusiasm in the government agencies. In the Legislature we had one real friend, Jim Martin, a Fulton County Representative of mid-town Atlanta. Brilliant as he is he was in no position to carry the whole Legislature. The Governor, who had previously been the Chairman of the Appropriation Committee in the House, told me that there was no use in trying to satisfy me, it was impossible.

I thought of the religious community. We were bleeding the individual churches and synagogues with cries for help. Mrs. Jones is hungry and cold and please give to widow Smith. They were wild and so were we.

The next visit I made was to Business. The Atlanta Gas Light Company's collection department had shown us courtesy in helping work out problems. They listened. I went on to the other utility companies etc. After innumerable visits, and it seems like hundreds of committee meetings, I gave up.

Then one cold December day, in 1982, I had a knock on the door of my home and it was a lovely lady from the Atlanta Gas Light Co. She said they had a plan and she wanted to talk about it. We talked at length. The Gas Company did not want to waste people's time. They wanted action.

HEAT was born. A couple of the Gas Company's V.P.s had visited Dr Ledbetter, the Commissioner of the Department of Human Resources, explained our idea and the fact the Gas Company would put in some seed money and begin to ask its customers to give regularly with their gas bills in order that those who could not pay would have heat.

The Commissioner was sold. On February 1, 1983, at his press conference, the Governor received a check for $50,000 from Mr. Joe LaBoon, the President of the Gas company, and announced the opening of the Emergency Fuel Fund with HEAT at its heart.

The Program is administered through the DFCS offices in every county, equitably throughout the state, on a year long basis.

FRANCES, PICTURED HERE WITH JIM MARTIN, A COLLEAGUE IN THE
GPRO, LAUNCHED AN EFFORT IN THE EARLY 1980S TO PROVIDE
ASSISTANCE WITH THEIR HEATING BILLS TO LOW-INCOME GEORGIANS.
(Photograph courtesy of Frances Pauley.)

There have been many snags and problems along the way.
But each year the program has gained strength . . .
Please know, we realize we are not nearly meeting
the need. But some 40,000 families have been helped
with emergencies because of the efforts of a whole
bunch of people. But if each one of [us] had gone out
with our tin cups and begged we could not have helped
so many families . . .
By the end of the year, I really believe we will
have the best program in the country. Too many people
for many different reasons want it to succeed . . .
I am convinced that we would have many less homeless
on the street, and no deaths from freezing if we could
combine our meager resources and Business and Government
and Just Plain People work together with a common goal.

BETSEY: This was really your idea, Frances. This is one that you took and absolutely would not let go of.

FRANCES: And it worked. A HEAT program is still going today. I think the main thing is to always be friends with all of your enemies. Don't ever bang the door shut. Don't ever go out in a fit of temper. Always leave the door open, so that you can come back, because you're lobbying on this subject this week and another subject next week. To leave friends is the main thing, which isn't always easy. It was good for my character to try to learn not to get angry with them. I think, as a whole, I built up respect from the legislators over time. Of course, there's the matter of just having to play your cards. I always felt, and still feel, play them straight, have them know where you stand. Don't be wishy-washy. You'll win in the long run. I still think that's so. I think I had their respect.

MURIEL: You earned their respect, particularly toward the end of your career over there. They knew they had to deal with you. They didn't have to do what you said, but they had to converse with you and be present with you.

FRANCES: Politicians have the same rule of thumb, that they want to make friends with everybody too. The politician isn't trying to make you angry. He's not trying to give you what you want, but he's not trying to make you angry. So usually he's leaving the door open too. I found them interesting and fun and pleasant. I guess you wouldn't be a politician if you didn't have a pretty good personality.

Some of the people who bothered me the most were the people who called themselves liberals. But they would go over there, and they would give in too much and play both sides. Those people bothered me worse than the people who just definitely believed the opposite from what I believed. I just don't think they were operating in a true manner. But they were trying to do what they considered politic, I'm sure. They felt that was the way you operated in the political arena. That *is* the way they operated in the political arena, but that isn't the way I did, and I think we'd get along better if people would just play it straight.

People are going to make a difference, and so is it going to be the good people or the bad people?

7 "Mother PUJ": Frances Pauley in Retirement

Within a few years of Bill Pauley's death in 1985, Frances moved into Wesley Woods, a Methodist retirement center just a few miles from the Georgia home she had moved to in 1908. Her transition to retirement, however, was only partial. Freed from the need to maintain a household, Frances rededicated her energy to civil rights and the needs of the poor, while developing her most recent interests in homelessness and AIDS. To these latest concerns, Frances brought personal convictions and political skills honed over five decades of activism.

The 1990s brought other challenges. By mid-decade, Frances had lost nearly all her eyesight. Doctors diagnosed the problem as macular degeneration, a common eye disease among the elderly that gradually leads to a loss in sharp central vision. Many of her favorite pastimes, notably reading, are no longer possible. Frances leaves Wesley Woods less often than in the past and relies on the phone to keep in touch with family and friends. The pleasure of remembering a lifetime of activism coexists with frustration that her current activities are so constrained. "It would be nice to be young again," she says.

Testimony before the Georgia Legislature Regarding AIDS Legislation

February 18, 1988

I shall not address HB 1281 in detail. I have read and listened to the discussions of the bill and have a concern that in producing the legislation, negativity and fear have replaced reason and sound judgment based on facts. As we face this most serious public health problem of my life time, I ask today what can you do and how can we help? What is your responsibility? How fast can you act?

You are politicians. Viewing the issue politically is difficult. It combines sexuality, a tragic disease with an unknown cure, and death. None of which are choice pieces to add to a successful campaign. But remember, this is a public health issue that you politically can-

not afford to ignore. Positive action is the only
answer.

Many things have been learned about AIDS. The first:
scientific studies have proven the effectiveness of
education in reducing the rates of infection. This
gives us a lead. Legislators can see that proper
directions and adequate funding are available throughout the state. I understand that the South Carolina
legislature, after much soul searching, passed only
legislation to further education to prevent the spread
of AIDS. Alabama's educational program in the schools
is under way. Georgia is already behind.

We know how the disease is transmitted. Casual
contacts do not constitute an exposure. We can help to
allay fears within the population through the
educational process. Never have I known of a problem
with such complicated emotional, moral, and even
constitutional overtones. Legislators must squarely
face the fact that this is a public health issue and
not a moral, emotional, or merely political problem.
Fear and anxiety are keeping us all from moving in a
positive fashion. It is no wonder that you have a pile
of strange bills and all sorts of voices shrieking for
you, our elected officials, to remove this unpleasant
danger from our midst.

We beg you to give calm compassionate leadership in
our state. See that needed programs are in place. The
hot potato must be dealt with through adequate funding
for education and funding for community based care for
the ill. Public health laws and criminal laws are
already on our books to protect the people of Georgia.

Due to the fear and prejudice many people in high
risk groups cannot obtain insurance, are evicted from
housing and refused employment. It just happened that
this new strange virus started in this country in the
homosexual community. Not true in every other country.
We must find ways to halt the discrimination. To
continue on a punitive, fearful, illogical path will
mean that the financial burden and human suffering in
the communities in our state will be astronomical.

In no way do I see that HB 1281 will help in this
public health issue.

I ask you to reconsider and say "no" to HB 1281 and
quickly devise ways for the legislature to lead the
way in seeing that we have the resources for the
education, and compassionate care for the victims of
this dread disease.

I got acquainted with gay rights through the board of the American Civil
Liberties Union, which I'd been serving on since the 1970s. They asked me
to come on their police committee in the 1980s, because it would be a help
to have somebody that looked as nice and old and proper as I, if we went
down to some police hearing. I began to hear in detail about police discrimination and brutality against gays. I'll tell you it just nearly drove me
up a wall. Anything that I could do, anyplace that I could be, anything
that I could say, I wanted to be there and say it. Because for me, for a man
not to be able to walk down the street—I don't care what kind of a man he
is—he's got a right to walk down that street without the police coming
and hitting him. There's just no sense in that. I think we have made lots of
changes, and things are better as far as the police in Atlanta go.

I became interested in AIDS in the 1980s when a very dear friend of
mine was the director of AID Atlanta. AID Atlanta is a service organization, providing assistance to people living with AIDS. I have worked on a
lot of things that have been controversial all my life, but with AIDS I had
no actual personal knowledge. I wasn't involved emotionally or personally with AIDS, because I didn't have a son or grandson or daughter with
AIDS. But it seemed to me it was the greatest discrimination that I've ever
heard of in my life.

The main thing I did for them was a lot of their legislative work and
lobbying. I was still working on the GPRO at this time, and I was involved
with the legislature. I knew the nuts and bolts of how to go about getting
a bill passed and how to get some money out of the budget. I knew the little fundamental details that I could help them with.

It wasn't easy. The one thing that you learn, after doing so many different things over the years, is you learn how to take it. Somebody can tell
me to go to hell in seven different languages, and my heart doesn't even
beat any faster. It doesn't upset me a bit. I think the only thing that really
bothers me is when my friends criticize me. When your enemies criticize
you, you know you must have been doing pretty well.

I worked on the hotline for AID Atlanta. The first day that I was on the
hotline, I came home and decided that I had learned more that day than I
had learned in the rest of my life put together. The contacts that I had
with mothers, with wives, with all the family of our people that were suffering with AIDS, and with the doctors—the whole scope of it was so

overpowering. I'll always be grateful to AID Atlanta because of what they taught me, not just about AIDS but how to deal with various people with various problems.

I hadn't been in Washington when they unfolded the AIDS quilt there, so I wanted to be sure and go here in Atlanta in 1988. I was so flattered that they asked me to be a reader. They read the names of the people who had patches on the quilt. It took from nine o'clock until one o'clock to read the names of people who died.

In the early 1980s, I started going over to the Open Door Community which, to me, of all the different agencies that I've come into contact with, and have worked a little bit with, and some of them a lot with, the Open Door I admire the most. I think the people that run Open Door are the most committed to their task. The Open Door Community is a residential community here in Atlanta, working to improve the lives of the homeless and poor.

The Open Door started with a couple of ministers at Clifton Presbyterian Church, and they decided that they would have to do something about the homeless. They went down and picked up homeless people and brought them to spend the night at Clifton, and the only place they had at Clifton was the area where they had their church services. They moved the chairs back and put the pallets down, and the men would sleep there. They would feed them supper and breakfast too, I think, before they were back out on the street again.

At that time, Ed Loring and Murphy Davis—husband and wife, both of them Presbyterian ministers—and another couple in their church decided that this wasn't enough, that what they needed was a place where people could really stay. They pulled out of Clifton and bought this apartment house down on Ponce de Leon Avenue, a big old apartment house, and opened up the Open Door Community.

Open Door is very democratically organized and run. It is fascinating in that respect. Ten or twelve people are partners, and the partners operate it. They meet for long periods of time and hash out what they're going to do. Then they all do it, and they really do it together. A lot of the time a conclusion they come up with is not what Ed and Murphy would have thought, but it's most beautiful. I think it's the reason that so many of the homeless people have become partners. They've developed because they are treated with equality and with respect.

The amount of pay that the partners take is fifty dollars a month. That's their spending money. They all eat in the common kitchen, they all sleep there, and they all dress out of the clothes that are given to them, even Ed and Murphy and their daughter. As I say, I think they come the nearest to really living their commitment.

People come into the house for various reasons. For instance, one man who is one of the real leaders now, he was literally in the ditch when Ed found him. He had broken bones, he had been in a fight, and he was drunk. Ed got him to Grady Hospital. When he was ready to leave Grady, he still had casts, and he didn't have anyplace to go. So Ed told him he could come to Open Door if he'd like to, and he said, no, that he wouldn't. They have certain rules at Open Door, although they don't have a lot of terribly rigid rules, but people don't stay on drugs and stay on alcohol and live at Open Door. That doesn't mean that if you have a drink you'd be put out; it's not that rigid. On the other hand, you couldn't continue to be an alcoholic and stay there indefinitely. This guy had said he just couldn't come. But he didn't have any other place to go, so he came. Well, that was about ten years ago and he's still there. He's just a wonderful leader.

They feed enormous numbers of people. For instance, they cook breakfast for about two hundred people and take it down to Butler Street to feed people that have literally been on the street all night. There's a church down on Butler Street, the Butler Street C.M.E. Church, that lets them use their basement, and the street people, the truly homeless, can come there and get a hot breakfast. Then every day at the house they serve lunch or dinner, and they have a regular soup kitchen to serve two or three hundred people. They try to serve times when other places don't. Open Door serves on Sunday mornings when other churches are having their services. We have our service on Sunday afternoon at five o'clock, because all the morning is taken up with feeding people. The formerly homeless people that live there are the ones doing the work, and then they have other volunteers that come in, a lot of wonderful, wonderful volunteers.

The kind of support that I have given them has been more in contacts with the government, the city or the state. They take no money from government agencies, no money from city or state or federal funds. It's all private money. That way they don't have a lot of strings attached. But there's always problems that they're having with the city, and so I've represented them in the government field.

I've also taken part in some of the social action sponsored by the Open Door and a related group, People for Urban Justice. I spent a lot of time down at the Imperial Hotel in downtown Atlanta when it was occupied by People for Urban Justice in 1990. This was to publicize the need for affordable housing. We brought food from the church for them. I sat in a chair at the front door, while the police surrounded the Imperial. I believe that's when I got my name, "Mother PUJ," for People for Urban Justice.

Just going to the Open Door to worship means so much, because when you leave, you really feel that they're so real, that nobody's come there just because it's the thing to do, to go to church. One day, in the course of

LEWIS SINCLAIR AND FRANCES PAULEY AT THE OCCUPATION OF THE
IMPERIAL HOTEL IN ATLANTA, JUNE 1990. THE OCCUPATION CALLED
ATTENTION TO THE NEED FOR AFFORDABLE HOUSING IN ATLANTA.

(Photograph courtesy of Gladys Rustay.)

their prayers, a man was saying what it meant to him to be there. He had never known what it was like to have a group that felt like a family, and now he had a family. He said, "I never thought in my wildest dreams that I would have a close friend, a white, middle-class woman like Frances Pauley." You know, that's worth a lot of work.

One time someone died in the backyard. People sleep in the backyard of the Open Door, because they're safe from the police back there. We were all upset about the death, because it was somebody who ate a lot in the soup kitchen. The next Sunday we had a memorial service. We had it out in the backyard, because the backyard was his last "home."

A couple of the homeless stepped forward, and one of them drew a circle on the ground and said, "You remember Bobby, the guy that died, how he used to be. He used to draw a circle like this. And then he'd say, 'All right, fellows, come and toss in your change,' and we would all toss in our change. Then we'd pick it up, put it together, and go across the street and get a bottle and come back and we'd pass the bottle around." And with that, this group of men stepped up to this circle and threw in red roses. Wasn't that beautiful? There's something about people that have suffered a lot. There's a depth of their feeling, and they're just so kind.

Thinking about the homeless, we don't realize that every homeless person is an individual, and that they're homeless for a different reason, their own reason. It seems to me—and I may be wrong because I certainly have not done any scientific research on it—but to me there seems to be no pattern. Each individual has his own reason that he has landed where he has, that he's lost hope to the extent that he's gone down that far. It makes you know that people must do everything they can to give people hope so that they won't sink into that.

A lot of them return to families and return to employment. They'll come back and worship with us and say what it's meant to them. I remember one mother coming and saying what Open Door had done for her son. She tried to do things for her son, but she seemed to be helpless, and yet Open Door had brought him back. And we gave a scholarship to a girl who had to pay her own way to get to college, and she was the daughter of one of the men there. You never saw anybody so proud in all your life as that man was of that daughter—as all of us were.

There are a lot of real, real success stories. But some people are so deeply damaged by poverty. Some of them turn to alcohol and drugs for solace. The drug problem we have today is different from what we had back a ways. There was a drug problem, but it was different from what we have now. To break that addiction takes a terrific commitment. It's just such a privilege to have a chance to know some of those people.

One Sunday there was a real big black guy who lives there who was sitting by me. There was some conversation about all the separation of blacks and whites, how actually now the African Americans and the whites are separating more. When they were talking about that, he reaches over and takes my hand and holds my hand in his two great, big hands. He just wanted me to know that it wasn't that way all over. That really did bring tears in my eyes.

I've been very, very lucky because I know a lot of different people. One of the payoffs about working hard in organizational work is that I knew wonderful people. Yet I've always lived in DeKalb County. That's one good thing about staying in one place and having my name in the telephone book. People locate me, people that I've met or have known sometime before now. I heard from a lady in Philadelphia recently. She called and said, "You probably don't remember me, but I lived in South Georgia, and I had a baby and my family turned me out. I didn't know what to do. I didn't have any money, and you took me to the welfare office and taught me about AFDC." She said, "I just wanted to call and tell you that my son graduated yesterday from the University of North Carolina." I think that was so thrilling. That was worth all the work I ever did, I think, if I just had that one case.

I've still got contacts all over the state. I had somebody call me from out of the state several years back, and he had a man on death row in his state whose family lived outside of some town in Georgia. And did I have any way at all of reaching them? They didn't have a telephone. I said, "Sure." I got out my cards and said, "Call so-and-so. They'll get them for you." And they did. So I get a lot of interesting calls like that.

I now live at a retirement community, Wesley Woods, affiliated with Emory University. One great thing about Wesley Woods is that there are so many interesting people here. Every single person here has such an interesting background; every person would make an interesting story. I suppose that the life of anybody, if they live to be eighty and eighty-five and ninety, enough has happened in the last ninety years to make an interesting story.

Over the last few years, my eyesight has gotten steadily worse. I never have had very good eyesight; I had glasses from the time I was seven years old. But now I've been pronounced legally blind. That's been hard to adjust to when I've been used to reading so much. It was funny because when I thought about what I was going to do when I got old, I always thought I wouldn't be able to walk. So I thought of all the things that I could do sitting down. But it never dawned on me that I wouldn't be able to use my eyes. I thought those would be the days that I'd enjoy

STUDENTS IN A TAI CHI CLASS AT WESLEY WOODS. DR. XU IS IN
THE FOREGROUND; FRANCES IS IMMEDIATELY TO THE LEFT
OF DR. XU.

(Photograph by Charlotte Teagle/The Atlanta Journal-Constitution.)

all of the handwork and knitting and the reading, all of the things that
you use your eyes for.

I've been fortunate to take up tai chi since coming to Wesley Woods, and
it has helped me improve my balance. The problem with most old people
is that we have a tendency to lose our balance and fall. You have broken
hips and broken arms; that's your main problem with old people. To do tai
chi takes some concentration as well as physical exercise, and for me that's
another thing that has helped. As I've gotten older, I've had less reason to
have to concentrate on anything, and I think the fact that you have to concentrate in order to do it is also beneficial for you as a total person.

It's been a pleasure, particularly to get to know Dr. Xu, who is our
teacher. I'm by far the most elderly student in the tai chi class; the next
oldest person is eighty-four. That makes me sort of teacher's pet. Consequently I get a great deal of attention. Dr. Xu says he's my adopted son.
Now I have various family members doing tai chi, including my great-
grandchild. Dr. Xu really got a big bang out of seeing my great-grandchild
doing tai chi.

I've been filmed for television doing tai chi. Every time I turn around, here's a reporter wanting a statement about this or a statement about that. It's interesting to me, because when I was working in civil rights, I used to try really hard to get publicity. We needed so much publicity about what was happening, because I don't think that people would have stood for some of the bad things that were going on, if they'd known about it. So there I was struggling and struggling to get something in the paper. In fact, not too long ago the man who had been the editor of one of the Atlanta papers at the time I was working on civil rights confided in me that he had told the staff not to print anything I asked them to because they wanted this image of Atlanta to be so good. They didn't want to have any bad race relations put in print. All the years that I needed the press, and wanted the press, and tried to get the press, and couldn't get them, and now that I'm not doing anything, why, the press is by my doorstep all the time. It's not the same people at all, this is a whole other generation of people that are interviewing me at this time, but sometimes it's almost hard to be decent.

I'm worried to death about some of the things that are happening today, and it makes me furious that I don't have any eyes and can't do anything much. I see us going back in a lot of ways. I see us going back in real integration. Separateness is increasing, and a lot of it is because of the blacks. And I don't blame them. If I were black, I'd have a hard time being an integrationist. But we tried "separate but equal" for a hundred, two hundred years, and it certainly didn't work. I don't think "separate but equal" is *ever* going to work. I wish that we had some really good human relations organizations intact that could be working to bring people together.

While it seems like we're getting more and more separated, in a certain way, in another way, not. I went to the Alvin Ailey dance company recently, and when I came out of the Fox Theater I'm sure that blacks outnumbered whites ten to one. It wasn't cheap, and these people were dressed so well. I thought as I went out, "Oh, my. There wouldn't have been that many well-dressed people in the whole city of Atlanta in 1960." I'm so glad that there are people now that don't remember that they had to sit on the back of the bus. We've just made an awful lot of progress.

It used to be that there must have been such a terrible feeling, a suppressed feeling of hatred to white people. It had to be so completely suppressed, and you had to teach your kid, "Yes, ma'am," "No, sir," no matter what, no matter how they were treated. You had to teach them that. If you didn't, they were going to be killed. It was a matter of survival. Now, I think this racial feeling has come out, and it's expressed when somebody pushes you out of line. When a black pushes me out of line, I'm always glad. I really am. It really tickles me. I've had it happen a few times. I don't think it's very nice manners, I admit, but it just tickles me that we've gotten that far, that people feel free enough to push a white person, to be rude to a white person.

Now, on the level of community cooperation, I don't know how much that has advanced. I think that we need to do more about seeing that poor people are properly represented. The poor just never have had anybody to lobby for them, never have had anybody to stand up for them. And they have even less today, I think. They certainly don't have any more today.

Welfare has not ever been very popular, I'm afraid. I can't understand it. It seems to me that people shouldn't want babies to starve, and that's what welfare is, feeding babies. All people think about is punishing the girl, an unmarried teenager, because she got pregnant. But why punish that baby? That baby needs to be fed and nurtured even more. But that isn't the way people see it. They don't see the baby as a future citizen.

We have far, far, far too many homeless. One of the worst things of all is that you can't live on the minimum wage. We have people sleeping in the backyard at Open Door who have jobs and minimum wage, but they can't rent a room. That's wrong to have it set up as such in a city, that the minimum wage in a city is not enough to pay rent. Rents go higher, minimum wage doesn't, and yet the authorities do nothing about rent control. So here's a man that makes more than minimum wage who is sleeping on the ground, because he's got to pay some alimony or child support. The courts make him pay the child support, and the child support takes so much that he hasn't got enough left on his little bit more than minimum wage to live on. Consequently, he sleeps on the ground and eats in a soup line, and yet he is working. The majority of the people who sleep on the ground in the backyard of Open Door have a job. They get up, and it's amazing how clean and decent they look when they get up and leave there and go off to work. This is a social problem that needs to be worked out.

When people say that not much change has taken place, I agree with them in the sense that we have such a tremendous way to go. I guess we always have had to fight the same fights over and over, haven't we?

"TALKING FOR A PURPOSE": STORYTELLING AND ACTIVISM IN THE LIFE OF FRANCES FREEBORN PAULEY

The life story of Frances Freeborn Pauley contained within these pages is that of a political activist whose career spanned the twentieth century. At the center of the story is a middle-class white woman, with northern roots and a southern upbringing, who carved out an ever-expanding role for herself in the social and political movements of this century. Hers is a political career, not in the traditional sense of office-holding and the formal exercise of power, but in a broader conception of politics in which the political efficacy of all citizens matters and the distribution of power and resources in a society is at stake. Frances's story communicates her deep commitment to meaningful democracy.

It was most often on the local level that Frances struggled to make democratic citizenship a reality, and there is in Frances's stories a remarkable measure of the quotidian. We are on the ground with Frances in the New Deal, in the civil rights movement, and in the struggle against poverty and homelessness. This local orientation also explains, in part, why Frances's story and the stories of other activists like her are little known. As U.S. political historians go about their work, they tend to construct a national history first, then a regional one, and only later recover the local stories. We are just beginning to understand the scope and significance of grassroots movements during the twentieth century. In our time, when many lament the lack of political leadership to tackle the social and economic problems around us, Frances offers inspiration that change can come from within communities.

In the struggle for social, racial, and economic justice, Frances exhibited a dogged determination and a willingness to learn by doing. "It's just a matter of starting, just putting your foot in the road and saying you're going to do something about it," she maintains.[1] Acting on that maxim, Frances made the extraordinary seem possible, even ordinary. Long after

Frances and I had embarked on the project of producing her life story, I came across her high school motto, printed alongside her graduation photograph, in which a much younger version of the ninety-plus-year-old face I've come to know looks straight into the camera with a small smile. "Common sense is instinct," she says, "and enough of it is genius." Her classmates added: "A girl who is not afraid of hard work."[2]

That Frances delivers a life story with politics at its center is an act of self-definition. She has thereby told us what she thinks is important about her life. I have followed her lead, explicating the logic and structure of her storytelling. A complex life deserves to be understood on many levels, but surely the first is that which the subject herself constructs.[3] Simultaneously, I chart a second, if related, course in order to contextualize her life story and thus to comment on Frances in relation to women's history, southern history, and civil rights history. In this I take the long view. Each phase of Frances's political life warrants extensive analysis, but this essay—which can only begin to comment on a lifetime of activism—looks at key developments over her lifetime. Perhaps the end of the twentieth century encourages reflection on the whole, and Frances, born early in the twentieth century and still alive at the turn of the next, is too tempting a subject to pass up. Frances's storytelling also urges me in this direction. Narratives delivered in later life tend to bring on retrospection, summation, and a definition of the whole.[4] The first of the oral histories on which this book is based was recorded in 1974, quite some time ago, but Frances was then already sixty-eight. She has since condensed and refined her stories further, clipping detail while emphasizing patterns, lessons, and meaning. I have helped Frances deliver her story, but in this essay I am also trying to do the historian's job of ordering, interpreting, and tracing change over time. Whereas Frances draws consistent meaning from her life, I try to locate the origin, development, and progression of that meaning over a lifetime. The logic of history comments here on the texture of story.

As befits an autobiography, the preceding compilation of stories is most revealing of Frances. It is her life that evolves and changes, she whom we come to know best. Nonetheless, Frances's story is also about many others, mostly southerners, who, community by community, made change possible.[5] In this, Frances's storytelling is true to her life's work; the life of an organizer turns, almost by definition, on enabling the actions of others. Her story is also about a century of social change in the South. As we travel with Frances from the early 1900s to the 1990s in Georgia, we see these changes through her eyes. Just as the old South, the slave South, gave way to the New South into which Frances moved in 1908, so the New South has given way to a somewhat different South that we have yet to define and fully explain. One way to examine this transition is through life stories. Many are needed; Frances's is one.

> One of my earliest memories is my mother telling me that when people call you a "damn Yankee," just smile. That was a good lesson for me, because I always talked too much. And I remember being proud that I was a "damn Yankee."

One of the hallmarks of Frances Pauley's storytelling is that small, simple vignettes often encompass a range of experience and meaning. This earliest memory is no exception. Frances takes the well-worn cliché of the damn Yankee and invests it with a great deal of personal significance. Condensed into these few words are her dual identity as both a northerner and a southerner, the importance of her mother's influence, and a hint that Frances, just like a damn Yankee, would try to leave her mark on the South. Much of the meaning she attaches to her growing-up experiences can be elaborated from this beginning.

During Frances's childhood, the Freeborn family shuttled between a new home in the South and a summer base in the Midwest. Around these annual migrations, Frances has built a body of regional comparisons. Her variations on the theme of North–South differences are numerous: her father's work helping southern farmers who "farmed so poorly in comparison with the way they farmed in Ohio"; a brother who was more "bothered" than Frances by their status as northerners in the South; her mother's disappointment at the differences in the Methodist faith as practiced in the North and the South; an aunt who, unlike the southern women they knew, worked outside the home for wages; and grandmother Freeborn, who hurried home one year to cast her ballot in Ohio. More often than not, the South suffered on these points of comparison, and Frances recounts with pride that her northern ancestors were pioneers, town founders, and early advocates of public education and women's rights.

In light of Frances's later activism, her mother's influence was pivotal, and Frances, in recounting her childhood, weaves a story of women, religion, and social change. In the church, Frances observed that women practiced the Social Gospel. Methodist women constituted the vanguard of southern white women's efforts to ameliorate the problems brought on by urbanization and industrialization: overcrowded cities, unsafe working conditions, and high rates of disease. Atlanta became the site of the earliest mission work of Methodist women in Georgia with the establishment of the Trinity Home Mission Society, a ministry to poor women and children, black and white, in downtown Atlanta in 1882. By the time the Freeborns settled in nearby Decatur, Methodist women sponsored settlement houses, homes for unwed mothers, kindergartens, and Sunday schools. In the broad-gauged reform movement of the early twentieth century known as progressivism, church women initiated many social welfare programs and worked with municipal officials to set up a rudimentary public health and welfare system in the metropolitan Atlanta area of Fulton and DeKalb Counties.[6]

Josephine Andrews Freeborn, visiting the day nursery at Atlanta's Fulton Bag and Cotton Mills and delivering medicine to the sick, was part of this tradition and imparted it to her daughter. Frances accompanied her mother on one occasion to visit the cotton mill's nursery school, and the memory remains vivid decades later: "I was so horrified. I still can smell how the room smelled, and I can see how dirty those children were. Cotton mills were awful, just awful. You know, poverty and its degradation are something you have to see and touch and smell." Josephine was also the source of several important childhood lessons. A woman with "leadership qualities," she taught Frances to stand her ground but pick her battles. Frances remembers feeling "awful" when her mother was dismissed from the church's Board of Stewards for not supporting segregation, but she admired her mother's principles and recognized that "it wasn't any use for her to fight at the level where she was."[7] Josephine's extended illness curtailed her activities, but Dorothy Tilly, an "organizer of women" in the Woman's Missionary Society of the Methodist Episcopal Church, South, and a notable southern reformer of the early twentieth century, nurtured Frances's early development in the church's youth group.[8] Frances recalls "trying to lead what I thought was a Christian life," and her models for that life were more individual and familial than institutional. The Methodist church in the South was too thoroughly implicated in segregation to serve as Frances's guide for a life of service and commitment. Nonetheless, her faith led Frances toward her principled positions and gave her the strength to stand by them, and she shared with some of the South's most outspoken white liberals a firm conviction that segregation was a violation of Christian faith. When Frances became disillusioned with her church, as happened frequently over the course of her life, it was because of the church's failure to live up sufficiently to its own ideals.[9]

Like many children raised in the South, Frances first learned about race relations in the domestic setting. The Freeborn family, however, hired African American domestic help not, as was common in their neighborhood, in the form of a nursemaid for Frances and her brother but rather a cook who also provided all-purpose domestic help. Frances's formative experience was with a day worker, not a "mammy," with all the complex connotations of racial intimacy and power that relationship called up. While the Freeborns enjoyed the same advantage as all southern, white, middle-class households—white domesticity and comfort were almost uniformly predicated on the low-cost labor of working-class blacks, especially black women—the distinctions the Freeborns drew mattered. Josephine did not expect such a thoroughly personalized and exploitative form of service. It would be some time before Frances developed a critique of southern employment patterns, but her childhood provided some of the ground on which she would later link poverty, labor, and racial practices.[10] Josephine Freeborn also paid a higher wage than prevailed in her neighborhood, required fewer hours of service, and had her domestic workers enter through the front door. For Frances, who devoted a lifetime to bringing injustice down to a level of personal understanding and responsibility, her mother provided an early example of individual courage. Such actions might even have unintended positive consequences. The family always had "the pick of the community" in terms of domestic help, although "that wasn't what Mama was thinking about."

Ultimately Frances concluded that she was "lucky" to have Yankee parents. Unlike many of her southern friends, she did not have the "handicap" of "the old master-servant mentality." Instead, Frances often experienced herself as an outsider to the South and an object herself of "discrimination" for "being from a northern family." As a result, she attributes to her childhood an instinctive understanding of discrimination that in turn paved the way for her racial liberalism. On this account, Frances differs from many of the southern white liberals with whom she otherwise shares the generational experience of being born into middle- or upper-class white families in the early twentieth century. Among the women of this group are Anne Braden, Virginia Foster Durr, Lillian Smith, and Sarah Patton Boyle, all of whom produced autobiographical works. Unlike Frances, each has needed to tell a conversion tale to explain how she overcame personal prejudice and left behind the privileges of race and class. Often their stories reveal a conflicted relationship with parents who are the objects of affection and yet also bear the responsibility of having taught the burdensome racial lessons of the white South, particularly that black inferiority justified white supremacy. Writer Lillian Smith is perhaps the best known of this group. Smith said she wrote her most famous work, the autobiographical novel *Killers of the Dream*, as "an act of penance" and "a step toward redemption."[11] Frances enjoys, by contrast, the luxury of unambivalent childhood memories. She remembers a secure and loving family life, yet one that planted the seeds of a quiet determination to challenge injustice. Perhaps most important for her later activist career, the price of dissent was not too high and far outweighed by the gain in personal integrity.

Frances passed from adolescence into adulthood during the 1920s, a time of increasing secularism and expanding models for female behavior. She was the first girl at Decatur High School to bob her hair, a momentous act at the time: "Boy, did it make a splash. That was my new freedom, to cut my hair." Frances narrates a time of growing independence as her own interests emerged, yet in rendering her life story, she describes these new influences as augmenting, rather than supplanting, the lessons of childhood. When she enrolled at Agnes Scott College in the fall of 1923, theater, and especially playwriting, captured her imagination. Other reform-minded women of her generation merged the new opportunities afforded by a college education with their Christian upbringing; many joined the student wing of the Young Women's Christian Association, with its roots in Protestant evangelical reform, and devoted their efforts to the labor movement and interracial reform.[12] Although Frances's choice was at once more secular and artistic, she too recalls her education as preparation for civic engagement: "Agnes Scott certainly taught me to be a serious student, a very serious citizen, that life is real, life is earnest. This was the attitude of the faculty as a whole." She was also surrounded by female role models, and the faculty members and administrators she cites as important to her education were all women.

Playwriting allowed Frances to give artistic expression to a growing social consciousness. Atlanta's Drama Workshop, a civic theater group she joined after graduating from college, was part of an effort to develop a "sectional drama" that reflected ordinary people and places in the South.[13] In the workshop's 1930 season, Frances presented "The Poor Farm," inspired by her church youth group's mission work at the DeKalb County Poor Farm. These visits helped Frances understand poverty on a personal level and avoid a reductionist view of the poor as social types: "I got to know the people a little bit, know them as individuals. I didn't look down upon them as cast-off folks." This insight animated her playwriting, and she sought to portray the poor as "very interesting people," "not as dregs or failures in life." Frances here introduces a core element of her activism: understanding precedes action. "It ought to be a required subject for everyone to take drama, to have to play a role, be somebody else. I think it teaches you so much," she says. Frances's later activism exhibited a flair for the dramatic, which she often attributes to her training in the theater, but as a formative experience the theater was about representing the diversity of the South in the spirit of social realism and, perhaps most fundamentally, about forms of artistic expression that encouraged empathy. As her activist career took hold, she moved increasingly toward a critique of the social structures that maintained poverty.

The onset of the Great Depression ended Frances's budding career in theater but launched her on a lifetime of political action. In 1930, the workshop lost its ticket receipts in a bank failure, and the group hobbled through its last season. As the Depression worsened, simply making do was challenge enough.[14] Recently married and raising two small daughters, Frances remembers the Depression as a "struggle": "How were you going to make ends meet, and how were you going to feed your family well, and how were you going to clothe the kids?" Like many families, the Pauleys fell back on local resources and bartered with neighbors for goods and services. They also relied on government assistance. Bill Pauley's landscape architecture business "had stopped dead" until he found work with several New Deal agencies, and Frances, in charge of a household that included her father and brother as well as her husband and daughters, was grateful for the "good eating money" that government work provided. Unlike many middle-class Americans who derived benefits from government programs, whether the direct relief of the New Deal or later government-subsidized housing and education during the economic boom of the post–World War II period, Frances acknowledges her debt to her government. She also reminds us that the benefits of a government-supported infrastructure (roads, airports, parks, recreation facilities) are shared by all: "We forget those good things that meant a lot to the state, a lot of that work was done in the Depression days."

The Depression encouraged Frances to view the causes of widespread social problems as systemic rather than individual. "Everybody was out of work," she maintains, "rich and poor, black and white, old and young. It was just what was happening in the world." Today Frances often despairs that the lack of will to do anything about poverty and homelessness stems from a tendency to attribute social problems to personal failings. She drew a different lesson from the Great Depression: if a problem was beyond individual control, then the solution required collective responsibility. That Frances is, in fact, incorrect about the leveling tendency of the Great Depression—in Atlanta blacks suffered worse effects than whites, and the Depression in general exacerbated class differences—only serves to highlight its meaning for her: everyone had hit rock bottom, and everyone needed to emerge together.[15] An analysis of the systemic nature of economic problems turned some socially conscious Americans toward socialism and communism, but Frances stopped short of those more radical solutions. She became, instead, a New Deal Democrat: "I was, of course, a great admirer of Roosevelt, as I still am."[16]

For southern white liberals, the New Deal era was a heady time. Roosevelt had declared that the South was the nation's number one economic problem, and liberals saw in his reform program not only a way to alleviate the immediate misery of the Depression but also a chance to build long-term solutions to regional problems that predated the 1930s. The cotton economy of the region had long been ailing, but the Great Depression hastened its collapse. In this time of economic upheaval, southern New Dealers hoped to wrest social and political control from the economic elite of the region and the politicians who served them. A number traveled to Washington to work in New Deal agencies, and they threw their weight behind developments, such as support of labor unions and racial liberalism, that had long been anathema in the region. Among the women of this group were Virginia Foster Durr, who championed voting rights, and Lucy Randolph Mason, a tireless advocate of labor reform and civil rights.[17] To their regional and national narrative, Frances adds a local story. She offers a view of the New Deal as its programs and funds insinuated their way into daily lives.

Frances has said, on many occasions, some version of the following: "The first thing I ever remember organizing was during the Depression." Occupied with two young daughters, Frances first noticed the suffering of families and children and directed her earliest efforts toward the health and welfare of the poor, which in Depression-era Georgia was one of the most pressing problems. Despite the inroads made by progressivism earlier in the century, Georgia's public health profile was dismal: the state ranked consistently in the top three for malaria deaths, only one town had a milk supply that met the standards of the U.S. Public Health Service, and much of the housing—in Atlanta, the majority—was substandard. Georgia's director of public health concluded that the state's most urgent need was additional funds for public health and medical care.[18] Frances's solution was to organize: "A couple of us ladies got together with the county's public health director and decided that we would try to set up a clinic." These "ladies" were the same church women who had taken the lead in establishing several private clinics for the indigent in DeKalb County, first made available to African Americans and later to needy whites as well.[19] Presbyterian women established a medical clinic for African Americans in 1919, and Methodist women set up a dental clinic in 1933. Over the course of the Depression, these church women laid plans for additional services, and the final consolidation of these independent clinics into the DeKalb Clinic occurred in 1939. Folded in from the public sector were the beginnings of municipally financed health care delivery, generally focused on disease prevention and maternal and child health. The DeKalb Clinic represented the culmination, aided by the New Deal, of women's progressive-era interest in health and social welfare.[20] Frances came of age as an activist in a time of growing public responsibility for social welfare. The local New Deal, which encouraged organized citizens to turn to their government for assistance in meeting social problems, became the blueprint for a life's work.

The story of the DeKalb Clinic has a personal dimension as well, and a hallmark of Frances's storytelling is that she weaves together a tale of her own development with a narrative of social change more generally. One of the keys to Frances's success as an organizer was her willingness— indeed, her eagerness—to learn. In the clinic, the lessons concerned the "myths" of race. Although Frances often emphasizes that her childhood differed from that of other white southerners, she nonetheless recognizes that she grew up in a world of thoroughgoing racial prejudice. The consequence may not have been a deeply ingrained belief in black inferiority, but it certainly was a large measure of ignorance. The clinic offered an opportunity for education. As she assisted on "well-baby day," Frances observed that the county's African American population took greater advantage of the clinic's services than did whites. Even more "surprising" to her was the fact that black fathers, rather than mothers, often brought the babies to the clinic. Frances came to realize that "the black mother was working, and the black father wasn't." In the South, where whites more typically viewed blacks as carriers of disease,[21] Frances noted instead that black families sought out preventive care. The lesson was profound: the prevalence of disease among African Americans was not the result of racial inferiority; rather, access to medical resources determined health. Frances took as her charge doing all that she could to make that care available. The organizing skills that were a hallmark of her work over a lifetime first became evident in the clinic. As vice-president she raised funds from the rich and powerful, and she traveled deep into neighborhoods to publicize the clinic's services.

Frances's work in the clinic likewise encouraged an understanding of health problems among poor whites. She found white mill villagers, malnourished and suffering from the harmful effects of harsh working conditions, to be "worse off than any blacks I have ever seen anywhere." Apart from the hyperbole—that blacks, concentrated on the lowest rungs of the occupational ladder, were somehow better off than whites (and Frances has been known to overstate her case to make a point)—when it came to health care, Frances was on firm ground. For all that Jim Crow had done to depress the standard of living for blacks in the South, working-class whites faced an equally daunting, if different, array of health problems.[22] Racial distinctions mattered to Frances insofar as they explained the origins and scope of a social problem, but the Great Depression drove home a far more important truth: suffering on both sides of the color line was deep enough as to be nearly equal. Anyone in that amount of need deserved sympathy and help. Much of Frances's life was devoted to racial

justice, but an even deeper structure of her political action was a commitment to help those in need.

The school lunch program, a direct outgrowth of her work in the
DeKalb Clinic, extended the education of Frances Pauley as she came to
know middle-class black social reformers of her day for the first time.
When malnourished children made their way to the clinic, the need to
provide proper meals became obvious at the same time that the federal
government provided the means to meet that need.[23] The story of bringing this New Deal program to DeKalb County is among Frances's
favorites, and she delivers it with relish, dwelling on the twists and turns
of plot development. It is also exemplary of another central tendency in
Frances's storytelling: she often attaches morals to her stories, ending
with an explicit statement of an implicit message.[24] After narrating her
discovery of Maude Hamilton, a black principal who first took advantage
of this government program, and the series of complications that ensued
as Frances sought to extend the program into white schools, she con-
cludes on this note of success: "It ended up that in six weeks we had hot
lunches in every school in the county. Children were getting not only hot
lunches but in many schools they were getting breakfast as well. The
school attendance just rose enormously. Kids were fed, and everybody
was happy." Then, this lesson: "The main thing about getting things done
is—and I think I still have a tendency to do the same thing—if you see
something that needs to be done, just go ahead and start. I think that's the
first lesson in organizing. Don't sit around until you get everything on
paper. Just go ahead and do it."

To this day, Frances rarely misses an opportunity to turn a personal
story into a political lesson, and the form of her storytelling style closely
resembles the parable.[25] Widely associated with the teachings of Christ, a
parable uses events and situations that are familiar to listeners to present
a deeper truth. Drawing on this tradition, Frances peoples her stories with
ordinary southerners going about their daily lives, but she asks them to
make a profound change in their world. Both the clinic story and the
school lunch story are about creating a more humane and just South. "Go
thou and do likewise," Frances in effect tells her listeners. Although
Frances's stories often reveal that she is being educated, she also encourages her listeners to imagine that they too can learn and change. Storytelling shades into political praxis, and is, for Frances, a political act.[26]

That Frances developed a storytelling style with close parallels to the
ministry of Jesus underscores the religious impulse for much of her early
activism. Certainly this was evident in her fundraising speeches for the
clinic, in which politics and religion, Roosevelt's reference to the forgotten
third of the population and Christ's injunction to charity commingled: "If

Jesus were to come to Decatur to-day would he not say, 'Give ye them to eat'? Did he not know the children? What would he do to-day about the ill clad, ill housed, ill nourished third?" Frances's growing disillusionment with organized religion in her later life has led her to diminish the explicitly religious content of her stories. In more subtle ways, however, her faith lingers in her storytelling. Frances speaks in parables.

The lesson Frances imparts to others is simple and clear, but the school lunch story reveals another side of the educable Frances. If the lesson Frances learned in the clinic was an unlearning of the myths of race, the racial learning of the school lunch program involved acquiring new knowledge, and the character of Maude Hamilton, who was "quite a woman," looms large in the story. Both the clinic and the school lunch program provided services to the needy of both races, but in the latter case the racial roles were reversed. Whereas the clinic was begun by white women as an act of benevolence toward African Americans, Hamilton, a black woman, led the way with the school lunch program. Even within the confines of segregation, Frances and the white principals were supplicants to the "superior" Maude Hamilton.[27] Similarly, it was the white population that lagged behind in deriving benefits from the New Deal. Despite the fact that the New Deal institutionalized racial discrimination in many of its projects, in Frances's experience it was not a government program that African Americans got belatedly, in half measures, if at all. Quite the opposite. Taking cues from black leadership was perhaps a strange set of circumstances for a white woman to find herself in, but Frances embraced it.

Nonetheless, such racial reversals had their limits; segregation was sidestepped, not confronted. When Maude Hamilton came to speak to the assembled school principals of DeKalb County, she waited in another room, "things were that segregated." Similarly, when a grand jury inspected the clinic and found that black and white patients shared a waiting room, it instructed the clinic to segregate the races. The staff complied. Frances also admits that the clinic readily accepted the "natural line" that separated blacks from whites in the clinic. "We were thinking about equality and justice," she says, "but weren't thinking about real desegregation and what that would require." For most southern white liberals of the period, integration was not yet thinkable; rather, they worked to improve the conditions of African Americans within the confines of segregation. Frances was no exception.[28]

Although neither Frances nor any of her white colleagues in the clinic and school lunch programs challenged segregation, change was under way, which can best be appreciated in generational terms. Frances went into the Great Depression under the tutelage of women like Dorothy Tilly who were imbued with the spirit of Christian charity, which, in the segregated South, amounted to no small measure of dissent within a discriminatory racial order. Nonetheless, most white women of Tilly's generation viewed African Americans as dependent on whites for leadership in challenging the racial status quo. For the next generation, the Great Depression opened up new vistas. The particular circumstances of a government program available to blacks as well as whites, an especially adept Maude Hamilton who first seized the opportunity, a young Frances Pauley open to new approaches—all of these conspired to position Frances as someone who could and would chart a different course. In this interaction with Maude Hamilton, it is possible to see how women of Frances's generation had formative experiences that, were they ready to accept them, moved them beyond earlier models of interracial reform.[29] In this the role of the federal government was critical. Although the New Deal did not intend to confront southern racial patterns, on the local and personal level it had unintended consequences. Frances Pauley's New Deal, it is no exaggeration to say, changed her life. Little wonder, then, that the Depression does not linger in Frances's memory as a negative experience; rather, it launched her on a career of social action.[30]

World War II, which pulled the country out of the Depression, changed the South profoundly. One of the most evident changes was a quickened struggle for civil rights and a marked increase in political participation among African Americans. During the war, the U.S. Supreme Court outlawed the white primary, a linchpin of white supremacy. This method of disenfranchisement, adopted throughout the South in the early twentieth century, limited participation in primary elections to white citizens at a time when the heavily Democratic political makeup of the South made the outcome of primaries tantamount to election. After the war, returning veterans, both black and white, translated the fight against fascism abroad into struggles for democracy at home. Those who had remained on the home front were also ready to challenge the racial status quo. Throughout the South, African Americans signaled a growing restiveness by joining the NAACP and registering to vote in record numbers, and Georgia had the highest rate of black political participation of any southern state. In metropolitan Atlanta, Frances's home, a massive black voter registration drive in early 1946 more than tripled the black voter registration count.[31] Black voting rights also increasingly became a cause supported by southern white reformers who saw in the postwar years an opportunity to expand political participation in the region, among white as well as black voters. They believed that the southern populace had too long been under the sway of the political demagogues for which the region was infamous, and they placed a large measure of their hope for change on the politicization of individual citizens. The intellectual underpinning for this shift was the development of a new liberal consensus in the postwar period, one that emphasized individual rights and the deleterious impact of racism. Eventually, these trends would lead into the civil rights movement, but the first step was political rights.

"I liked politics, and I really did want to run for the legislature. I just thought it would be more fun to be in the legislature than anything," says Frances of her growing interest in electoral politics in the postwar period. She did not, however, run for political office, not in the 1940s, nor later. Instead she channeled her political interest into the League of Women Voters, that little-studied outgrowth of the much-studied women's suffrage campaigns of the early twentieth century.[32] Frances found the league to be "one of the few ways that women could work" in a time when neither political party, whether in the South or elsewhere in the nation, paid much attention to developing leadership potential in women. The league, by contrast, provided women with an education in politics. Active membership in the league required managing a portfolio on one of the critical issues of the time, and league women were often better informed than many elected representatives. This "very sophisticated leadership," Frances notes, would "go to the league office and stay all day." From the mid-1940s through the early 1960s, the League of Women Voters was Frances's avenue into the critical questions of democracy and desegregation as they moved to center stage in the political life of the South and the nation after World War II. As a member, then officer, and finally president of the Georgia League of Women Voters from 1952 to 1955, Frances helped open up Georgia politics.

When Frances joined the Georgia league, a citizen had to put up a good fight simply to learn what was happening in the legislature: "We had to do a lot of the stuff that now you can just walk in a clerk's office and get. To get a roll call vote you would have to get permission to read the journal, and to get permission to read the journal was kind of like getting in Heaven." The league's most basic tasks, then, were observing and reporting. Frances began her tenure with the league as a legislative monitor, and she spent many hours leaning over the railing of the visitors' balcony, simply recording votes. The league's goal was "to get the facts out—how was the government run, what was happening, just the plain nitty-gritty facts." In the league, Frances further developed a sense, shared by many American progressives, that information and education were critical starting points in addressing social and political problems. The facts, once widely known, would move people to action. She also learned to do her political homework and developed a knack for detailed research. For the rest of her career, Frances would use this skill to good effect, particularly as she worked on controversial or unpopular measures. Factual information—plenty of it, carefully marshaled—might sway the more rational members of her audience, while her gift for storytelling moved others. Frances learned to deploy both strategies adeptly, often in tandem.

The centerpiece of the league's program, locally and nationally, was voter education and citizenship training.[33] This seemingly innocuous program was neither routine nor accepted by many Georgia politicians in the 1940s. When two political commentators surveyed the political landscape of Georgia in 1947, they concluded that the League of Women Voters was one of a very few organizations making a serious effort at voter education, and it was the only one with a year-round program.[34] The league met with a great deal of resistance from legislators on this account. As Frances recalls, "They didn't like us meddling in their business."

Despite its emphasis on fact-finding, the league aimed to effect political change, and in the 1940s this meant "meddling" with Georgia's county unit system, which V. O. Key, in his classic study of southern politics in the late-1940s, described as "unquestionably . . . the most important institution affecting Georgia politics."[35] In what was essentially an indirect system of election, each county in the state carried two, four, or six unit votes, depending on its population. Candidates who won a majority of votes in a county garnered all of its unit votes, and victory went to those who amassed the most unit votes rather than the largest popular vote. The practical impact of the system was to weigh heavily the vote in Georgia's numerous rural counties and to diminish significantly the political clout of the much smaller number of urban counties. For the league, with its commitment to representative democracy, this was a critical matter, and the imbalance of political representation only intensified during Frances's time with the league as Georgia continued a trend toward urbanization that the Depression and World War II had fueled. Who got to vote and how those votes counted was also a racial issue, because most of the state's politically active African Americans resided in urban areas.

The League of Women Voters had been working against the county unit system for some time, but the issue came to a head in 1952 when Governor Herman Talmadge, himself a beneficiary of rural rule in Georgia, sought to institutionalize the county unit system by writing it into the state constitution. To oppose Talmadge, the league joined a coalition of organizations representing liberal forces in Georgia to form Citizens Against the County Unit Amendment. Their goal was to influence the public to reject the amendment when it came up for a popular vote on the November ballot. It was an exhausting and exhilarating fight, one that Frances still remembers clearly: "It was the first time I had just worked day and night without making the bed, without doing anything, just putting my whole self into it. We just simply had to win, and we did, but by a hair." Of the league's and Frances's leadership, Pulitzer Prize–winning journalist Julian LaRose Harris enthused, "It was inspiring to meet women who were providing leadership for both men and women in what proved to be an astonishingly successful effort to save Georgia from political bankruptcy . . . As for yourself, I have seldom seen an iron hand so effectively masked by a glove so seemingly soft and pliant."[36] Frances, with her tendency to state matters more prosaically, found the origins of her leadership in the realities of intergroup conflicts within the coalition: "Finally they decided that the only trustworthy group was the league. That's one thing, the league has always kept its skirts clean."

The image of a squeaky-clean League of Women Voters, echoing as it does the claims of early twentieth-century suffragists, the foremothers of the league, that women would clean up politics with their votes, suggests an intriguing connection between gender and politics in postwar Georgia. Political corruption—buying votes, bribing officials, tampering with electoral returns—extended into the 1940s and 1950s.[37] Frances attributes her later defeat on the 1954 private school amendment to electoral irregularities. More generally at stake in postwar Georgia was the basic issue of democratic citizenship in a complex society: which individuals and groups have access to the political process and to political power? Citizens Against the County Unit Amendment brought together predominantly urban interests, including city mayors, urban legislative delegations, organized labor, and newly re-enfranchised black voters, all of whom stood to benefit from adherence to the "one man, one vote" principle. These were often perceived to be special interest groups that marshaled their vote as a bloc. The league, by contrast, presented itself as an advocacy organization for good government that stayed above the political fray. "In the public interest" was a favorite league phrase to describe the character of its work. It did not seek to be, nor did it present itself as, a special interest group for women. Instead, informed and responsible action by all citizens was its mission.

Despite its carefully honed neutrality, the league was quite plainly throwing its weight behind certain political tendencies in Georgia. The opposition, well aware of this, often responded to the league's rhetoric by identifying women in the league as the so-called good government crowd and by tarring it with guilt by association. If the league supported organized labor, then it was communist inspired; if it advocated black voting rights, then it was led by "nigger lovers." In this climate, the league directed its efforts at the public at large, toward the court of public opinion. League women were rarely the first or the most outspoken advocates of reforms such as the abolition of the white primary or the county unit system. But when the league, with its educated, well-heeled, and hardly radical membership, spoke in its measured and reasoned tone, the tide of racial hyperbole ebbed just a bit. In the early 1950s, on the eve of the civil rights movement, while black activists were registering black voters and demanding access to the ballot, and while the courts were chipping away at racially discriminatory voting regulations, the League of Women Voters helped cast these changes as reasonable, even desirable. The uncoupling of skin color from the capacity for citizenship required activists on the one hand and, on the other, advocates who simply made the proposition look reasonable. The irony, however, was that the league, by not calling attention to itself as a women's organization representing women's interests, seems as a result to have disappeared somewhat into the historical woodwork. Then, as now, women's politics, when lacking an explicit gender ideology and rhetoric, tended to go unnoticed.

Even as the league joined the battle over the county unit system, it confronted its own internal conflicts over race and democracy. Frances, who believes that personal change must accompany social change, worked to make the league itself more democratic. One of the achievements of which Frances is most proud was opening the membership of the league to nonwhite women. At a time when many state and local members of the league resisted admitting black women, believing it was "right" but not "expedient," Frances and a core group of like-minded women pushed ahead.[38] At her first convention as president of the DeKalb League in 1947, the membership accepted new bylaws eliminating the clause that limited membership in the league to white women.[39] Over the next decade, as Frances moved into more active service in the state league, she pushed the desegregation agenda forward, despite—but also in part because of—growing racial tensions in the South. "A lot of people like to join something," she maintains, "if it's doing something. So we got good people in the league."

More generally, Frances sought to expand the membership of the league in Georgia. In the 1940s, the tendency of the national league was "to stretch out," Frances remembers, and "that same feeling got into our state league."[40] With a group of fellow renegades, Frances helped elect a state league president who resided outside the metropolitan Atlanta area, a new departure for the league, which was dominated, as Frances put it, by Atlanta-area women who felt "superior," "a little snooty." Frances, first as vice-president and later as president of the state league, "pushed organization," and the League of Women Voters established itself as a presence in a number of smaller cities and towns across the state. Frances remained for the rest of her life committed to making meaningful participation in democracy possible for an ever-expanding range of citizens.

Over time, she moved beyond the league's limited constituency toward an increasingly grassroots and participatory model of citizenship. That said, the work of the league years was important on its own terms. Frances's aim was to make one of the few women's organizations that was committed to women's political participation stretch its own thinking about representative democracy. To do this, Frances implemented the league's program of voter education and citizenship training on a scale that most women in the organization were unprepared, at least initially, to countenance. Furthermore, in leading the league into the county unit fight and the desegregation of its own ranks, Frances also took the membership of the league into the very real political fights of the 1940s and 1950s, where they stood a chance of making a difference. In this period, and throughout most of her career, Frances chose not to align herself exclusively with the most radical spirits but rather to move the South's ordinary citizens along, encouraging them to learn by doing, by acting politically. This was especially true for the school desegregation fight.

Frances's three-year term as president of the Georgia league coincided with the U.S. Supreme Court's decision on *Brown v. Board of Education*, delivered on May 17, 1954.[41] The ruling is often cited as the single most important Supreme Court decision of the century. In one stroke, the court outlawed the doctrine of "separate but equal" in public services and institutions for blacks and whites, holding instead that separate was inherently unequal and that African Americans had suffered grievously under the laws and customs that segregation enforced. The import of *Brown* reverberated across the South. For African American families and communities, it represented an opening wedge for dismantling the injustices wrought by segregation. To segregationists, the ruling was equally momentous, but they met it with alarm. Integration, they charged, promised to shake southern society to its foundation. "I suppose you want your daughter to marry a 'nigger'?" was one of the incendiary questions Frances faced when called to testify before Georgia's segregationist politicians. These two forces would face off time and time again across the South. Among the most memorable images of the civil rights movement are those of stoic black school children, walking toward the entrances of their new schools, as crowds of angry whites taunted them. What followed in the wake of these tumultuous scenes was the closing of public schools, in some places for several years. Georgia was spared this fate. Desegregation took hold in Atlanta in August 1961, and its schools remained open. The extent of desegregation, however, was token; nine African American students enrolled in four previously all-white high schools. How *Brown* came to mean neither equal education nor social dissolution is a central question in the history of school desegregation.

Frances's story sheds light on the crucial but little recognized role of women in Georgia's transition.

Frances devoted two decades to school desegregation, but her years with the League of Women Voters were the first and most charged. In 1953, Governor Herman Talmadge, with whom Frances had tangled in the county unit fight, proposed a constitutional amendment that would allow the state to divert public funds to private schools in the event of a court order to integrate. Talmadge's action signaled his intent to circumvent a court order, but for supporters of public education his private school amendment represented obstruction and much more. Georgia's educational reformers, including many women in the league, believed that the state had only come to have a respectable public school system in the late 1940s. In 1947, Georgia instituted a compulsory twelfth grade for the first time, and in 1949 the state passed a law, the Minimum Foundation Program for Education, that established a basic level of funding for all of Georgia's schools. These reforms had been the culmination of decades of struggle to increase funding for teacher salaries, for school construction to alleviate overcrowding, and for educational instruction. The private school amendment threatened all that had been accomplished.[42] Frances set out to reassemble the coalition that had defeated the county unit amendment, but she found that school desegregation was an entirely different matter. Whereas the problem of the county unit could be approached as "governmental philosophy" around which many constituencies had rallied, the private school amendment was "nothing but a race issue." Those who persevered were advocates of public education, and these were largely women, the leadership of several statewide women's organizations, spearheaded by the League of Women Voters. "At that time, even more than now," Frances observes, "women arranged for the children." Whereas the coalition to defeat the county unit succeeded in its campaign, Frances and her colleagues failed with the private school amendment. When it passed in November 1954, Georgia went into the post-*Brown* era with a legislature and a citizenry that appeared ready to resist federal law to preserve Jim Crow.

School desegregation reached a crisis point in Georgia in 1958. A school desegregation suit for the Atlanta schools, filed by the local NAACP on January 11, was working its way through the courts on a collision course with state laws that made it a felony to spend tax money for integrated public schools and vested the governor with the power to close any public school upon its integration, thereby setting in motion the transfer of public funds to private schools. These laws, passed in 1955 and 1956, further signaled the depth of political resistance to *Brown* in Georgia. In an atmosphere of impending doom, a group of white moderates who named themselves HOPE set out to preserve the public school system in Georgia. It was, Frances says, "another very, very hot fight," and her narrative documents the extraordinary scope of HOPE's campaign, which ranged from dramatic political theater—such as dropping a trail of petitions from the top balcony of the capitol to the floor below—to "nitty-gritty" organizing—such as providing members with stickers to place on their checks that declared: "If schools shut down this account may also close." In the end, HOPE rallied thirty thousand white Georgians around a campaign for "children's rights to an education." HOPE's achievement was to turn a "race issue" into a public education issue and thereby defuse some of its emotional charge.[43] It was an unusual campaign in Georgia's history, in that women provided an unprecedented degree of leadership for such an important political issue. Nowhere was the success of HOPE's strategy more evident than in the terms by which Governor Ernest Vandiver, who had declared previously that "not one" black child would sit next to a white child in a Georgia school, announced his retreat. "We cannot abandon public education," he declared, and he called one piece of his legislative package a "child protection amendment."[44] On August 30, 1961, the Atlanta public schools desegregated peacefully, and the schools remained open. Locally and nationally the news media reported extensively and favorably on Atlanta's achievement, and President John F. Kennedy issued a proclamation praising the city. Others, however, noted how far Atlanta was from the ideal of an integrated society. Rev. Martin Luther King, Jr., recently relocated from Montgomery, Alabama, to his native Atlanta, cautioned that "token integration is not a solution, it is a sign of a start. We still have a big job to do here."[45]

The onset of school desegregation in Atlanta was at once a victory and a defeat for advocates of school desegregation. In retrospect, that moment throws into high relief how much and yet how little had changed with *Brown*. Measured against the very real possibility of school closures and violence, the achievement was remarkable. For many in HOPE, it was more than they had dared hope for. Measured against the hope of equal educational opportunity, however, the victory was shallow. Most African American school children remained in segregated schools in 1961, as they would for many years. What is all the more striking is that so many in Georgia labored tremendously to achieve even token desegregation. The Atlanta NAACP called forth legal, financial, and organizational resources to carry forward a suit, while HOPE struggled to rally white public opinion around the lowest common denominator of keeping the schools open. When that happened on August 30, it was the moment when outright resistance to segregation passed from the scene but a more passive form of resistance was born. What was put in place then, and what still prevails today, is a public school system that is nominally desegregated but still unequal for most black school children. Frances was among that much smaller number of white Georgians who dedicated themselves to the next stage of the struggle to claim for *Brown* a meaning more in line with the potential it held for equality and justice.

The years in which Frances joined the debate over school desegregation marked a turning point of a more personal nature in her activist career. "I had made a resolve within myself in 1954," she remembers, "that I was not going to belong to, give my efforts to, give my money to, or support in any way anything that was segregated. That's what I believed, and I decided that I'd better live up to it." To meet this personal commitment, Frances set about a program of interracial self-education, taking advantage of the resources of nearby Atlanta University, a prestigious complex of black colleges and universities. She joined the integrated Women's International League for Peace and Freedom, whose Atlanta chapter was predominantly black; she began attending the weekly lecture series, known as the Hungry Club, at Atlanta's black YMCA; and she organized interracial political discussion groups through the American Fund for Political Education. Frances also put herself under the tutelage of Sadie Mays, an African American social reformer and the wife of Benjamin Mays, president of Morehouse College, who was willing to "correct a white person": "That was wonderful to have a friend like that because it meant well for my education. She never minced words."

Wonderful, yes, but more so in retrospect. The early 1960s were a turbulent period for Frances, during which the moorings that had sustained her activism over the 1940s and 1950s no longer held firm. Her commitment to desegregation required not only learning new lessons from new friends but also constructing a new identity as an activist. Frances's storytelling bears only traces of the turmoil that accompanied this transition, but her personal writings from the 1960s record the difficulty. In a letter to her children, Frances wrote, "I have always tried to be of service. But I am sensitive about this. Because the Negroes have shown me how awful paternalism is—so I hesitate to say—or think—that I want to be of service. But anyway I still do." Frances struggled to find her role, as a white woman, in a black-initiated and black-led movement. Turned away by an official of her church who told her that "anything that was connected with the kinds of things that I had done were evil in the eyes of the church," Frances searched beyond the traditions of her Methodist upbringing for a new ground for her actions. She wondered, "can't you help with—and not for—I would like to work shoulder to shoulder." Over the course of the 1960s, Frances answered her own question by taking her cues increasingly from African American activists. The road to that answer, however, was hardly an easy one, and she experienced guilt and shame over white privilege: "I know I am in a superior position because I am white. But that makes me feel inferior. I know I have hated my white skin many times. I could go—and maybe help work—if only I weren't white." Ultimately she turned her insecurity into a deepened sense of responsibility to act as a southern white woman, whatever advantages and disadvantages that social role afforded her. This new orientation to her activism, which included a willingness to take unpopular stands, would sustain Frances in the years ahead.

Humor was one key to Frances's success in this transition. To this day, Frances leavens her stories with laughter and jokes, even in the midst of quite serious matters. Often the humor is at her own expense, delivered with a light, self-deprecating tone. Describing her decision to work only on an integrated basis, Frances pauses and notes this consequence: "So we dropped our membership at Druid Hills Country Club, and that was bad because we lived across the street and it was easy to take guests over there to eat. It meant I'd have to cook more. But my cooking didn't improve much, I'm afraid!" Frances, well aware that her actions were unusual among whites of her time, uses humor to convey that she was nonetheless a quite normal person with her own shortcomings. You need not be perfect, she implies, to take the kind of actions she had.

The ability to laugh was even more important: "I began to learn—and I found laughter is the greatest relief in the whole wide world. Crying is a relief too. But then you have a head ache—and your eyes burn—and you have made people unhappy. Laughter gives the same relief and no one suffers—in fact they relax and maybe laugh too." When her work became especially difficult, Frances found that laughter released pent-up emotions, bound people together and allowed them to move forward. It also signaled that a measure of control had been established over a painful situation. In her storytelling about these events, Frances makes similar use of humor to establish rapport with her audience. There is some danger, however, that her humorous stories transport her listeners too quickly from difficulty to mastery. Frances, while she readily admits the challenges of her activism, usually ends her stories on a note of success. The pain, she implies, was all to the greater good. She thus encourages her audience to dwell on a successful outcome rather than an uncertain process. In light of this central tendency in her storytelling, I have taken to reading Frances's humor as suggesting precisely those times when her work threatened to overwhelm her. Laughter marks the very pain and frustration it helps to overcome.[46]

Frances's tenure as executive director of the Georgia Council of Human Relations in the 1960s provided the context for applying these lessons. It also took her squarely into the civil rights movement, where she would participate to an unusual degree for a white woman who was already looking, if not acting, quite grandmotherly. Like many who immersed themselves in the day-to-day struggles of the movement, Frances has no doubt that the 1960s were qualitatively different than the years that came before and after. "To me," she says, "the movement means pretty much the sixties." Frances finds it difficult, however, to convey with words what it meant to experience the movement from the inside, as when she struggles to describe the mass meetings of the early 1960s in Albany, Georgia:

That singing was so tremendous that now I get quite emotional sometimes when I hear some of the songs. I don't think that there's any way of ever reading or seeing on television or ever getting a real feeling of what some of those mass meetings were like, and some of that singing was like. Sometimes when I hear those songs again, they're almost hollow in comparison with the way they were when those audiences sang them. It was something about that, the movement and the feeling of the movement, that was just so compelling. I suppose that's the reason that you always stick with it and keep on trying to do something about it.

Albany has been called the "singing movement," the place where black activists harnessed the tradition of African American music to civil rights protest. Out of Albany came Bernice Johnson Reagon and the Freedom Singers, and their musical repertoire spread throughout the movement.[47] It is a testament to their artistry that Frances associates singing with "the feeling of the movement," a phrase that connotes both emotional response and physical sensation. That experience almost defies translation into words. Singing, like laughter, constitutes its own language, one that keys the depths of the most evocative stage of Frances's career. It inspired her to "keep on trying" and extended her commitment to building a desegregated society. Her narrative brings together the black and white stories of the civil rights movement.

The Georgia Council on Human Relations was Frances's organizational home during the movement. When she took over the council, Frances set about establishing local interracial groups across the state and implementing a program of desegregation activity. It is difficult for those who were not raised under Jim Crow to appreciate the enormity of these tasks. "It's not just a matter of casually asking a few people in for tea," Frances reminds us. In many towns, Frances found herself planning the first interracial meetings that any of her participants had attended, and finding a place to meet was often as difficult as locating willing recruits. Before the Civil Rights Act of 1964 was passed, this was illegal activity, and Frances was asking her fellow citizens to break the law. Law-abiding southerners, black and white, might understandably hesitate on that account alone. Beneath the legal obstacles lay the human dimension: "We were all trying to make sense out of this thing called *racism* and *prejudice*."

Frances summarizes her role as being a "bridge," a term that captures the intermediary nature of her role in the movement. She was the bridge between blacks and whites in local councils, but she was also a bridge between black activists and white officialdom in many small towns, and occasionally a bridge between various black-led organizations in the shifting combination of cooperation and competition that characterized the movement at the organizational level. At its worst the work was tiring and discouraging. "Albany is a sick, sick, sad, sad town," Frances sighed in 1963, when the hope of an interracial council seemed dim. Nonetheless, Frances had a gift for enjoying the process and relishing the victories. Three years later she rejoiced: "Had good meeting in Albany at the Court House. A real wonderful occasion—over 100 present. Visited the integrated nursery—17 Negroes, 14 whites—Unbelievable in Albany." Frances's strength as an organizer lay in searching out the possible in a time when many southerners, black as well as white, believed that change was impossible: "Wherever the local group wanted to start, that's where we would start." A skillful organizer, Frances enabled the participation of others, helping them make decisions and take action. The goals of her work were clear—"every one was a plan for action"—but she let others, with some judicious prodding, determine how they would reach their specific goals. Effective organizers, of which Frances is an exemplar, work at the juncture of the leaders and the led, blurring the distinction between the two as they develop leadership in others. In this regard, she shares much with a number of African American women, most notably Ella Baker and Septima Clark, who similarly left their mark on the movement through their effective leadership as organizers.[48]

Such was the general nature of interracial organizing for the movement, but Frances's involvement in the Albany Movement, one of the more storied chapters in the history of the civil rights movement, allows us to compare her view to the volumes that have been written on Albany and examine what her memories can teach us about the civil rights movement. Albany, a small city in the southwest corner of Georgia, became a center of movement activity in the fall of 1961. A coalition of local organizations, aided by activists from SNCC, launched a citywide campaign for integrated public facilities and voting rights. In a few short months, more than one thousand activists headed to southwest Georgia's jails. In December 1961, the arrival of Martin Luther King, Jr., and his SCLC, followed by his well-publicized arrest, transformed Albany into a national symbol of the movement in the deep South—and eventually a symbol of its failure. By most accounts, the Albany Movement collapsed in 1962 when sustained mass protests did little to undermine Jim Crow. Laurie Pritchett, Albany's police chief and himself a symbol of white intransigence, reportedly crowed that the city remained as segregated as ever.[49]

For Frances's perspective we have two distinct but reinforcing sources: writings from the period (letters and a diary) and retrospective oral history interviews. The diary is a chronicle, Frances's ordering and interpretation of events as they unfolded.[50] It reflects the often chaotic nature of the civil rights movement and the day-to-day shifting of forces and fortunes. Frances records the strengths and frailties of many activists, only some of whom, such as Andrew Young of SCLC and Charles Sherrod of SNCC, are well represented in the literature on the civil rights movement. Charles Jones of SNCC, an accomplished orator, moved hundreds at mass meetings, but Frances found him to be a bundle of contradictions: "Sensitive, sweet, bitter, full of hate, talking love your white brother." Perhaps because Frances herself was a female observer and participant, many more women appear in her chronicle than is typical of accounts of Albany, a reminder of the great deal of research yet to be done before we will understand women's participation in the civil rights movement as fully as men's. In relation to the existing literature on the Albany Movement, which emphasizes the role of Rev. Martin Luther King, Jr., perhaps the most interesting aspect of Frances's diary is that it records King's presence only once, almost in passing: "July 9–10, 1962: Court—verdict of King and Abernathy." The weight of Frances's chronicle is with local people, the movement on the community level.

Frances's retrospective assessments of the Albany Movement are shaped by the passage of time and by the debate among participants, journalists, and scholars that has swirled around those events ever since.[51] Cognizant of the controversy over King's role, Frances devotes far more time to him in her oral histories than in her diary. She has stated emphatically, on numerous occasions, that King was called to Albany by the Albany Movement. "Well, I'll have you know," she insists, "SNCC asked him. I heard it." Frances characterizes the events of 1961–62, in which King figures prominently, as a "fizzle," and King's departure left the movement adrift, with "various factions blaming each other that they hadn't succeeded." Still, she says pointedly:

The thing that people don't realize is that King played such a small part. He came in and he didn't really stay so very long. It wasn't such a big part that he played. The whole Albany Movement was the people there, and the same thing was true of the whole movement. It was a grassroots movement. It's overrated, King's influence, just because he spoke so beautifully and wrote so beautifully.

Frances, who treasures her friendship with Coretta and Martin Luther King, nonetheless objects to the "great man" theory of history, not because King is in any way undeserving of the attention he has received, but because that attention has tended to obscure the collective nature of the movement and the thousands of communities transformed in its wake. Famous individuals pass on Frances's stage, but they matter because of what they bring to a local struggle.

When Frances describes her work in Albany, the events to which King was central serve as prelude to the heart of her own story. She takes pride in having "stuck it out," and she offers a perspective on social change in the area that reaches well beyond the King years. Indeed, her work in Albany began in earnest in 1962 and extended until 1967, as she slowly built a viable local council. This was no easy task. Frances's diary is a record of the fits and starts of organizing, and her oral histories describe some painful failures. When she sent a letter to white households in Albany, urging white citizens to acknowledge the legitimacy of African American grievances, the response was overwhelmingly negative. Initially, Frances had trouble rustling up even a handful of sympathetic whites.

Slowly, however, the rewards of having "stuck it out" emerged. Indeed, by 1965 Frances had contacts not only throughout southwest Georgia but in each of Georgia's 159 counties.[52] Through a series of vignettes, Frances sketches a portrait of positive, if slow, social change. The Southwest Georgia Council on Human Relations, availing itself of new resources made available by the federal government's War on Poverty, launched basic education and job training programs that were "useful" and "successful," as well as "integrated." The desegregated day care that Carol King, wife of Albany's most famous black attorney, established in the late 1960s eventually became one of the first Head Start programs in the country. And Frances's struggle for civil rights grew to encompass welfare rights, as the Georgia council began organizing recipients of aid to address the discriminatory provisions of the state's welfare policies. While she acknowledges obstacles and difficulties, Frances suggests that Albany was indeed changing in the late 1960s, a marked contrast to most studies, which suggest a dispirited movement, fundamentally unable to alter the deeply racist patterns of the city.[53]

Frances's narrative reveals, by contrast, the halting actions by which white and black Albanians slowly began to build a desegregated society.

Her story of Carol King's day care program freezes a moment in time and provides a telling snapshot of social change: "One day I was riding down a white street in Albany and noticed both black and white mothers and children going into the front door of a very attractive, well-kept house. I saw one lady let a little white boy out of her car, and she said to him, 'Be good, son, and don't play with those nigras.'" Lest the import of this simple scene go unnoticed, Frances adds, "But this was an integrated group of kids with an integrated committee of mothers, in Albany, Georgia, in the sixties." Little in the historiography of the civil rights movement prepares us to understand this scene. The event is so much smaller in scale, so much less dramatic than a mass march or a sit-in. The action is fleeting, merely the parting comment of a mother to her son. The people are ordinary, indeed nameless. The outcome is at once completed and open-ended. The mother enrolled her child in a desegregated program, but we are left to wonder: Is this as far as this mother would go, to combine desegregated behavior with racist cant? What would her child grow up to believe and do? This scene might be taken to represent as much the aftermath of the movement, what followed in the wake of the events that have defined the movement for us. Yet it is better understood *as* an event of the civil rights movement, for here was a step toward formal desegregation and a hint that, beneath a shifting color line, hearts and minds may have been changing too. Stories such as this one reveal Frances's gift as a storyteller of social change: she enables us to see it as it happened—step by step, person by person, day by day. A view of the civil rights movement that looks only at large-scale events misses this critical dimension. Similarly, studies that overly emphasize the actions of well-known figures often misrepresent the motives of organizers such as Frances, who undertook their work not to draw attention to themselves but to change the world.

Frances's stories of Albany are peopled by black and white southerners, the famous and the ordinary, but given the lack of attention to the white response to the civil rights movement, her narrative is most revealing of the range of white southerners whose actions and reactions must be accounted for in any effort to understand the complexity of the movement.[54] There are activists, like Frances herself, who worked for social change, as well as those who resisted, spewing racial hatred. All are important, but interesting to Frances, the organizer, only insofar as they could be moved from hatred or indifference to understanding and action. Frances's stories flesh out the middle ground, offering a portrait of whites who, like the mother at the day care center, were capable of change. Taken together, these stories present a somewhat startling view of white southerners—startling, that is, in light of the prevalent view of a nearly monolithic white racism in the South. "People are born into a certain way of living," Frances says, "It takes a jolt to get out of it. It doesn't really mean that they're all that mean and bad, but it takes a jolt to make them see that maybe they could make a change." To the extent that Frances helped bring about social change in Georgia, it was because she respected white southerners enough to believe that they had the capacity to change. Frances took as her task creating the circumstances for that to happen. Frances believed in the rule of law and supported the judicial activism of the courts as a means of changing behavior, but she worked on the more intangible terrain of intellect and emotion. Hers is an organizer's (and an optimist's) perspective, but Frances had seen just enough change to believe that more was possible.[55]

But what of Frances herself? How did a white woman in her fifties and sixties experience the movement? This is an especially intriguing question because women of Frances's age and race are little represented in the literature on the civil rights movement. The young white women who supported the movement are somewhat better known, although interest has focused on their sexual relations as much as their political action.[56] Frances's story, for better or worse, offers none of that titillation and is, it must be said, simply less dramatic. Although Frances participated in demonstrations and mass meetings, she studiously avoided arrest and was arrested only once—in Albany. She says, still with some relief, that she never spent a night in jail.

Just how unusual, and consequently alone, Frances felt at times is revealed in a lengthy story about Baker County, a place so racist that activists labeled it "Bad Baker." Frances begins on a humorous note. Describing her efforts to ascertain the response among white business owners to the civil rights demonstrations in Newton, a small town in Baker County, Frances remembers, "I went into each of the stores. I would chat with people, all of them just as friendly as they could be. I very easily passed for a very nice white southern lady. Being fat and old, you can get by with a lot!" In a twist on the phenomenon of interracial passing, Frances tried, and sometimes succeeded, in passing for an elderly white southern lady, or, more precisely, what was expected of a woman of her race, region, and generation.

When Frances's effort was exposed for what it was—infiltration—the situation became more perilous than comical. As the march started, several whites began to say "ugly things" to her. Frances was caught between two worlds: "I was by myself, in between the group of whites on one corner and the blacks on the next corner. I didn't want to go over to the blacks, because I didn't want to get them in trouble by being with them." Frances describes moving from one side of the street to the other, one storefront to the next, until "I ran out of places to stand." "I didn't know what else to do except to leave, but I didn't want to leave. I just felt like it was cowardly to go, but I didn't know where to go. I didn't have a motel room, a friend's house, anyplace. There wasn't anyplace I had to go," she recalls. Unlike southern black activists, Frances was not sustained by a civil rights organization or a community network. She worked with these groups, but she did not belong to them. In relation to liberal whites in the Southern Regional Council, her institutional base, Frances ventured well beyond the support they were willing to offer the movement and was often urged to temper her remarks and behavior. And, unlike the student generation that came to the South, she was not enveloped in a youth movement that created a home and family for participants, sometimes quite literally, as in the freedom houses. Frances was on her own as she traveled the state.

Personal support came from other quarters. Like-minded friends in Atlanta, such as Father Austin Ford, provided much-needed encouragement (and sometimes accompanied Frances), and her home life in DeKalb County also provided an anchor. Frances traveled for only a portion of each week, returning home to tend to the house, to Bill, and to her father, who, although elderly, enjoyed good health until his death in 1972. The letters Frances wrote to her children intertwine news of her organizing activity with updates from the home front: "Must be off to the kitchen— I'm doing extra cooking for a change"; "Papa loused up my Saturday shopping but he enjoyed it"; "I must get to my mending. What happens to my clothes is a miracle. They disintegrate."[57] From a distance of thirty years, these remarks read as a counterpoint to political turmoil. I suspect that Frances's routine responsibilities at home interjected a degree of normalcy into her often chaotic activist work.

Frances was also able to carry on because she had done much to prepare for her activities in southwest Georgia. During her league years, Frances had faced down many a racist, albeit of a fairly genteel variety. Her HOPE activities brought crank phone calls late at night, seemingly harmless, although one could never be sure. The threats she encountered in southwest Georgia were more frequent and direct, but they were no surprise. Frances's sixty-plus years served her well in this respect, and her life story stands in contrast to many movement lives marked by tragedy. The record of the civil rights movement is filled with the broken bodies and crushed spirits of those, especially the young, who undertook too much, too soon, for too long. Frances had readied herself for several decades, and she reserved some parts of herself from the movement. This saving grace helped her sustain her involvement beyond the 1960s.[58]

The next phase of Frances's career took her, for the first time, away from the volunteer sector. In 1968, at the age of sixty-two, Frances became a "fed," taking a position as a civil rights specialist in the Atlanta regional office of the Office of Civil Rights within HEW. She joined HEW at an exciting time, a time, she hoped, of promise. The Civil Rights Act of 1964 had banned discrimination in schools and other institutions receiving federal funds, and the expanding Office of Civil Rights aimed to implement the law with rigor. At the same time, the U.S. Supreme Court undermined the systematic evasion of the *Brown* decision that prevailed across the South. In the *Alexander v. Holmes County* decision of 1969, the Court mandated that desegregation take place "at once." In this context, Frances approached her work with a "real mission": "It was a matter of giving everybody an equal chance for education, no matter what the color of their skin. We were working our tails off to put that into effect." HEW was frustrating at times, and Frances, whose tolerance for bureaucracy extends only as far as she sees some good in it, struggled with the "limits of regulations." Nonetheless, the work had sweet rewards: "We had the law, and if you discriminated you did not get federal funds. That was what the law said and what the government meant. So it was a lot of fun, because you had some power behind you, which I had not ever had before."

Frances spent the bulk of her HEW years as coordinator of operations for the state of Mississippi. In many ways the work was quite familiar, as it involved extensive travel and endless rounds of meetings and negotiations, but her constituencies now included school boards and school personnel. Frances's goal was to urge voluntary compliance, and to prepare the way she did her "homework" in advance. She presented the authorities with workable plans and then nursed them through the process. Somewhat to her surprise, this was possible even in recalcitrant Mississippi, the state that many civil rights workers deemed the most racist. Frances would not deny the racism of Mississippi ("some powerfully mean segregationists"), but she found an ironic benefit: "It was easier to work with white people in Mississippi, because you knew what side they were on." Frances even came to empathize with Mississippi school officials: "A lot of these men were in terrible situations, and some of them weren't so prejudiced, really deep down in their hearts, as they appeared to be."

Despite the need to spend most of her time in negotiations with school personnel, Frances was and remained a community organizer, and her sympathies derived from her years in the movement. Before meeting with school officials in a community, she first sat down with local African American leaders to get "the dirt," and their complaints and suggestions informed the plans she developed. Frances is an example of a civil rights activist who took the organizing impetus of the movement into the federal bureaucracy, "the giant," as she called it. What were the possibilities for working in the spirit of an organizer within the government? Could the movement be sustained by "going inside?" For some movement activists, such behavior was, by definition, selling out. Many younger black activists, such as those Frances had worked with in southwest Georgia, had a skeptical, if not negative, view of the federal presence. At best, their national government had not protected them from the reprisals of racist state and local officials during the 1960s. At worst, they faced repression, especially at the hands of the Federal Bureau of Investigation. For Frances, the question did not resolve itself so easily.[59] As a bureaucrat, she was forced to leave behind the grassroots-organizing strategy that shaped her work with the Georgia council. With the council, she enjoyed the luxury of setting her own schedule and returning time and time again to groups and communities that sought her help. HEW was a different matter: "I never had as much time in a place as I needed to really do the job as I felt it needed to be done." That her HEW work was more hurried and routinized is reflected in Frances's storytelling as well. Her descriptions of the Georgia council years are most often stories of individual people and places, rich in specificity. By contrast, Frances describes her HEW work as a standard operating procedure, and indeed she most often had to apply a template, rather than respond to local circumstances.[60] Yet even as the character of her work changed, Frances believed her goals for HEW were consistent with her years in the movement. She was still seeking to be a bridge, but with HEW the span was even wider, reaching from black communities, through local school boards, to the federal government, in order to harness the energy of the movement to the world of public policy. Frances had a long memory of the federal government, reaching back to the Depression, and she brought to HEW a sense that the government, when influenced by "good people," could be a positive force.

Frances believes that she was part of the "most successful team in the country," an assessment that flies in the face of the now prevalent view of school desegregation as failed policy. From this perspective, desegregation, and busing in particular, only led to white flight and the eventual resegregation of schools, with predominantly white schools in suburbs and largely black school districts in many urban centers. Now, almost a half-century after *Brown*, other educational problems, such as lower graduation rates and a persistent lag in academic achievement among black school children, loom as far more important to many early supporters of desegregation. What black children need, in this view, is better teachers, smaller classes, and programs designed for their educational needs. Furthermore, many now contemplate the losses of desegregation: black teachers and administrators were dismissed or demoted and black schools, the incubators of black community leadership for students and adults alike, were closed.[61] Frances understands this point of view, admitting that she'd have a "hard time being an integrationist" if she were black, but she remains an advocate of desegregation as it might have been.

To return with Frances to the early 1970s is to be reminded of the promise of *Brown* at high tide and to consider desegregation not as failed policy, but as policy that never was given a chance to succeed. For many in HEW, school desegregation was only beginning in these years to deliver on its potential as an effective policy to bring about equal educational opportunity and break down the barriers that separate blacks and whites. By 1973, the eleven southern states had achieved the most significant degree of desegregation of any sector in the nation, with nearly one-half of black children attending desegregated schools.[62] Frances, with her tendency to make a point with a story rather than a statistic, often tells the story of visiting a Mississippi school that was "beautifully integrated." Tears came to her eyes as she watched black and white school children engaged in marching band and other extracurricular activities. Frances's enduring hope for school desegregation was not only that black and white children would sit side by side in classrooms but also that their contact would bring mutual respect and affection. She approached her work with a stubborn faith that adults might change, but she believed that children were the South's best hope. Although her chief concern was to see that black children received an equal and high-quality education, she dared hope that the benefits of desegregation would accrue to white children as well. She left HEW in 1973, when she realized that the Nixon administration would not enforce vigorous desegregation policies.

In the ensuing years, little has happened to encourage her, as the federal courts have also retreated from enforcement. But Frances has yet to see an alternative to desegregation that produces equality of opportunity for black children, much less delivers on the hope of an integrated society. Neither politicians nor the public at large have exhibited a willingness to devote resources to programs aimed specifically at improving the quality of education for minority children.[63] Failing that, Frances remains committed to the desegregation agenda.

When she left HEW, Frances was sixty-seven, an age at which most people would have retired. Instead, she turned her formidable political skills to poverty; she founded the GPRO in 1975 and coordinated its efforts with and on behalf of the poor for the next dozen years. Frances and the cadre of friends and associates who launched the GPRO did so under inauspicious circumstances. In the mid-1970s, the U.S. economy experienced a period of malaise that combined recession with high rates of inflation and unemployment. Economists inelegantly labeled the problem "stagflation." An increasingly conservative political climate compounded the effects of economic downturn. Soon after Nixon's election in 1968, the federal government began a retreat from the Great Society and its War on Poverty, and government services to the broad range of the populace, and particularly to the poor, lagged. In the South, some parts of the region enjoyed a much-ballyhooed "sunbelt boom" in the 1970s and 1980s, but the poor saw inflation cut into meager wages and welfare subsidies. The benefits of sunbelt growth extended primarily to corporations in the form of low taxes and a pro-business environment and secondarily to workers in urban, professional occupations. In Georgia, the surge of employment and wealth was concentrated in metropolitan Atlanta, while the rest of Georgia was poorer than Mississippi, long the bellwether for poverty and discrimination in the region.[64]

The context was daunting for advocates of the poor, but the poverty rights years were an especially creative period in Frances's activist career and all the more striking because she undertook this work in her seventies and eighties. Although advancing age slowed her pace, the freedom of founding, rather than joining, an organization allowed Frances to concentrate on what she did best: grassroots organizing, research and education, and legislative lobbying. The GPRO was a synthesis of four decades of political experience, and Frances deployed those techniques that had been most effective in the past.[65]

The most basic task of the GPRO was to preserve the gains of the 1960s, specifically the welfare stipends to which many poor Georgians, especially African Americans, had only recently gained access. The GPRO labored to convince the legislature and the Department of Human Resources to raise the standard of need for determining benefits and increase payments to keep pace with inflation, and it protested changes in eligibility requirements that removed many needy Georgians from the welfare rolls. This was a decidedly uphill battle, with more defeats than victories, but Atlanta legislator Jim Martin summed up the impact of the GPRO's efforts: "Because Frances made us try, Georgia moved from the bottom of the states to close to the middle in the level of Aid to Families with Dependent Children benefits."[66]

In its campaign for welfare rights, the GPRO refused to adopt a solely defensive posture. Instead, it countered with an expansive vision: it made basic human needs—adequate food, clothing, and housing—a fundamental right and a paramount obligation of the state. The GPRO extended its efforts on behalf of the poor, whether black or white, but a disproportionate share of welfare recipients in Georgia were African Americans. Implicit in its program was a continuing struggle against racism as well as poverty. Moreover, the GPRO worked to establish the right of the poor to effective participation in the political system that determined their fate. Toward that goal, Frances and her colleagues organized poverty rights chapters in numerous cities and towns, provided education on Georgia politics, and facilitated lobbying activities (including an annual Poor People's Day at the capitol). By involving the poor in the practices of representative democracy, the GPRO transformed them from mere clients of the state and recipients of its charity into political actors on a par with other citizens. This sort of activity had engaged Frances since her years with the League of Women Voters. In the 1970s and 1980s, however, she took as her constituency those Georgians who were viewed by politicians and the public as least capable of participation in the democratic process.[67]

Into the late 1980s, Frances continued to be a voice for the poor and disenfranchised in the legislative halls of Georgia. Her ongoing activism raises the question of the decline of the civil rights movement in the 1970s and 1980s. Both scholarly and popular assessments most often lament a movement in disarray, especially following Martin Luther King's death in 1968. According to this interpretation, the movement had lost its signal leader, the major civil rights organizations could not unite around a common program, and the federal government had retreated from the field.[68] All of this is true, but such an assessment also signals that we know much more about the *dis*continuous history of the civil rights movement, the stories of the organizations and individuals, such as King and SNCC, that did not survive the 1960s. What we are in danger of neglecting is a parallel history of continuity. In Frances's case, all the strands of her previous activism can be traced into the 1980s: her organizing style of leadership, her commitment to democratic practice, and her interest in linking political education to activism. The life stories of activists who worked beyond the 1960s suggest the potential of a fuller history of these years, one that respects the unique character of the civil rights movement but also recognizes ongoing activism.

The case for continuity is even stronger if we view the GPRO not as a turn to poverty, but as a return. Frances's work in the poverty rights years is most reminiscent of her Depression-era activism. In both of these stages, Frances emphasized advocacy for the poor, and she organized concerned citizens to attend to the state's needy. With the 1930s and 1980s as anchor points, the centrality of poverty to her fifty-year activist career comes into focus. Even as voting rights and desegregation dominated the agenda of the Georgia League of Women Voters during Frances's presidency in the 1950s, the league also studied the state's welfare program and advocated for the needs of welfare recipients in Georgia. While she traveled the state for the Georgia Council on Human Relations in the 1960s, Frances also established welfare rights groups in numerous communities. Her first assignment with HEW involved enforcing welfare regulations. The civil rights movement, seen through the trajectories of lifelong careers that began in the early twentieth-century, may be much more centrally about addressing the needs of the poor than we have believed to date, which the extended framework of the 1930s to the 1980s enables us to appreciate.[69]

It is hard to pick a retirement date for Frances Pauley, but certainly the pace of life slowed for her in the latter half of the 1980s, and as the 1990s progressed, her visits to the legislature became less frequent. Even so, Frances added new concerns, such as homelessness and gay rights and AIDS activism, to her portfolio, and new organizations, such as AID Atlanta and the Open Door Community, benefited from her advice and counsel. Although Frances threw herself into the work, with still-considerable energy as she aged, her activism has mattered as much as an example and inspiration for others as for those things that she herself did. Frances no longer had to "do"; she could simply "be."

When she looks about her today, Frances is of two minds, concerned about where the nation is headed, yet mindful of progress. On the one hand, southern society was transformed over the course of her lifetime. On the other, the problems of poverty and homelessness in the present can sometimes seem all too much like the Great Depression. Frances is among those who believe that the economic problems of our society loom largest, even wrapped up, as they are, with matters of race. For the new New South, the South of the emerging twenty-first century, this is the challenge. Like many, Frances is unsure of what exactly needs to be done but wishes for "some really good human relations organizations" to "bring people together." For herself, Frances says, "It would be nice to be young again."

Thus far, I have followed Frances closely, melding explication of her life story with commentary on its significance. To fully examine Frances's narrative, however, it is necessary to attend to her silences and omissions—at least some of them—for they are, in their own way, just as revealing.

In this day and age, it is nearly impossible not to comment on Frances as a woman and not to undertake an analysis of her life story that attends to gender. But it is equally important to note that Frances most often does not. She has never defined herself as a feminist, nor commented to any extent on the larger framework of women's political development. She speaks of women *as women* largely in regard to her years in the League of Women Voters, and she contrasts the league's seriousness of purpose with the "ridicule" league women faced from male legislators, "mainly because we were women." She also describes the league as "the best training ground" for women in politics. Still, she seems to have happily acknowledged that training and moved on; she does not dwell on the feminist implications of the league's program. When I asked about the gender composition and gender relations within some of the organizations to which she belonged, Frances, on more than one occasion, replied, "I hadn't thought about that." Then, after a bit of reflection, she might elaborate, as she did with HOPE:

> I can't remember any place where the men took the leadership in HOPE. We did have a good many men in HOPE, and they did so much, so that's unfair to say. But I also think that the women had the time to do it for free, and the men didn't. HOPE was also about children and education, and at that time, even more than now, women arranged for the children.

Much that women of Frances's generation, race, and class took for granted, including that "women arranged for the children," only became the subject of widespread social debate in the later stages of Frances's activist career, and she has not joined that debate with any more than a passing interest.

Frances's story, however, made its way into my hands, and my influence comes into play. For me, attending to Frances as a woman and an activist is the intellectual ground on which I picked up this project, and feminism is central to my inquiry into the significance of Frances's life. These concluding remarks represent a conversation between generations, between a historian who came of age with contemporary feminism and a narrator from an earlier generation.

Frances has this to say about the rise of the contemporary women's movement of the 1960s and 1970s: "Now I never have been really active in some of the women's stuff. I hope I've been active as a woman trying to do a substantial job in things, but I never have been active in things like NOW [National Organization for Women] and all. I don't mean I'm opposed to them."[70] This retrospective nonchalance is born out by the historical record that Frances created. I have come across only one instance in which she signaled a particularly feminist consciousness. In 1966, Frances wrote, in a letter to her counterparts, the other state directors of Councils on Human Relations:

> I wish to enter a complaint. The Civil Rights Act of 1964 says in Title something that there shall be no discrimination against sex. I consider it a grave discrimination that women always have to be the secretaries. At one period in my long career as a professional (5 yrs., 7 mos., 2 days) I found myself the secretary to some ten varied groups. Why? I cannot write well nor type well and the mimeo machine jumps at me when I go toward it—nothing, except

I was the only woman present—and me being desperately afraid of being asked out of the pipe smoking group, I smiled and nodded—yes, oh, yes.[71]

Frances's complaint about the sexual division of labor within organizations was common among feminists of the late 1960s, but it was unusual for Frances. Although a feminist consciousness weighs in, the council's work on desegregation remained her central concern. "How, in Heavens name," Frances continued, "can we keep in the fold that white _____ who has taken a first wee step on the road to understanding and help him progress without losing all the truly committed folk—both white and black???" The letter also indicates that Frances called and ran the meeting, hardly subordinate tasks, much less secretarial. By the late 1960s, Frances was leading a mixed-sex organization and her staff at the Georgia Council included a number of men. Although she had certainly experienced sexism, she was at the height of her organizing powers, confident of her mission and abilities. Feminism, it seems, had less to offer Frances than it did women who felt the sting of discrimination on many levels. Thus Frances, who caught many other waves of social change as they came along in the twentieth century, let feminism largely pass her by.

Frances seems, moreover, to have viewed feminism as somewhat of a distraction from the community organizing that engaged her in the 1960s and 1970s. In our most recent interview, I asked Frances directly about feminism, and she elaborated:

I don't have a very good feeling about it. If you were working in a community, how could you work just with women? Just the same as how can you work just with the blacks, or just with the preachers? I was trying to get different parts of the community together, to understand each other and work, like the rich and poor, the black and the white, get the different people together enough so that they could understand other people. It [feminism] didn't bring people together. It seemed to me that the feminist groups were more the elite women, the educated, white, kind of upper group, rather than a group with rich and poor, educated and uneducated.[72]

For a self-described organizer who worked to "bring people together," this is a damning charge. Frances levels a critique much like that of black feminists of the 1960s who viewed the women's movement, particularly in its earliest stages, as ignoring women's relationship to families and communities and as lacking concern over the problem of poverty. The trajectory of her own career had little to do with contemporary feminism as it evolved in the 1960s and 1970s; instead, Frances had more in common with those civil rights activists who continued to work on poverty in these decades and with predominantly white women's organizations, such as the League of Women Voters, that insisted that the government accept greater responsibility for the well-being of the poor. Feminism is a missing dimension from Frances's life story in part because self-consciously feminist organizations, such as the National Organization for Women, did not address themselves to poverty in the years that Frances was launching the GPRO, and feminism's coming to terms with women's poverty happened only as Frances's activist career was winding down.[73]

Frances is similarly uncomfortable identifying herself as a leader. Although she describes her activities in detail, she only casually and in passing refers to herself as a leader. Like many women of her generation, Frances shies away from that label, which, like feminism, does not have good connotations for her. Some of this is a result of modesty; Frances has never made much of her accomplishments. Of her years in the civil rights movement, she says explicitly that she did not take a leadership role, characterizing her role as "helping" the movement. Frances perceived herself to be an ally to the black-led movement. More generally, however, Frances believes that the civil rights movement has too often come to be viewed solely from the perspective of its leaders.

> The one thing that I think is so important about the movement is that it was a *movement*. It was not an organized effort of one person or a few people or a board's decision. It wasn't any high-powered organization. It wasn't Madison Avenue. It seemed to be a grassroots movement that was coming up all over the United States, and particularly all over the South. Now, certain leaders emerged, like James Farmer and Martin Luther King and so forth, but there were a tremendous number of heroes and heroines on a local level that really were the movement.

Like many organizers, Frances is well aware of the politics of knowledge that surrounds the civil rights movement. Local people "were the movement," but in insisting on this, Frances also acknowledges that it was not widely understood in the 1960s, nor is it now.

For myself, I respectfully disagree with Frances on the question of her leadership. I do believe she should be recognized as a leader, and it is the logic and language of feminism that allows for such an interpretation. Feminist scholars of social movements have taken up the question of leadership, and their deliberations are rooted in fundamentals of feminist thought. Simply put, feminism challenges the definition of what constitutes politics and leadership. The work that women, such as Frances, did as organizers, behind-the-scenes workers, and—in a word that Frances herself often uses—"bridges" is being redefined as a form of leadership, albeit previously underappreciated.[74] This discussion, moreover, is not limited to scholars. At reunions of movement participants, questions of gender and leadership are among the most hotly debated; writers and documentary filmmakers are increasingly drawn to female subjects; and teachers on all levels of education search out materials that raise these issues. We live in a world whose very definitions have been reshaped by feminism. Frances is concerned about the politics of knowledge regarding the civil rights movement, as am I. But I am also concerned about a feminist interpretation of the history of leadership in the civil rights movement. Where Frances shared concerns with black feminists of the 1960s and 1970s, I share mine with feminist scholars of the 1980s and 1990s who analyze the means by which particularly female forms of leadership have been rendered historically invisible.[75] The two agendas dovetail nicely. By recognizing organizing and bridge-building as leadership, we follow organizers back to the communities of local people whose activism and leadership were critical to building a mass movement.

The relationship between Frances's family life and her activism is another area of particular interest to feminists, given the central place that feminism accords to the intersection of public and private lives. When she speaks directly on this, Frances emphasizes the encouragement she received. Of Bill, she says, "I was very lucky with my husband, because he thought that people ought to do what they wanted to do. He was proud of the things that I did. He was always interested in what I was doing and always supportive, or I couldn't have done it." Frances also admits, however, that she took pains to keep some parts of her activism hidden, particularly its dangers. Following her arrest in Albany, she asked for assistance from a reporter, saying, "Please call Southern Regional Council and tell them to get me a lawyer and a good one, fast. And for goodness sake, don't tell Bill or Papa." Frances implies that conflict would have followed from this disclosure, had Bill known about this turn of events. Her view of Bill's support is predicated on a separation of family and work. While Frances enjoyed the benefits of a supportive home life, she managed this relationship with some care, avoiding the potential for conflict.

The rise of the feminist movement has led Frances to comment on her role as wife and mother, although more out of interest than critique. It was, quite simply, another time. When I asked Frances a basic, although clearly feminist inspired, question about how she and Bill divided up household responsibilities, she replied: "The household was my entire responsibility. That was women's work. I'm still surprised when I see men cook and wash dishes and baby-sit. Housework wasn't man's work, just like I never mowed the lawn or worked in the garden, except to grow a few flowers here or there. The whole society was regimented as far as what men did and women did." For Frances, it was important to be home for her children, and while her daughters were young, the rhythms of family life determined how and when she worked. She set "a few real guidelines" for herself, which included being at home when her daughters returned from school. Only after her daughters were grown did she feel able to pursue her career on a "regular basis." Thereafter (and, given the longevity of Frances's activism, this amounted to another thirty years), she enjoyed greater freedom, but her responsibilities included caring for her father into the early 1970s and for Bill into the mid-1980s.

The sum total of Frances's storytelling, however, indicates that family life is not what she deems to be most significant about her life. Although she speaks with ease and affection about her family, she does not make them central to the story of her activism; rather, they play supporting roles and generally appear offstage. Her story of traveling to Albany to join SNCC in a time of crisis is a case in point: "Bill and I were over in Brunswick, vacationing with our kids and grandchildren at the beach, at St. Simons, and I got a call from SNCC, this was Albany SNCC, asking me to come over. So Bill and I raced over there, drove from Brunswick over to Albany, getting there at about two o'clock in the morning." From this point, Frances narrates a dramatic mass meeting, including SNCC's decision to invite King to Albany, for which the family vacation in Brunswick serves only as prelude. In her storytelling, the self that Frances constructs measures its importance by political acts and by degrees of change in southern society. The family is static, while the world of Georgia and the South changes around it, much as Frances organized for social change in the world, not in the home. Family remains outside of politics. Seeing Frances through feminist eyes helps establish what her story is about, by helping to define what it is not about.

Although Frances casts her family members in supporting roles, one might wonder: What impact did Frances's activism have on their lives? Frances does not dwell on such matters. When I asked her about this, she demurred, "We'll have to ask them about that."[76] These are, rightly, questions that only others can answer. Nonetheless, Frances, who in other contexts will speculate on people's motives and perspectives, draws a clearer line when describing her family. The drama and conflict of her life story remain outside the family. This reticence reflects, in part, Frances's generational experience. In the late twentieth century, autobiographies that delve deeply into family matters, even of the most intimate sort, are commonplace, but women of Frances's age were unlikely to air such matters in public or in published forms.[77] Frances's storytelling, taken in its entirety, provides its own clues to her reticence. A happy, secure, and supportive home life, one that was relatively free of conflict, undergirds her entire activist story. Her narrative of childhood features loving parents who taught her the importance of activism. Her narrative of adulthood features flexible family arrangements that allowed her to pursue her interests. These views dovetail with Frances's general tendency to tell stories with positive outcomes. To narrate any significant degree of difficulty or conflict in her personal life would distract from a life story that tends toward stories of success. We do not know the price that Frances and those close to her paid to support her activist career, but there would be a certain narrative price for the telling of a story that otherwise has such unity and purpose.

These perspectives on work and family, seemingly contradictory to a younger feminist but to Frances simply the way she lived her life, help situate Frances in the history of women's activism. They date her as having come of age between the suffrage generation and the generation that grew up with contemporary feminism, both of which focused attention on gender in ways that Frances's cohort did not. The economic concerns of the Depression era, followed by the changing race relations of the postwar period, shaped her outlook on politics. Nonetheless, Frances's life is not without feminist import. Throughout her activist career, Frances worked with women who fully believed that they, along with men, should define and shape the social and political world. She tried, as she says, "to do a substantial job in things." Frances sought out allies wherever she could find them, and more times than not, especially in her early career, these were women. In mixed-sex groups as well as in women's organizations, Frances and her colleagues implicitly developed leadership potential in women.[78]

Moreover, others can and should offer different interpretations of Frances's life than she herself does. Many of Frances's younger female friends view her as a role model. Betsey Stone describes Frances as "a remarkable feminist," a model for how to live a life defined by meaningful work.[79] In this sense, too, Frances's life story can have feminist import, even while she does not define herself as a feminist. Indeed, as much as feminists must interrogate the relationship of family and work, family and politics, there is also something refreshing about Frances's decision to tell a life story with activism at its center. Although she lived and worked through the heyday of resurgent domesticity after World War II, she overthrows the "marriage plot" in her life story, defining herself instead by politics.[80] Frances's life can and should have many meanings, particularly as her own ability to tell it fades, and as it passes from one generation to the next.[81] Finally, I'm reminded that Frances has nothing but praise for those who live to tell the tale and show up for the next struggle, a struggle which, she also understands, they will have to define and determine.

NOTES

[1] Frances Pauley, interview by author, tape recording, June/July 1995, Atlanta, Ga., in author's possession. All quotations in this essay, unless otherwise noted, are taken from the preceding text of Frances Pauley's life story. As the editor of that text, I have taken additional editorial license when pulling quotations into this essay: I have not included ellipsis points where I eliminated a phrase or sentence. Ellipsis points are necessary when working with texts created by others, but as I was the creator of this text, I continued that practice when pulling material into this essay. Throughout, my goal has been ease of reading. Furthermore, to retain the immediacy of storytelling, I have used the present tense when writing about Frances's storytelling ("Frances says . . . ") and the past tense when describing events that took place in the past ("Frances organized . . . ").

[2] *Caveat Emptor*, Decatur High School yearbook, 1923.

[3] On life stories as constructions of self, see Daphne Patai, "Introduction: Constructing a Self," in *Brazilian Women Speak: Contemporary Life Stories* (New Brunswick: Rutgers University Press, 1988), 1–35; Kim Lacy Rogers, *Righteous Lives: Narratives of the New Orleans Civil Rights Movement* (New York: New York University Press, 1993); Susan E. Chase and Colleen S. Bell, "Interpreting the Complexity of Women's Subjectivity," in *Interactive Oral History Interviewing*, ed. Eva M. McMahan and Kim Lacy Rogers (Hillsdale, N.J.: Lawrence Erlbaum Associates, 1994), 63–81.

[4] As Kim Lacy Rogers puts it, this is a "past that anticipates its own future." *Righteous Lives*, 193. The field of narrative psychology examines life stories to illuminate the function of storytelling in human development. For the argument that life stories provide life with unity and purpose, see D. P. McAdams, *The Stories We Live By: Personal Myth and the Making of the Self* (New York: Morrow, 1993). On life review among the elderly, see Robert N. Butler, "The Life Review: An Interpretation of Reminiscence in the Aged," *Psychiatry* 26 (1963): 65–76, and "The Life Review: An Unrecognized Bonanza," *International Journal of Aging and Human Development* 12 (1980–81): 35–38.

[5] For a discussion of the social and collective nature of oral history material, see Samuel Schrager, "What Is Social in Oral History?" *International Journal of Oral History* 4 (1983): 76–98. See also Cedric N. Chatterley and Alicia J. Rouverol, with Stephen A. Cole, *I Was Content and Not Content: The Story of Linda Lord and the Closing of Penobscot Poultry* (Carbondale: Southern Illinois University Press, 1999).

[6] Thomas Mashburn Deaton, "Atlanta during the Progressive Era," (Ph.D. diss., University of Georgia, 1969), chap. 7; Workers of the Writers' Program of the Works Projects Administration in the State of Georgia, comp., *Atlanta: A City of the Modern South* (New York: Smith & Durrell Publishers, 1942), 72–80; Mary E. Frederickson, "'Each One Is Dependent on the Other': Southern Churchwomen, Racial Reform, and the Process of Transformation, 1880–1940," in *Visible Women: New Essays on American Activism*, ed. Nancy A. Hewitt and Suzanne Lebsock (Urbana and Chicago: University of Illinois Press, 1993), 296–324. The involvement of church women in social welfare was a South-wide phenomenon; see Anne Firor Scott, *The Southern Lady: From Pedestal to Politics,*

1830–1930 (Chicago: University of Chicago Press, 1970), chap. 6. African American women were also undertaking social welfare work at this time. For one treatment of such work, also in the metropolitan Atlanta area, see Jacqueline Anne Rouse, *Lugenia Burns Hope: Black Southern Reformer* (Athens: University of Georgia Press, 1989). Frances, however, was socialized into a white women's network of reform and only later began to learn of interracial work.

[7] The context for Josephine's dismissal was a merger movement that was under way within the Methodist Church in the 1920s, an effort to reunite the northern and southern wings of the church. The denomination had split in the 1840s over slavery. Bishop Candler organized opposition to the merger through the local conferences of the church, but ultimately he only delayed reunion. In 1939, the northern and southern branches united to create the United Methodist Church. See Martin E. Marty, *Pilgrims in Their Own Land: 500 Years of Religion in America* (Boston: Little, Brown, 1984), 382–85.

[8] Arnold Shankman, "Dorothy Eugenia Rogers Tilly," in *Notable American Women: The Modern Period: A Biographical Dictionary* (Cambridge: Harvard University Press, 1980), 691–93.

[9] Morton Sosna, *In Search of the Silent South: Southern Liberals and the Race Issue* (New York: Columbia University Press, 1977), 173.

[10] For a description of the typical patterns of black-white relations in domestic service, from which the Freeborns varied, see David M. Katzman, *Seven Days a Week: Women and Domestic Service in Industrializing America* (New York: Oxford University Press, 1978), 194–95, 202, 274. On the political economy of domestic service in the South, see Tera W. Hunter, *To 'Joy My Freedom: Southern Black Women's Lives and Labors after the Civil War* (Cambridge: Harvard University Press, 1997), esp. 111.

[11] Fred Hobson, "The Sins of the Fathers: Lillian Smith and Katharine Du Pre Lumpkin," *Southern Review* 34 (1998): 755–79. Anne Braden, *The Wall Between* (New York: Monthly Review Press, 1958); Sarah Patton Boyle, *The Desegregated Heart: A Virginian's Stand in Time of Transition* (New York: William Morrow & Company, 1962); Hollinger F. Barnard, *Outside the Magic Circle: The Autobiography of Virginia Foster Durr* (New York: Simon & Schuster, 1987); Lillian Smith, *Killers of the Dream* (New York: W.W. Norton, 1949).

[12] Jacquelyn Dowd Hall, *Revolt Against Chivalry: Jessie Daniel Ames and the Women's Campaign against Lynching* (New York: Columbia University Press, 1974), 82–83.

[13] Playbill, "Four One-Act Plays," Drama Workshop, Atlanta, Ga., n.d., in Frances Pauley's possession, used by permission.

[14] On the Great Depression and the New Deal in Georgia, see Numan V. Bartley, *The Creation of Modern Georgia*, 2d ed. (Athens: University of Georgia Press, 1990), 172–77; Kenneth Coleman, gen. ed., *A History of Georgia* (Athens: University of Georgia Press, 1977), 263–66, 310–18; Clifford M. Kuhn, Harlon E. Joye, and E. Bernard West, *Living Atlanta: An Oral History of the City, 1914–1948* (Atlanta: Atlanta Historical Society, and Athens: University Press of Georgia, 1990), chap. 7; Douglas Lee Fleming, "Atlanta, the Depression, and the New Deal," (Ph.D. diss., Emory University, 1984).

[15] Fleming, "Atlanta, the Depression, and the New Deal," 289, 295–303. On the value of inaccurate memories as "errors, inventions, and myths [that] lead us through and beyond facts to their meanings," see Alessandro Portelli, *The Death of Luigi Trastulli and Other Stories: Form and Meaning in Oral History* (Albany: State University of New York Press, 1991), chap. 1; quotation on p. 2.

[16] Frances's response to the Great Depression stands in contrast to many others who did view their own suffering as the product of individual failure. See Studs Terkel, *Hard Times: An Oral History of the Great Depression* (New York: Simon & Schuster, 1970), and Michael Frisch, "Oral History and *Hard Times*: A Review Essay," in *A Shared Authority: Essays on the Craft and Meaning of Oral and Public History* (Albany: State University of

New York Press, 1990), 11–12. Virginia Foster Durr is an example of a contemporary who, like Frances, witnessed the human misery of the Depression and turned toward social activism. Barnard, *Outside the Magic Circle*.

17 Barnard, *Outside the Magic Circle*; John A. Salmond, *Miss Lucy of the CIO: The Life and Times of Lucy Randolph Mason* (Athens: University of Georgia Press, 1988).

18 T. F. Abercrombie, "History of Public Health in Georgia, 1733–1950" (Atlanta: Georgia State Board of Health, n.d.); Kuhn, *Living Atlanta*, 32.

19 By 1918, white southern Methodist women had made work with African Americans the focus of their domestic program. Frederickson, "'Each One Is Dependent on the Other,'" 310.

20 The Junior Service League of Decatur, Annual Report, 1938–39, in Frances Pauley's possession, used by permission. Mary Walker Fox, *The Sesquicentennial Celebration, 1823–1973, The First Methodist Church, Decatur, Georgia* (Decatur, Ga: First United Methodist Church, 1973); J. R. Evans, "Annual Report of the DeKalb Clinic, Inc.," [1940?], in Frances Pauley's possession, used by permission; Social Planning Council, *A Report on Health and Welfare in DeKalb and Fulton Counties* (Atlanta: Social Planning Council, 1943). The literature on women and the rise of the welfare state in the United States is vast and growing. For an overview, see Seth Koven and Sonya Michel, "Womanly Duties: Maternalist Politics and the Origins of Welfare States in France, Germany, Great Britain, and the United States, 1880–1920," *American Historical Review* 95 (1995): 1076–1108.

21 This was the prevalent view in the white South, including among reformers. See Glenda Elizabeth Gilmore, *Gender and Jim Crow: Women and the Politics of White Supremacy in North Carolina, 1896–1920* (Chapel Hill: University of North Carolina Press, 1996), 170; Hunter, *To 'Joy My Freedom*, chap. 9.

22 Edward H. Beardsley, *A History of Neglect: Health Care for Blacks and Mill Workers in the Twentieth-Century South* (Knoxville: University of Tennessee Press, 1987), vii.

23 Research suggests that the school lunch programs of the New Deal were a vital link in women's New Deal activism. See Martha H. Swain, "A New Deal for Southern Women: Gender and Race in Women's Work Relief," in *Women in the American South: A Multicultural Reader*, ed. Christie Anne Farnham (New York: New York University Press, 1997), 252, and *Ellen S. Woodward: New Deal Advocate for Women* (Jackson: University Press of Mississippi, 1995), 336–37.

24 On the moralizing tendency of narrative, see Hayden White, "The Value of Narrativity in the Representation of Reality," in *On Narrative*, ed. W. J. T. Mitchell (Chicago: University of Chicago Press, 1981), 1–23. For the argument that endings of stories relate to their lessons, and that "a narrative is a good story that makes us care about its subject," see William Cronon, "A Place for Stories: Nature, History, and Narrative," *Journal of American History* 78 (1992): 1370, 1374, quotation on 1374.

25 For a brief introduction to the parable, see Tom McArthur, ed. *The Oxford Companion to the English Language* (New York: Oxford University Press, 1992), 747. See also John Dominic Crossan, *The Dark Interval: Towards a Theology of Story* (Niles, Ill.: Argus Communications, 1975), 56–57, 87, 121–22. My thanks to Tami Specter, my colleague at the University of San Francisco, for first suggesting that Frances speaks in parables, and to my father, John Nasstrom, for helping me develop this idea.

26 On the multiple levels on which narratives can be analyzed, from text to political praxis, see Kristin Langellier, "Personal Narratives: Perspectives on Theory and Research," *Text and Performance Quarterly* 9 (1989): 243–76.

27 On white women learning from black women, see Frederickson, "'Each One Is Dependent on the Other,'" 308, 311–12, and Gilmore, *Gender and Jim Crow*, chap. 7.

[28] For the argument that white liberals of the 1930s emphasized economic and class issues over race but still made significant steps to include blacks in government programs, see Peter J. Kellogg, "Civil Rights Consciousness in the 1940s," *The Historian* 42 (1979): 21–22; Morton Sosna, *In Search of the Silent South: Southern Liberals and the Race Issue* (New York: Columbia University Press, 1977), 60–64; Tracy Elaine K'Meyer, *Interracialism and Christian Community in the Postwar South: The Story of Koinonia Farm* (Charlottesville: University Press of Virginia, 1997), 18–19. Frances's assertion that the clinic organizers "hadn't thought about" segregation invites incredulity. It is, however, consistent with her general sense of the Depression. Frances remembers the Depression as a leveling experience for "rich and poor, black and white, young and old." Her memory of Bill's work for the PWA is that "it paid only a little bit more than it paid for manual work," and indeed the PWA was among the least racially discriminatory of the New Deal programs in the Atlanta area. See Ann Wells Ellis, "'Uncle Sam Is My Shepherd': The Commission on Interracial Cooperation and the New Deal in Georgia," *Atlanta Historical Society Journal* 30 (1986): 50–51, 58.

[29] My analysis here is informed by several treatments of white women's interracial reform. The questions being explored concern the scope and pace of social change, rather than how racist white women were or were not. See Frederickson, "'Each One Is Dependent on the Other,'" and Gilmore, *Gender and Jim Crow*. My analysis of a generational perspective was aided by Jacquelyn Dowd Hall and Anne Firor Scott's review essay "Women in the South," in *Interpreting Southern History: Historiographical Essays in Honor of Sanford W. Higginbotham*, ed. John B. Boles and Evelyn Thomas Nolan (Baton Rouge: Louisiana State University Press, 1987), 495–505.

[30] On racial discrimination within the New Deal in Georgia, see Kuhn et al., *Living Atlanta*, 214, and Ellis, "'Uncle Sam Is My Shepherd,'" 47–63. Even though much of the New Deal was discriminatory in both intent and practice, in other ways it encouraged a growing challenge to the southern racial order among both politically active African Americans and some white liberals. See Douglas L. Smith, *The New Deal in the Urban South* (Baton Rouge: Louisiana State University Press, 1988).

[31] Patricia Sullivan, "Southern Reformers, the New Deal, and the Movement's Foundation," in *New Directions in Civil Rights Studies*, ed. Armstead L. Robinson and Patricia Sullivan (Charlottesville: University Press of Virginia, 1991), 94–95. For a description of Atlanta's 1946 voter registration drive, see Kathryn L. Nasstrom, "Women, the Civil Rights Movement and the Politics of Historical Memory in Atlanta, 1946–1973" (Ph.D. diss., University of North Carolina at Chapel Hill, 1993), chap. 2.

[32] Historians are only now beginning to explore the general significance to twentieth-century politics of the League of Women Voters, apart from its role as the successor to the women's suffrage campaign. See Susan Ware, "American Women in the 1950s: Nonpartisan Politics and Women's Politicization," in *Women, Politics, and Change*, ed. Louise A. Tilly and Patricia Gurin (New York: Russell Sage Foundation, 1990). The league's own historians have placed more emphasis on the years before World War II, but good overviews of the league's history can be found in Louise M. Young, *In the Public Interest: The League of Women Voters, 1920–1970* (Westport, Conn.: Greenwood Press, 1989), and League of Women Voters of the United States, *40 Years of a Great Idea* (Washington, D.C.: League of Women Voters of the United States, 1960). On the league's significance in relation to the county unit fight and school desegregation in Georgia, see Paul E. Mertz, "'Mind Changing Time All Over Georgia': HOPE, Inc., and School Desegregation, 1958–1961," *Georgia Historical Quarterly* 77 (1993): 41–61; Nasstrom, "Women, the Civil Rights Movement, and the Politics of Historical Memory," chap. 3; Matthew Lassiter, "The Rise of the Suburban South: Race,

Education, and the Middle Class, 1945–75" (Ph.D. diss., University of Virginia, in progress). Sometimes references to the league's importance are mentioned only in passing or are well buried in footnotes. Numan V. Bartley notes that the league led the civic groups that opposed the private school amendment in Georgia in *The Rise of Massive Resistance: Race and Politics in the South During the 1950's* (Baton Rouge: Louisiana State University Press, 1969), 55, n. 21. Harold Paulk Henderson describes the importance of the League to the poll tax issue in *The Politics of Change in Georgia: A Political Biography of Ellis Arnall* (Athens: The University of Georgia Press, 1991), 85–86. Martin Gruberg notes that the Georgia League of Women Voters was credited with eliminating the poll tax in *Women in American Politics: An Assessment and Sourcebook* (Oshkosh, Wis.: Academia Press, 1968), 90.

[33] Ware, "American Women in the 1950s," 282–83.

[34] Calvin Kytle and James A. Mackay, *Who Runs Georgia?* (1947; Athens: University of Georgia Press, 1998), 54–55.

[35] V. O. Key, Jr., *Southern Politics in State and Nation* (New York: Vintage Books, 1949), 119.

[36] Julian LaRose Harris to Frances Pauley, letter, January 8, 1953, Frances Freeborn Pauley Papers, Special Collections Department, Robert W. Woodruff Library, Emory University, Atlanta, Ga. Frances's papers contain numerous letters praising her work on the county unit fight.

[37] Kytle and Mackay, *Who Runs Georgia?*, 79–85.

[38] "Brief Stating Georgia's Position Re 'White' In By-Laws," October 23, 1946, Papers of the League of Women Voters of the United States, Manuscript Division, Library of Congress, Washington, D.C.

[39] Annual Meeting Minutes, DeKalb County League of Women Voters, November 6, 1947, League of Women Voters of DeKalb County (Ga.) Records, Special Collections Department, Robert W. Woodruff Library, Emory University, Atlanta, Ga.; Lenecia L. Bruce to author, June 27, 1997.

[40] In 1944, the League of Women Voters underwent a significant restructuring intended to place more decision-making in the hands of local leagues. The League of Women Voters, which had been a federation of state leagues, became an association of individual members. At the same time, the league changed its name from the *National League of Women Voters* to the *League of Women Voters of the United States*. League of Women Voters of the United States, *40 Years of a Great Idea*, 36–37.

[41] For a history of the *Brown* decision, see Richard Kluger, *Simple Justice: The History of Brown v. Board of Education and Black America's Struggle for Equality* (New York: Knopf, 1976).

[42] The Minimum Foundation Program was a case of odd political bedfellows. Segregationist politicians supported it in the hope of staving off desegregation by beginning to deliver, at long last, on the "equal" component of "separate but equal." Educational reformers supported the program because it promised increased funding for public schools, which they viewed as a positive development under any circumstances. Bartley, *Creation of Modern Georgia*, 206.

[43] This interpretation of HOPE's central role in Georgia's desegregation struggle is based on Mertz, "'Mind Changing Time All Over Georgia'"; Nasstrom, "Women, the Civil Rights Movement, and the Politics of Historical Memory," chap. 3; Lassiter, "The Rise of the Suburban South." For a similar argument on the importance of white moderates in the state of Virginia, see Matthew D. Lassiter and Andrew B. Lewis, *The Moderates' Dilemma: Massive Resistance to School Desegregation in Virginia* (Charlottesville: University Press of Virginia, 1998).

[44] Vandiver quoted in Nasstrom, "Women, the Civil Rights Movement, and the Politics of Historical Memory," 197.

[45] King quoted in Nasstrom, "Women, the Civil Rights Movement, and the Politics of Historical Memory," 116.

[46] On the meanings and functions of laughter, see Jeannie B. Thomas, *Featherless Chickens, Laughing Women, and Serious Stories* (Charlottesville: University Press of Virginia, 1997), especially 45–48, 71, 116, 137, 186, and 202, n. 16.

[47] Clayborne Carson, *In Struggle: SNCC and the Black Awakening of the 1960s* (New York: Harvard University Press, 1981), 63–64.

[48] For a fuller discussion of organizing and leadership, and a brief review of the literature on the subject, see Kathryn L. Nasstrom, "Down to Now: Memory, Narrative, and Women's Leadership in the Civil Rights Movement," *Gender & History* 11 (1999): 113–144. On the concept of "bridge leadership," see Belinda Robnett, *How Long? How Long? African-American Women in the Struggle for Civil Rights* (New York: Oxford University Press, 1997), 19–23. Joanne Grant, *Ella Baker: Freedom Bound* (New York: John Wiley & Sons, 1998); Septima Poinsette Clark, *Echo in My Soul* (New York: Dutton, 1962).

[49] Participants, journalists, and scholars have all written extensively on the Albany Movement. For two reviews of the literature on Albany, from very different perspectives, see Michael Chalfen, "'The Way Out May Lead In': The Albany Movement beyond Martin Luther King, Jr.," *Georgia Historical Quarterly* 79 (1995): 560–67; Joan C. Browning, "Invisible Revolutionaries: White Women in Civil Rights Historiography," *Journal of Women's History* 8 (1996): 186–204. For a detailed account, with an emphasis on King and SCLC, see Taylor Branch, *Parting the Waters: America in the King Years, 1954–63* (New York: Simon & Schuster, 1988); on SNCC, see Clayborne Carson, *In Struggle*, chap. 5; and, for a perspective on white southerners, David L. Chappell, *Inside Agitators: White Southerners in the Civil Rights Movement* (Baltimore: Johns Hopkins University Press, 1994), chap. 6.

[50] On the distinction between a chronicle, which has a simple ordering relationship of ". . . and then . . . and then . . . and then . . .," and a narrative, which has "many ordering relations," see Louis O. Mink, "Narrative Form as a Cognitive Instrument," in *The Writing of History: Literary Form and Historical Imagination*, ed. Robert H. Canary and Henry Kozocki (Madison: University of Wisconsin Press, 1978), 144.

[51] The wide-ranging, interdisciplinary study of the nature of memory has clearly established that memories are not reconstructions of past events but, rather, constructions of those events in which the concerns of the present reshape understandings of past events. For an introduction to historical memory, see David Thelen, "Memory and American History," *Journal of American History* 75 (1989), 1117–29, especially 1119–21.

[52] Frances Pauley to Maxwell Hahn, letter, July 8, 1965, Southern Regional Council Papers, microfilm edition, Series IV, State Councils, Reel 142 (Ann Arbor, Mich.: University Microfilms International, 1984).

[53] As David Chappell notes, the central question asked of the Albany Movement was whether or not it was a failure. Chappell comes down on the side of failure. Chappell, *Inside Agitators*, 220–21. Michael Chalfen, by contrast, suggests notable successes in "'The Way Out May Lead In.'" Significantly, Chalfen also follows developments in Albany beyond 1962.

[54] For a notable work that looks carefully at the role of white southerners, see Chappell, *Inside Agitators*. For Albany, however, Chappell focuses mainly on police chief Laurie Pritchett.

[55] I am indebted to Charles M. Payne who stated this matter, in reference to the organizers in SNCC, with unusual clarity. "In the movement's sense of 'organize,' in the transformative sense, it is probably safe to say that you cannot organize people you do not respect." *I've Got the Light of Freedom: The Organizing Tradition and the Mississippi Freedom Struggle* (Berkeley: University of California Press, 1995), 365.

[56] While interest in these questions runs high, and memoirs and scholarly works are in progress, very little analysis has been done on the roles or perspectives of young white women. Sara Evans has produced the standard scholarly treatment, although a number of her interpretations are much criticized by movement participants. *Personal Politics: The Roots of Women's Liberation in the Civil Rights Movement and the New Left* (New York: Vintage Books, 1979). For one memoir, see Mary King, *Freedom Song: A Personal Story of the 1960s Civil Rights Movement* (New York: William Morrow and Company, 1987).

[57] Frances's letters to her children are available in Pauley Papers, Series 1 (Personal Papers) Box 1. Quotations drawn from three letters: Dear Children, n.d.; [no salutation], March 2, 1969; and [no salutation], April 20, 1962.

[58] My thanks to Murphy Davis for helping me understand the significance of Frances's age and experience when she joined the movement, and to Joan Browning for reminding me of the terrible personal price paid by many movement activists.

[59] Charles M. Payne has a subtle discussion of both ongoing resistance and co-optation among activists who sought to work within the power structure beginning in the 1960s in *I've Got the Light of Freedom*, chap. 12.

[60] My thanks to Paul Rilling, who helped me understand that Frances's different storytelling style for the HEW years reflects the different character of her work in those years.

[61] The debate within the NAACP, the organization that initiated the legal challenge to segregation, over the value of desegregation is especially significant. See "At N.A.A.C.P., Talk of a Shift on Integration," *The New York Times*, June 23, 1997. For one take on the debate, see both Glenn C. Loury, "Integration is Yesterday's Struggle," and Paul Ruffins, "Segregation is a Sign of Failure," in *The New Crisis* 104 (1998): 22–24. For a longer treatment of many of the key issues, see James Traub, "Separate and Equal," *The Atlantic* 268 (1991): 24–37. On the losses that one black community experienced with desegregation, and its effort to prevent these losses, see David S. Cecelski, *Along Freedom Road: Hyde County, North Carolina, and the Fate of Black Schools in the South* (Chapel Hill: University of North Carolina Press, 1994).

[62] Gary Orfield, Susan E. Eaton, and the Harvard Project on School Desegregation, *Dismantling Desegregation: The Quiet Reversal of* Brown v. Board of Education (New York: The New Press, 1996), 8. See also, for reminders of progress in the early 1970s, Kluger, *Simple Justice*, 767–68.

[63] Orfield et al., *Dismantling Desegregation*, viii; Waldo E. Martin, Jr., ed., Brown v. Board of Education: *A Brief History with Documents* (Boston and New York: Bedford/St. Martin's, 1998), 230–37.

[64] Bartley, *Creation of Modern Georgia*, 233. For an overview of southern economic development and its relation to poverty in this period, see David R. Goldfield, *Black, White, and Southern: Race Relations and Southern Culture, 1940 to the Present* (Baton Rouge: Louisiana State University Press, 1990), 244–55.

[65] We know far too little about the activist careers of the elderly, but there is reason to believe that later life can be an especially creative period. See Butler, "The Life Review: An Unrecognized Bonanza," 38. On later-life creativity in the careers of writers and the need for theories of creativity among the elderly, see Anne M. Wyatt-Brown and Janice Rosen, eds., *Aging and Gender in Literature: Studies in Creativity* (Charlottesville: University Press of Virginia, 1993).

[66] Jim Martin, "Afterword," in Murphy Davis, *Frances Pauley: Stories of Struggle and Triumph* (Atlanta: The Open Door Community, 1996), 84.

[67] For this interpretation of the poor as more than clients of the state, and on a definition of a just society as one that attends to human needs, see Nancy Fraser, *Unruly Practices: Power, Discourse, and Gender in Contemporary Social Theory* (Minneapolis: University of Minnesota Press, 1989), and Temma Kaplan, *Crazy for Democracy: Women in Grassroots Movements* (New York: Routledge, 1997). For case studies of grassroots organizing in the 1970s and 1980s, see Ann Bookman and Sandra Morgen, eds., *Women and the Politics of Empowerment* (Philadelphia: Temple University Press, 1988).

[68] For an overview of this question, see Goldfield, *Black, White, and Southern*, 212–27. For two recent perspectives on this question from historians who have studied the grassroots movement, see John Dittmer, *Local People: The Struggle for Civil Rights in Mississippi* (Urbana and Chicago: University of Illinois Press, 1994), 423, and Payne, *I've Got the Light of Freedom*, 360.

[69] For a fuller discussion of Frances's life story and the chronology of the civil rights movement, see Kathryn L. Nasstrom, "Beginnings and Endings: Life Stories and the Periodization of the Civil Rights Movement," *Journal of American History* 86 (1999): 700–711. August Meier argues for seeing the movement as spanning the twentieth century in "Epilogue: Toward a Synthesis of Civil Rights History," in *New Directions in Civil Rights Studies*, ed. Armstead L. Robinson and Patricia Sullivan (Charlottesville: University Press of Virginia, 1991), 211–223.

[70] Frances Pauley, interview by Paul Mertz, transcribed interview, June 10, 1988, Atlanta, Ga., Pauley Papers, 14.

[71] Frances Pauley to "Dear Directors," letter, October 18, 1966, Southern Regional Council Papers, Reel 155.

[72] Frances Pauley, interview by author, tape recording, March 24, 1998, Atlanta, Ga., in author's possession.

[73] For an introduction to black feminism, see Patricia Hill Collins, *Black Feminist Thought: Knowledge, Consciousness, and the Politics of Empowerment* (New York: Routledge, 1991). For the argument that the League of Women Voters, in contrast to the National Organization for Women, displayed a great deal of interest in welfare rights, see Marisa Chappell, "Welfare is a Feminist Issue: Second-Wave Feminism Confronts Women's Poverty, 1968–1982," (Paper presented at the Eleventh Berkshire Conference on the History of Women, Rochester, N.Y., June 6, 1999).

[74] Charles M. Payne, "Ella Baker and Models of Social Change," *Signs* 14 (1989): 885–99, especially 897–99, and *I've Got the Light of Freedom*, 3–4; Bernice McNair Barnett, "Invisible Southern Black Women Leaders in the Civil Rights Movement," *Gender and Society* 7 (1993): 162–82; Karen Bodkin Sacks, "Gender and Grassroots Leadership," in *Women and the Politics of Empowerment*, 77–94; Robnett, *How Long? How Long?*

[75] See Robnett, *How Long? How Long?*, 203–209, and Nasstrom, "Women, the Civil Rights Movement, and the Politics of Historical Memory."

[76] Frances Pauley, taped conversations with author, May/June 1997, Atlanta, Ga., in author's possession.

[77] Estelle C. Jelinek, ed., *Women's Autobiography: Essays in Criticism* (Bloomington: Indiana University Press, 1980), 10.

[78] For a very similar perspective on women in the Young Women's Christian Association and the American Friends Service Committee, see Susan Lynn, "Women, Reform, and Feminism: The Young Women's Christian Association and the American Friends Service Committee, 1945–1960" (Ph.D. diss., Stanford University, 1986), chap. 5 and 235–39.

[79] Betsey Stone, conversation with author, April 13, 1997, Durham, N.C.

[80] Sara Alpern, Joyce Antler, Elisabeth Israels Perry, and Ingrid Winther Scobie, eds., *The Challenge of Feminist Biography: Writing the Lives of Modern American Women* (Urbana and Chicago: University of Illinois Press, 1992), 9.

[81] For another perspective on a younger generation reading feminist import into a life story that, for the narrator, is not centrally defined by feminism, see Katherine Borland, "'That's Not What I Said': Interpretive Conflict in Oral Narrative Research," in *Women's Words: The Feminist Practice of Oral History*, ed. Sherna Berger Gluck and Daphne Patai (New York: Routledge, 1991), 63–75.

EDITORIAL METHOD AND COMMENTARY

Everybody's Grandmother and Nobody's Fool: Frances Freeborn Pauley and the Struggle for Social Justice is based on two documentary records of Frances Pauley's activist career: a body of oral history material recorded over the last twenty-five years and her personal and professional papers on deposit in the Special Collections Department at Emory University.[1] The first-person narration of oral history constitutes the bulk of this book's content; it is augmented by autobiographical writings from her papers. These are Frances's words, as I selected and edited them, and a description of my editorial choices and some indication of their consequences are in order.

Frances had been speaking retrospectively about her life's work for quite some time before I picked up the threads of that practice and wove them into this narrative. The earliest interview to which I had access was recorded in 1974. Frances had left the federal government and her work with HEW a year earlier, and the GPRO was still in its formative stages. She was then sixty-nine years old. The last interviews are those I conducted with Frances between 1995 and 1998. We began working together in the summer of 1995, when Frances was just a few months shy of her ninetieth birthday. All told, seven interviewers contributed to this project, resulting in more than one thousand pages of transcripts and a number of untranscribed interviews.[2]

As Frances and I set to work in 1995, my first task was to take stock of existing interviews. Frances provided me with several in her possession, and I quickly realized that this material, when combined with interviews already on deposit in oral history collections in the Atlanta area, amounted to more than enough to begin a book-length project. I began to work as an editor and interviewer almost simultaneously. As interviewer, I drew up a series of follow-up questions for those activities Frances had already narrated at length and a more detailed set of questions for those she had not yet discussed. As editor, I began to take note of patterns in

Frances's storytelling style. Knowing that I had an unusually rich body of material, spanning a quarter-century, I was as interested in the form of Frances's stories as their content.

One of my initial and enduring impressions was that Frances had been quite consistent over time in her storytelling. The narrative of her arrest in Albany, Georgia, during the civil rights movement, for example, is virtually the same in interviews dating from 1974 and 1994. Moreover, I found Frances to be a wonderful interviewee: a good storyteller, happy to speak at length, and someone who enjoys the give and take of the interview setting. My appreciation for Frances as a narrator deepened as I worked with the interviews conducted by others. Although she was usually willing to follow the lead set by her questioner, Frances would direct the flow of an interview when she saw the need. I noticed instances in which she would not move on to a new subject if a topic had been missed or not sufficiently elaborated. If an interviewer was unfamiliar with some aspect of Georgia history or politics, Frances would fill in the necessary background information before interjecting her own story or assessment. Her friends have told me that Frances, as a public speaker, was quite adept at gauging her audience and tailoring the content, tone, and level of her remarks accordingly, and I observed much the same in Frances the interviewee. This tendency also made it possible for me to step in only rarely to add a phrase of clarification or to annotate Frances's remarks. Usually I could find an instance where Frances stopped and explained some basic information to the uninitiated.

This was especially true of a distinctive set of recordings from the late 1980s and 1990s. These were not interviews, in the sense that oral historians understand and create them, but rather recordings of Frances's spoken remembrances as delivered yearly between 1987 and 1996 to a small audience at the Open Door Community, a residential Christian community serving the homeless and hungry in Atlanta. For ten years, on the occasion of her birthday, Frances spoke about her life's work and answered questions. Unlike the oral history material, which was generated in one-on-one conversations, the Open Door material is more like a set of speeches, albeit informally delivered, before a familiar and congenial audience.[3] Despite these differences, the Open Door material and the oral history interviews are quite similar. Frances's distinctive storytelling style is evident throughout.

Frances's consistency and her care as an interviewee led me to an early editorial decision not to include questions in the text of her life story. Oral historians recognize that the interviewer's questions shape the information recorded, but the number of interviews used to create this narrative and the consistency of Frances's stories over time minimized the influence of any single interviewer. Finally, Frances is a consummate storyteller, and the question-and-answer format, which interrupts even as it guides, is not as well suited to conveying that quality in her speech.[4]

Despite the consistency of Frances's storytelling over the years, subsequent experiences have, quite naturally, altered her memories. Frances recalls the Albany Movement, a critical series of events in the civil rights movement in Georgia, in greater detail in her 1974 interview than in any subsequent recordings. Over time, the significance of a story became more salient than the details within the story. A process of distilling events into a highly clarified memory set in, as the events themselves receded further into the past.[5] When Frances and I began working together in 1995, she often found herself unable to provide a detailed answer to a question that I posed, but she always called up a story that illustrated her general response to the particular issue I was raising. Frances has told me some of her stories many times now, and her favorites are, in a fashion, a way to answer a question faithfully, even if she cannot answer it directly.

As I worked closely with the interviews I inherited, my initial sense of the remarkable consistency of Frances Pauley the storyteller gave way to a more nuanced reading of differences among her interviews. Frances was noticeably edgy in two interviews conducted in 1988, more apt to show her disappointment over recent developments in Georgia politics. The same sentiment was evident in documents from the mid-1980s in her collection. In a piece unusual both for its self-revelatory and deflated tone, Frances recorded her thoughts as she packed up to move from her home. Her theme was loss—loss of her mother at a young age, loss of her father, loss of husband Bill, loss of friends: "I am tired, tired, tired of giving up, giving up, cutting back, cutting back. I guess that's what life is. So, it is correct to say that I am tired of life."[6] The contrast to the more typically energetic and upbeat Frances is striking. I have preserved some of this contradictory material, but the text as a whole favors the Frances who always found a way to persevere and, I think, favors the way that Frances wants to be remembered.

The consistency of Frances's memories over the years makes this her book; my role as editor marks the text in less obvious ways. As I assembled the oral history material, I often added a word or phrase for clarity, changed tense and usage for agreement, and inserted dates to mark the passage of time. I also smoothed out the fits and starts of speech to make oral material recorded in a conversational setting flow as written words on the page. On occasion, I inserted entire sentences as transitions from one topic to the next. To indicate emphasis and humor in Frances's speech, I ended sentences with exclamation points, rather than using bracketed remarks, such as [laughter].

The documents from Frances's papers I treated somewhat differently. I sought to reproduce them as faithfully as possible, but I balanced accuracy with readability in my editorial choices. I corrected obvious typographical errors and altered usage and punctuation when necessary for clarity. Punctuation was a particular challenge with Frances's letters, which she tended to pepper with three, four, and sometimes more ellipsis points between sentences. I transposed these into hyphens so as to avoid the impression of omission of material where none was eliminated. The ellipsis points that do appear in the documents indicate places where I have omitted material. For the diary entries in chapter four, however, I deviated from this standard practice. These excerpts represent a small fraction of the entire document, and I reorganized entries from a strict chronological order in the original to the geographic organization represented by the sections on Savannah, Albany, and Southwest Georgia. For this reason I have not inserted ellipsis points, as virtually every entry would have been followed by ellipsis points.

With the documents, as with the oral history material, my editorial practices have been more on the order of selection and arrangement than alteration. I sought to preserve the structure and tone of the documents, and for this reason I chose not to standardize usage. Frances produced most of this documentary material for use at the time, with no idea that it might see its way into print. The documents should be read in this light. Frances's first priority was to get something done, whether it was making a speech, running a meeting, or swaying a legislator's vote. Many of these activities did not require careful written presentations, certainly not at the time, much less for the historical record. I laughed out loud when I came across Frances telling an interviewer about her attitude toward her collection of papers: "I wasn't interested in it, and I'm not now. I mean I'm not a historian; I admire historians, but there's so much you've got to get done, like correlating."[7] Frances's documents should be taken in the spirit of Frances on the run, which she usually was, while the oral history material reflects my greater tolerance for "correlating" and editing.

I became a more aggressive editor on matters of organization.[8] Although I put very few words in Frances's mouth, I freely moved her words around. As I worked with material gathered by seven interviewers, I mixed elements of the same story to create a single version. My standard practice was to find the best rendition of a story (from often as many as five different versions) and build on it. "Best" was clearly my subjective judgment, but I looked for the clearest narrative flow and the greatest impact—the "punch" of the story. Once I had the best version, I incorporated additional elements from other versions, sometimes as little as a phrase, other times as much as an entire paragraph. On a few occasions, I found I had no best version to build on, and I collected and assembled sentences and paragraphs from various interviews to create a whole.

My chief contribution as editor was to take many stories and weave them into an extended narrative. We cannot know how Frances would have produced her life story in book form, only that she has not. As often as possible, I took my cue from Frances, observing which stories she placed in which order and how she made a transition from one aspect of her life to the next. I also sought to preserve the hallmarks of Frances's storytelling, such as a tendency to compare the past and present and to attach a moral to the end of her stories. I have heard Frances say, many times, some version of the following: "The main thing about getting things done is—and I think I still have a tendency to do the same thing— if you see something that needs to be done, just go ahead and start. I think that's the first lesson in organizing."[9] Frances rarely missed an opportunity to turn a personal story into a political lesson, and this is the central characteristic that I sought to preserve.

My arrangement combines the simple chronological ordering of a life story, from childhood to the present, with both topical and chronological organization within chapters. This seemed the best way to reveal a life story unfolding, while keeping related material together and avoiding repetition. This pattern is especially evident in the first chapter. I gathered all the material on Frances's mother and her religious experience (two closely related matters in Frances's storytelling) into one section, and followed that with all the material about Frances's education. I continued this practice with material about family life in subsequent chapters. Frances did not speak at length about her family. Rather, she most often constructed a political self and measured the meaning of her life by changes in the social and political world. In each chapter, a section focused on her family serves as a counterpoint to the political material and indicates the family influences that shaped her activism. Family members appear in supporting roles in the text I assembled, just as they did in Frances's stories.

Omissions within and additions to the body of oral history material further illustrate our mutual yet different influences on this book. Several notable aspects of Frances's political work are not addressed here. There is no reference, for example, to her service on the Georgia Advisory Committee to the U.S. Commission on Civil Rights, which Frances joined in 1964, nor material on her extended interest in the Atlanta school desegregation suit beyond the initial desegregation of the schools in 1961. As the last interviewer to work with Frances on an extended basis, I broached these subjects, but our conversations did not generate material that I warranted sufficiently detailed to include. Ultimately I let stand Frances's neglect of these (and other) subjects.[10] Knowing Frances, I'm not at all surprised by these omissions. Both the work of the U.S. Commission on Civil Rights and the Atlanta school case had a much heavier bureaucratic content than Frances takes to naturally. Her primary activity in the 1960s was the organizing work that she loved; bureaucracy in memory, as in life, garnered as little of her attention as she could afford to give it. Frances is also less likely to tell stories of campaigns with ambiguous outcomes, much less those that ended in failure. And the Atlanta school case, which was in litigation for nearly two decades and ended more in compromise than victory, is surely an instance of a less-than-satisfactory ending from Frances's point of view.

There is, however, one instance in which I did *not* follow Frances's lead, nor accept her reticence. When I embarked on this project with Frances, I immediately noticed that none of the previously recorded material covered in any detail the GPRO, which Frances launched in the mid-1970s and sustained for well over a decade. I have puzzled over and worked on that silence ever since, for this last major project of Frances's career was far too important to omit. How to explain Frances's omission of the activities that represented the culmination of a lifetime of activism? The research agenda of the scholars who had previously interviewed Frances provided part of the answer. They had not asked Frances about this—a painful reminder of just how much the interviewer shapes the historical record. Yet this explanation was not sufficient, as Frances had on occasion set the agenda in her interviews, and she could have chosen to discuss the GPRO years when she told her stories at the Open Door Community. The key to Frances's reticence, I believe, lies in the nature and timing of her work with the GPRO. Much of the GPRO's work verged on drudgery: following bills through the legislature; buttonholing recalcitrant representatives to lobby for an unpopular measure to benefit the poor; and constantly doing battle with government bureaucracy. Frances had done similar work for decades, but those tasks had previously been leavened by a strong dose of organizing, an activity that she enjoyed tremendously. With advancing age, Frances was less able to travel the state to organize GPRO chapters, and her husband's lengthy illness during that period placed additional demands on her. Then, in the late 1980s, the impetus for much of the organization's work passed to other individuals and groups. Leaving the work of the GPRO was an admission that her life of activism was winding down. Frances wrote to her good friend Paul Rilling in 1986: "To tell you the truth, Paul, I am sick of the whole thing. I think ten years is enough. A lot of people are picking up. If they can carry it, O.K. If not, O.K., also. . . . If we had done better, the children of Georgia wouldn't be so bad off today."[11] There is acceptance in these words, but a grudging acceptance, and there is a clear recognition of how much more needs to be done. In the mid-1980s, the problems of poverty and homelessness weighed on Frances, as they do today. These are also issues about which it is difficult to tell stories of success, or even of the virtues of perseverance. Frances has not turned this information into stories, I suspect, because it is still painful.[12]

Although I worked with Frances on several occasions to record material about the GPRO years, we generated far less detailed material, relative to the oral history documentation of her earlier activities. Frances's daughter, Marylin Pauley Beittel, and her good friend, Lewis Sinclair, helped me chart a different course. Frances and I were in the habit of conducting our interview sessions in the mid-morning and then breaking for lunch. Frances would often invite Lewis to join us, and it was Lewis who mentioned other GPRO members who might help, in particular pointing me toward Muriel Lokey and Betsey Stone. Over time, a plan to involve others in recording the history of the GPRO evolved. The form and content of the chapter on the GPRO, so different from the rest, reflects these circumstances. The chapter contains not a first-person narrative but a conversation between Frances and friends, and it relies more heavily than the others on documents to provide details of the GPRO's advocacy on behalf of the poor and disenfranchised.

When it came time to edit the material generated by these joint interviews, I faced a dilemma. To continue my practice of combining material from various interviews would create the false impression of a single conversation when, in fact, several separate conversations had taken place. Ultimately, however, I decided to maintain the editorial practices I had established in earlier chapters. The information recorded with Muriel Lokey concerning the early years of the GPRO is concentrated in the first half of the chapter, and that with Betsey Stone concerning the later years in the second half. In one or two places, however, the imperative of bringing related information together leaves the impression that Frances, Betsey, and Muriel were all in the same room at the same time, which is not the case. I also decided not to insert my questions as interviewer, even though the more conversational form of this chapter invited that approach. Again, I decided to maintain previous practice, by allowing the arrangement of material to function as the transitional links that an interviewer's questions often provide. I admit, however, that this chapter contains some especially aggressive editing.

Once all chapters of the manuscript were in draft form, Frances and I embarked on the final stage of our collaboration. Frances now suffers from macular degeneration, a common eye disease among the elderly that gradually leads to a loss in sharp central vision, and we knew that she would not be able to read the manuscript in its entirety. That task fell to Marylin, who reviewed my work and improved it with her suggestions. Still, some decisions and corrections remained that only Frances could make. In June of 1997 and March of 1998, Frances and I reviewed each chapter. First, we addressed minor factual inconsistencies. Frances is a gift to an editor in that she usually gets her facts right, a tendency that she attributes to her training in the League of Women Voters. Like everyone, she has a selective memory, but when Frances remembers details, she is remarkably accurate. Nonetheless, by working in Frances's papers and other documentary sources, I found a number of places where Frances's memory and the recorded facts varied, and I brought these to her attention. To help us with the chapter on Frances's work on school desegregation compliance in Mississippi for HEW, Paul Rilling came over from Anniston, Alabama, in June of 1997. He helped us verify the existing material and add to a chapter already in draft form. Where Frances's memory and the factual record differed, I allowed her to correct her memory, and most often she chose to set her "memory" straight. For my part, although I share the oral historian's hesitancy to change material previously recorded, I saw no reason, given Frances's preference, to argue that the spontaneous memories of conversation should take precedence over the more carefully considered recollections of the revision process. Frances takes some pride in getting her facts straight—"I always tried to be accurate"—and I chose to honor that aspect of her work.[13] This is not to suggest, however, that every point of fact in this book has been checked. Quite the contrary. Most have not, and many of them—such as how many people attended a particular meeting—would be impossible to verify.

Interpretation is another matter. How Frances perceived events, reported on the actions and motivations of others, and more generally selected what was and was not important enough to comment on—all of these reflect her world view, and I have left them alone. In its entirety, this book represents Frances's construction of a political self, and it contains a description of the social and political world of twentieth-century Georgia and the South that she helped shape. Therein lies its value. I did, however, call to Frances's attention those places where she had made a particularly critical comment about another person. On more sober reflection, not to mention the impending reality that her words would appear in print, Frances toned down some of the offhand language of the interview setting, while keeping the essential meaning of her remarks. These discussions were great fun for me, partly because we enjoyed many a chuckle over some colorful figures in Georgia politics, but also because they gave me an opportunity to tell Frances about the choices I had made and why I thought some stories were particularly important from my perspective as a historian of women's politics and the civil rights movement. I also told Frances about some stories that I had decided to leave out; Frances generally agreed with my choices, but on one occasion insisted that a story be added to the manuscript that I had considered superfluous.

Most of our decision-making is recorded on tape. According to standard oral history practice, these tapes will be made available to researchers, along with the other interviews for this project. Some of the simplest corrections and verifications, however, were done by phone. As I worked from my home on the West Coast, I would often call Frances, while having my morning coffee, to chat and do a bit of business. These phone conversations were not recorded, but the corrections made at this stage were minor relative to the corrections made during our meetings in Atlanta.

In a final, mutual decision, Frances and I agreed on the words that now close her narrative. The initial decision was mine, but I read the last several paragraphs to Frances. She agreed that, yes, she liked the way I had ended her story—with a question: "When people say that not much change has taken place, I agree with them because we have such a tremendous way to go. I guess we always have had to fight the same fights over and over, haven't we?"[14]

Notes

[1] Frances Freeborn Pauley Papers, Special Collections Department, Robert W. Woodruff Library, Emory University, Atlanta, Ga.

[2] For a list of the interviews, see "Notes on Sources."

[3] For a compilation of these stories, see Murphy Davis, ed., *Frances Pauley: Stories of Struggle and Triumph* (Atlanta: The Open Door Community, 1996). The original tapes are on deposit in the Pauley Papers.

[4] My decision in this regard stands in contrast to much late-twentieth-century practice in editing oral history for publication. For the argument that questions should be included, see, for example, Michael Frisch and Milton Rogovin, *Portraits in Steel* (Ithaca: Cornell University Press, 1993), 21.

[5] See Paul Thompson, *The Voice of the Past: Oral History*, 2d ed. (New York and Oxford: Oxford University Press, 1988), 137. On the synthesizing quality of memory, and for an introduction to historical memory generally, see David Thelen, "Memory and American History," *Journal of American History* 75 (1989): 1117–29.

[6] Frances Pauley, "The Lightning Struck," August 1988, Pauley Papers.

[7] Frances Pauley, interview by Paul Mertz, transcribed interview, June 10, 1988, Atlanta, Ga., Pauley Papers.

[8] For an argument for "an aggressive editorial approach," see Michael Frisch, "Preparing Interview Transcripts for Documentary Publication: A Line-by-Line Illustration of the

Editing Process," in *A Shared Authority: Essays on the Craft and Meaning of Oral and Public History* (Albany: State University of New York Press, 1990), 84.

[9] Quotation from chapter 2.

[10] The fullest documentary record of Frances's work is contained in her personal collection at Emory University and, for the 1960s, in the files of the Councils on Human Relations of the Southern Regional Council, which are available on microfilm. Southern Regional Council Papers (Ann Arbor, Mich: University Microfilms International, 1984).

[11] "History of work on increasing benefits for AFDC—as I remember it," [addressed to Paul Rilling], January 1, 1986, Pauley Papers.

[12] My thanks to Murphy Davis of the Open Door Community for helping me understand Frances's reticence. Conversation with author, Atlanta, Ga., June 11, 1997.

[13] Quotation from chapter 6.

[14] Quotation from chapter 7.

Notes on Sources

Seven sets of interviews, some edited by the interviewer, constitute the core of Frances Pauley's life story. Within these notes, they are identified, unless otherwise indicated, by the interviewer's name and the date of interview (when needed to distinguish multiple interviews by the same interviewer). They are (in chronological order, with joint interviews listed last):

Frances Pauley. Interview by Jacquelyn Hall. Southern Oral History Program, Interview no. 4007, July 18, 1974. Southern Historical Collection, Library of the University of North Carolina at Chapel Hill, Chapel Hill, N.C.

Frances Pauley. Interviews by Paul Mertz. August 1, 1983, and June 10, 1988. Frances Freeborn Pauley Papers, Special Collections Department, Robert W. Woodruff Library, Emory University, Atlanta, Ga.

Frances Pauley. Interview by Lenecia L. Bruce. September 20, 1983. League of Women Voters of DeKalb County (Ga.) Records, Special Collections Department, Robert W. Woodruff Library, Emory University, Atlanta, Ga.

Frances Pauley's spoken remembrances, delivered at the Open Door Community between 1987 and 1996, as edited by Murphy Davis in *Frances Pauley: Stories of Struggle and Triumph* (Atlanta: Open Door Community, 1996), cited in these notes as *Stories of Struggle and Triumph*. The tape recordings on which this publication is based are in the Frances Freeborn Pauley Papers, Special Collections Department, Robert W. Woodruff Library, Emory University, Atlanta, Ga.

Frances Pauley. Interviews by Cliff Kuhn. Georgia Government Documentation Project, April 11 and May 3, 1988. Special Collections Department, Pullen Library, Georgia State University, Atlanta, Ga.

Frances Pauley. Interviews by Kathryn L. Nasstrom. 1991 to 1998. In author's possession. Tapes and transcripts for these interviews will be deposited in the Frances Freeborn Pauley Papers, Special Collections Department, Robert W. Woodruff Library, Emory University, Atlanta, Ga.

Frances Pauley. Interviews by Albert McGovern. February 1994. In Frances Pauley's possession. Tapes and transcripts for these interviews will be deposited in the Frances Freeborn Pauley Papers, Special Collections Department, Robert W. Woodruff Library, Emory University, Atlanta, Ga.

Frances Pauley and Harry Boardman. Interviews by Kathryn L. Nasstrom. June 5, 1996, and March 29, 1998. In author's possession. Tapes and transcripts for these interviews will be deposited in the Frances Freeborn Pauley Papers, Special Collections Department, Robert W. Woodruff Library, Emory University, Atlanta, Ga.

Frances Pauley and Muriel Lokey. Interview by Kathryn L. Nasstrom. January 23, 1997. In author's possession. Tapes and transcripts for these interviews will be deposited in the Frances Freeborn Pauley Papers, Special Collections Department, Robert W. Woodruff Library, Emory University, Atlanta, Ga.

Frances Pauley and Betsey Stone. Interview by Kathryn L. Nasstrom. May 31, 1997. In author's possession. Tapes and transcripts for these interviews will be deposited in the Frances Freeborn Pauley Papers, Special Collections Department, Robert W. Woodruff Library, Emory University, Atlanta, Ga.

Frances Pauley and Buren Batson. Interview by Kathryn L. Nasstrom. June 11, 1997. In author's possession. Tapes and transcripts for these interviews will be deposited in the Frances Freeborn Pauley Papers, Special Collections Department, Robert W. Woodruff Library, Emory University, Atlanta, Ga.

Frances Pauley and Paul Rilling. Interviews by Kathryn L. Nasstrom. June 13, 1997, and March 29, 1998. In author's possession. Tapes and transcripts for these interviews will be deposited in the Frances Freeborn Pauley Papers, Special Collections Department, Robert W. Woodruff Library, Emory University, Atlanta, Ga.

Most of the documentary material derives from the Frances Freeborn Pauley Papers, Special Collections Department, Robert W. Woodruff Library, Emory University, Atlanta, Ga., and is cited in these notes by series and box number. Full citations for documentary material from other collections appear within these notes.

CHAPTER 1

The most detailed interview concerning Frances's life before 1930 was conducted by Albert McGovern in 1994. Most of the material for this chapter derives from his interview. Additional information was culled from chapter 1 of *Stories of Struggle and Triumph*, and from my 1995 and 1996 interviews with Frances. Some of this information was expanded on in our taped conversations of May and June 1997. Passing references to these years can be found in the early portions of Mertz (1988) and Kuhn (April 11, 1988).

CHAPTER 2

The speech that opens this chapter can be found in Series Nine (Other Affiliated Files), Box 75, Pauley Papers. This series contains additional documentary evidence for Frances's work with the DeKalb Clinic.

Information on the Pauley family, the Great Depression, and Bill Pauley's work was culled from McGovern, Hall, Kuhn (April 11, 1988), and from my 1995 interview with Frances.

For the Junior League, the DeKalb Clinic, and the school lunch program, see McGovern, Hall, Kuhn (both interviews), and my 1995 interviews. I also touched on these matters in my earliest (1991) interview with Frances.

The World War II years are covered in my 1995 interviews and in *Stories of Struggle and Triumph*, chapter 2.

CHAPTER 3

The bylaws for the DeKalb County League of Women Voters are in the League of Women Voters of DeKalb County (Ga.) Records, Special Collections Department, Robert W. Woodruff Library, Emory University, Atlanta, Ga.

On Frances's involvement in the League of Women Voters, see Hall; Bruce; Kuhn (April 11, 1988); Mertz (1988); McGovern; and my 1991, 1995, 1996, and 1997 interviews. The most detailed interview on this subject is that conducted and edited by Lenecia L. Bruce, a league member herself, in 1983. Of the joint interviews I conducted with Frances Pauley and others, the interview with Betsey Stone, which is primarily about the Georgia Poverty Rights Organization, also contains some information on the league. The most extensive discussion of the desegregation of the League of Women Voters can be found in Bruce, Kuhn (both interviews), and in my 1995 interviews.

The documents on the county unit fight, tolerance pledge, and private school amendment can be found in Series Two (League of Women Voters Records), Box 5, Pauley Papers.

Frances has discussed the political activities of her league years extensively. See Hall, Kuhn (both interviews), Bruce, Mertz (both interviews), McGovern, and my 1991 and 1995 interviews. On the county unit fight, the most detailed treatments are in Hall, Kuhn (both interviews), and my 1995 interviews. The most detailed discussion of the tolerance pledge is in my 1995 interviews. The white primary is touched on only briefly in Kuhn (April 11, 1988) and Mertz (1988). The private school amendment is covered in Hall, Kuhn (April 11, 1988), and in my 1991 and 1995 interviews. Only the interview by Bruce has information on the league's work on welfare in the 1950s and Frances's interest in serving on the national board of the League of Women Voters of the United States.

The letter that opens the section on Frances's own education about race and race relations is an undated letter to her children. Series One (Personal Papers) of the Pauley Papers contains the small amount of personal and family material in her collection. The letters are in Box 1. Several interviews touch tangentially on this topic (Hall, Kuhn [April 11, 1988], and Mertz [1988]), but the only extended treatments of these topics are in McGovern and in my 1995 interviews.

The HOPE statement of purpose is from a HOPE press release, January 19, 1959, Box 3, HOPE (Help Our Public Education) Papers, Atlanta History Center, Atlanta, Ga. Frances's own papers are also a source of documentary material on HOPE specifically and school desegregation generally. See Series Four (HOPE Records), Pauley Papers. All of the interviews touch on school desegregation in some manner, and several have extensive treatment: Hall, Kuhn (both interviews), Mertz (both interviews), McGovern, and my 1991 and 1995 interviews.

The text from the world politics brochure is from Series Three (Fund for Adult Education Records), Box 6, Pauley Papers. The Hall interview has a brief mention of the world politics groups, as does my 1995 interview. Most of this material, however, was recorded in my joint interview with Frances and Harry Boardman in 1996 and in a follow-up joint interview with Frances, Harry, and Paul Rilling in 1998.

The reference to Governor Vandiver that closes this chapter is from an undated letter to Frances's children, Series One (Personal Papers), Box 1, Pauley Papers. Based on the content of the letter, I have dated it January 1963.

Chapter 4

The letter that Frances refers to as the "occupant mailing" to white citizens of Albany can be found in Series Five (Georgia Council on Human Relations Records), Box 9, Pauley Papers.

For the early period of Frances's tenure with the Georgia Council on Human Relations, including her fundraising activities, see Hall, Mertz (1983), Kuhn (both interviews), McGovern, and my 1995 interview. McGovern treats this period in the greatest detail. A small piece of information came from a letter Frances wrote to her daughter Marylin and son-in-law Jim, dated March 5, [1961?], Series One (Personal Papers), Box 1, Pauley Papers.

The story of Coretta Scott King and the Bible School is from Kuhn (April 11, 1988).

General information on organizing local Councils on Human Relations can be found in Hall; Kuhn (May 3, 1988); Mertz (1983); McGovern; and in my 1991, 1995, and 1996 interviews. The most detailed information is in Kuhn (May 3, 1988) and McGovern.

From *Stories of Struggle and Triumph*, I pulled the information on the Dorchester Academy, Frances's young friend Inman, and the story of Oliver Wendell Holmes and the dogs at Franziska Boas's home.

The dated excerpts that open the sections on Savannah, Albany, and southwest Georgia are from a diary that Frances kept during her tenure with the Georgia Council on Human Relations. The diary is a fairly recent addition to Frances's collection at Emory and is, as of publication of this book, within the unprocessed portions of her collection. A small amount of this dated material derives from letters to her children, Series One (Personal Papers), Box 1, Pauley Papers. These letters are those dated March 1, 1961; March 5, 1961; Sunday, n.d. [which I believe was written May 3/4, 1962]; March 26, [1961]; April 20, 1962; and November 3, 1963.

For the oral history material on Savannah, see Kuhn (April 11, 1988) and McGovern. On Albany, see Hall, Kuhn (both interviews), Mertz (both interviews), and McGovern. My 1995 interviews make a brief mention of it. On southwest Georgia, see Hall, Mertz (both interviews), Kuhn (both interviews), and McGovern. The Hall and Kuhn interviews have the most thorough treatments of Albany and southwest Georgia. The story of Carol King's integrated day care is from a speech titled "African American Women in the Civil Rights Movement," which Frances presented at the University of Georgia on March 7, 1991 (in Frances Pauley's possession, used by permission).

For the end of Frances's tenure with the Georgia Council on Human Relations, see Hall, Kuhn (May 3, 1988), and my 1995 interviews.

CHAPTER 5

The letters to Frances Pauley's children and cousins, dated March 2, 1969, and [December 13/14, 1969], are in Series One (Personal Papers), Box 1, Pauley Papers.

Brief references to Frances's first tasks with HEW involving welfare compliance can be found in McGovern and in my joint interview with Frances and Paul Rilling.

The transition from the Georgia Council on Human Relations to HEW and the nature of work in HEW are covered in Mertz (1988); Kuhn (May 3, 1988); McGovern; and in my 1991, 1995, and 1996 interviews with Frances and my joint interview with Frances and Paul Rilling. Additional information, especially concerning Frances's continuing work in Georgia, came from *Stories of Struggle and Triumph*, chapter 7.

Specific stories about HEW work (as opposed to its general nature) and Frances's decision to resign are covered in Mertz (1988); McGovern; my 1995 and 1996 interviews; and a letter, dated January 15, 1974, to Anna Lord Strauss, Series Eight (Georgia Poverty Rights Organization Records), Box 32, Pauley Papers.

I recorded Frances's retrospective appraisal of school desegregation in my 1996 interviews.

CHAPTER 6

Frances's observation concerning the parallels between racism and discrimination based on poverty is contained in her testimony before the Georgia legislature, June 20, 1979, Box 1 of September 1995 additions to the collection, Pauley Papers.

The letter that opens this chapter is the same letter to Anna Lord Strauss cited for chapter 5.

Most of the interview material for this chapter derives from my joint interviews with Frances and Muriel Lokey and Betsey Stone. Additional interview material came from McGovern; my 1995, 1996, and 1997 interviews; and (a brief reference) Bruce.

The documents for this chapter are all from Series Eight (Georgia Poverty Rights Organization Records), Pauley Papers: the bylaws and statement of purpose for the GPRO are in Box 32; the position paper is in Box 37; "History of work on increasing benefits for AFDC, as I remember it" is in Box 47; and the narrative of the history of HEAT, which is untitled, is in Box 55. For details of the history of Poor People's Day at the Capitol, I culled additional information from "Bits of Rememberances of the History of Poor People's Day at the Georgia Legislature" in Box 68.

CHAPTER 7

Frances's testimony regarding AIDS legislation is in Series Ten (AIDS Files), Box 78, Pauley Papers.

Interview material concerning AIDS activism comes from Mertz (1988) and from my joint interview with Frances and Buren Batson.

On the Open Door Community, see McGovern and my 1995, 1996, and 1997 interviews.

On events and issues at Wesley Woods, see Kuhn (April 11, 1988), my 1996 and 1997 interviews, and a brief mention in my joint interview with Frances and Betsey Stone.

For Frances's assessments of current affairs, see Kuhn (May 3, 1988), McGovern, and my 1995 and 1996 interviews. For the purposes of establishing Frances's beliefs in the present, I pulled information from interviews between 1988 and 1998, looking for consistency of opinion.

Index

Page references in *italics* indicate photographs. Those followed by n indicate endnotes.